Parker Gillmore

Through Gasa Land, and the Scene of the Portuguese Aggression

The Journey of a Hunter in Search of Gold And Ivory

Parker Gillmore

Through Gasa Land, and the Scene of the Portuguese Aggression
The Journey of a Hunter in Search of Gold And Ivory

ISBN/EAN: 9783744761918

Printed in Europe, USA, Canada, Australia, Japan

Cover: Foto ©Andreas Hilbeck / pixelio.de

More available books at **www.hansebooks.com**

Through Gasa Land,

AND THE

Scene of the Portuguese Aggression.

THE JOURNEY OF A HUNTER IN SEARCH
OF GOLD AND IVORY.

BY

PARKER GILLMORE ("UBIQUE"),

*Author of " Days and Nights by the Desert,"
" The Great Thirst Land," " Gun, Rod, and Saddle,"
&c. &c. &c.*

London:
HARRISON AND SONS, 59, PALL MALL,
Booksellers to the Queen and H.R.H. the Prince of Wales.

HARRISON AND SONS,
PRINTERS IN ORDINARY TO HER MAJESTY
ST. MARTIN'S LANE

PREFACE.

THE claim that Portugal has made to the possession of Gasa Land is preposterous : that it be deemed the owner of Mashoona Land, is ridiculous. My reasons for saying so are that, it has only two ports along the sea-board of the first-mentioned, beyond the limits of which it dare not go ; while for permission to trade at Senna, Tete, and Zumbo, stations on the Zambesi river, it annually paid to the Suzerain of Mashoona Land—the Matabele King—a large subsidy, which, if not forthcoming at the stipulated date, was enforced by an army.

Even under such unfavourable circumstances these trading posts might have flourished, but for the Portuguese being incorrigible slave-dealers, not only preying upon the population in their vicinity for compulsory domestic service, but yearly sending thousands and thousands to Brazil, and such other markets as could be found for the unfortunate captives. Even at the present day, slavery exists in all these out of the way, insignificant trading stations.

The bondsmen are generally brought from north of the Zambesi, and entrapped by bodies of armed men, under the command of half-breeds, these expeditions being fitted out and subsidised by Portuguese merchants. The horrors that the unfortunates have suffered in their journeys down country can neither be imagined nor described.

The perpetuation of the accursed institution of slavery is the desire of the Portuguese subjects resident in Austral Africa, and the Boers of the Transvaal; hence their sympathy with each other. Since our late policy was to conclude a disgraceful peace with those descendants of the Dutch who form the population of the so-called South African Republic, they and the Portuguese have made common cause to oppose British interests in every possible way, and it is an ascertained fact that, but for the counsel and advice of the authorities at Pretoria, we should never have had the insolent pretensions of the Court of Lisbon made in reference to the Mashoona and Mocololo countries. If actual hostilities should occur between us and these allies, many of our late rebellious subjects will be found fighting in the adverse ranks. The culpable partition of Zululand, the destruction of Secocomie's tribe, the restrictions placed upon the Swazie race, combined with the recall and disgrace of the true patriot and able statesman, Sir Bartle Frere, have directly been the cause of the difficulties which we now have to face; and I very much fear that the task before us will be found far more onerous than at present anticipated, for, blink the matter as we will, disloyalty is rampant all over South Africa, not even excepting the Old Colony.

Gold is to be found in great abundance in Manica and other adjoining parts of the Matabele country; but care must be taken that the working of these valuable mines do not fall into the hands of unprincipled companies, as much misery will be inevitably entailed upon the natives if such should occur. Only lately I "interviewed" the directors of an embryo company, who coolly informed me that, they were about to work mines of the valuable metal in Manica and Mashoona Land, having obtained a permit to do so from the Portuguese Government. Doubtless the new South African Company will be able to deal with such pretenders. If not, I should advise that Lubengulo, King of the Matabeles, be told off to settle with them ; after he has done so, if I am not much mistaken, they will give little further trouble.

It is impossible in this narrative to state the correct names of stations and rivers, for the inhabitants change them with the accession to office of every new chief.

The positions of my camps, hunting grounds, and gold-fields are only approximately correct, for I had no instruments to enable me to lay down exactly their latitude and longitude.

The reminiscences added at the termination of my journey " Through Gasa Land, and the scene of the Portuguese Aggression " are experiences which I think will give the reader a fair idea of the life of a hunter, and the people that dwell upon the western side of Matabele Land, familiarly designated as the " Hight Veldt."

PARKER GILLMORE ("UBIQUE").

" LAND AND WATER,"
    58, PALL MALL, S.W.

CONTENTS.

Chapter I.
The Start. A South African Coaster

PAGES
1—4

Chapter II.
Our Zulus. Buffaloes killed. Our Batteries

5—10

Chapter III.
Great Variety of Game. Elephants. A Perplexing Position ... ...

11—16

Chapter IV.
A Dangerous Situation. Crocodiles ...

17—20

Chapter V.
A Gun set. Snakes. A Forehead Shot. Bad Shooting ...

21—28

Chapter VI.
A Mangy Hyæna. A Free Fight. Ivory Trading ...

29—33

Chapter VII.
The Mantatees. Skilful Spooring. Formidable Bush

34—38

Chapter VIII.
Game in Sight. A Grand Old Man. Hunted

39—44

CHAPTER IX.

A Disagreeable Experience. A Java Saurian. An Outcry in Camp ... ... 45—50

CHAPTER X.

Hippopotami. A Precious Drink. Nervousness. Oh! what a Surprise ... 51—57

CHAPTER XI.

A Bonne Bouche. Cruel Work. An Unexpected Charge. Half-a-pint of Nectar ... ... 58—63

CHAPTER XII.

An Exciting Night. A Weird Situation. The Irrepressible. A Mother's Boy ... 64—69

CHAPTER XIII.

A Dark Night. A Ludicrous Scene. A Great Naturalist. Leopards. A Summary Proceeding 70—77

CHAPTER XIV.

Giraffes. A Black Cobra. Gordon Cumming. The Rhinoceros Bird. Ready for the Fray ... ... 78—85

CHAPTER XV.

My Left Barrel. The Second Dish. Laid by the Heels. Time an Object. A Fine Race. Riding down Giraffe. Who missed? ... 86—99

CHAPTER XVI.

Weapons. Proper Charges. Sympathetic Music. A Midnight Visitor ... ... 100—105

Chapter XVII.

The Cyclone. Drowned out. Zulus as Soldiers   106—110

Chapter XVIII

Dillon's Departure. Fishing. A Novel Capture. An Invalid Companion ...   111—118

Chapter XIX.

A Crafty Old Buffalo. Where to Aim. A Pet Crane. A Formidable Reptile. Sight or Scent   119—127

Chapter XX.

Not Unattractive Harmony. Christianising the Natives. The Death Bed. Pursuit of the Maneater ...   128—133

Chapter XXI.

A Trying Search. Carrion Feeders. Funeral Service. A Truce to Moralising ...   134—139

Chapter XXII.

Tropical Flora. Sun-birds. Ourebi and Duyker. Weaver-birds. Good Luck ...   140—148

Chapter XXIII.

A Narrow Escape. Dangerous Attendants. Native Carelessness. Order and Cleanliness ...   149—156

Chapter XXIV.

Trip to the Lagoon. Sloane's Rhinoceros. A Rebellious Infant ...   157—162

Chapter XXV.

An Enchanting Scene. Large Mushrooms ...   PAGES 163—166

Chapter XXVI.

An Uncommon Pet. Two Marauders. An Accident. No Surrender ... ... 167—173

Chapter XXVII.

An Unwilling Capture. A Spoilt Child. Vultures and their Prey ... ... 174—177

Chapter XXVIII.

The Soothing Pipe. Lonely. A Black Child ... 178—182

Chapter XXIX.

A Satanic Yell. A Wonderful Tale. A Sturdy Ox 183—188

Chapter XXX.

Once more Afloat. A Strange Bird. Surgeon-birds. Game to the Last... ... ... 189—195

Chapter XXXI.

An Unfortunate Calf. The Lion's Food. Exercising my Patience. Camp Comforts ... ... 196—201

Chapter XXXII.

Floating down Stream. Suckled by a Lioness. Building the Raft... ... ... 202—206

Chapter XXXIII.

A Life on the Ocean Wave. An Error in Natural History. A Happy Past... ... 207—212

Chapter XXXIV.

Robbing a Crocodile's Nest. Maternal Affection of Crocodiles. Home, Sweet Home. The Great Mashoona Race. Subsidies to the Matabele King .. 213—222

Chapter XXXV.

Game worthy of a Sportsman's Skill. A Dangerous Mother. Gold! Gold! ... . 223—227

Chapter XXXVI.

My Black Baby. A Child's Pluck. The Portuguese as Tenants. Slavery and its Results ... 228—234

Chapter XXXVII.

A Discovery in Natural History. Preparations for a Start. Dillon's Prowess ... ... 235—239

Chapter XXXVIII.

A Rat Hunt. A Fortunate Escape ... ... 240—241

Chapter XXXIX.

On the Line of March. Peculiarities of the Tetze Fly. A Land of Promise for Emigration. Treatment of the Natives. Native Ingenuity .. 242—249

Chapter XL.

A Grand Country. The Food Supply. Bad Shooting. Gluttony at the Mansion House. Abundant Spoor of Game. A Pugnacious Old Cow. A Veteran Soldier. Portuguese Tabooed. Ancient Stone Works. Rejoin Dillon. Livingstone's Description of Tete. Tete and its Environs. Slavery. Coal. Convict Soldiers ... 250—280

Life on the Hight Veldt and Country West of Matabele Land 281

Hunting Favourites in Austral Africa ... 291

A Hottentot Patriot 319

Female Heroism 329

Belief in Ghosts ... 337

THROUGH GASA LAND,

AND

The Scene of Portuguese Aggression.

CHAPTER I.

THE START.

My first experience of big game shooting in South Africa I am not likely to forget, although it occurred some years ago, for, let me tell the reader, it was not sport at all, but the most harassing, trying work, without break or cessation ; and it would have, had it continued for any length of time, certainly made Jack a dull boy, or driven him stark, staring mad, and sent him into a premature grave.

Shooting and hunting are delightful amusements when you have food in abundance and rest at night, but when you have a scarcity of both and no shelter, and often a most malarious climate, then I say most emphatically "the game is not worth the candle."

The exploits of Gordon Cumming, Andersson, Sir Cornwallis Harris, and other mighty Nimrods had created within my bosom an unquenchable desire to become their rival; but, alas! my purse was far from a long one, so, instead of marching into the interior of the country "with all the pomp and circumstance of war," in the way of waggons, horses, hounds, and innumerable attendants, I had to pursue my game on foot with what natives I could pick up as associates, and sleep upon the open veldt or under the spreading forest, with the heavens for my canopy, and mother earth for my mattress. However, I consoled myself that my knowledge of field sports, particularly in elephant hunting—for I had shot several of these animals in Ceylon—would make up for these drawbacks; but never, as in this instance, was the adage of "counting your eggs before they are hatched" so thoroughly verified.

Few men were ever blessed with a better constitution than I possessed at the age of twenty-five years. Moreover, I was, at that period of my life, as hard as nails; could walk from morning till night, day after day without fatigue, and, on a push, run a mile or more without having to cry "Bellows to mend." I never was very fast on foot, it is true, but what I lacked in speed I made up in staying power.

Such was the state of my affairs, bodily and financially, when I found myself in Natal, prepared to go forth and do battle with the wild beasts of the earth. The hotel at which I put up was the resort of numerous elephant hunters, who made an annual visit into Zululand for skins and ivory. These gentry had wonderful stories to tell of their exploits, which added only fuel to the fire that was burning within me.

While gathering what information I could pick up about the interior, I met two gentlemen emulated by the same desires as myself, and situated in the same way in respect to *l'argent*.

There is no harm in mentioning their names— more particularly as I can assert that two better, more genial, and Mark Tapley-like chums I never had—for they have long joined the vast majority.

Selwin was quiet, unassuming, and courageous; Dillon was fiery and impulsive, but generous to an excess. The first would have made a model clergyman if his heart had been in his work; the latter the *beau idéal* of a light cavalry officer.

With these I took counsel, and without dissent it was resolved that we should break new ground in our projected shooting trip, and proceed to the north of Zululand.

A dirty, ill-found, and worn-out little top-sail schooner was in Durban harbour; her destination was Delgoa Bay, and in her we determined to ship. Her appearance did not promise well for comfort or sea-going qualities; but we argued that the passage was very short, and that if she had kept afloat to such a venerable age she was not likely to go to pieces on this voyage.

In both these opinions we were correct, but the question has often since arisen in my mind, why did this wretched craft not go ashore or founder? I can only ask why? Her skipper—I think his name was Drake—appeared to have no idea of taking an observation, so consequently hugged the land, seldom, or never, losing sight of it, while the craft's gear was everlastingly giving way. The weather was not really bad; still, we had a stiff breeze, and as our schooner was very light, it may be imagined how the little vessel jumped about on the anything but placid Indian Ocean. Moreover, a more inutile crew never hauled on a brace, and never were at hand when wanted to do so; so Selwin, who had great yachting experience, and I, who had much boating knowledge, not figuratively, but literally did all the work of the vessel. But let me skip over the dangers by sea, and the horrors we encountered from cockroaches and other gruesome and uncanny beasts by night. In due course of time we landed at Lorenzo Marquez, the vilest, filthiest, and most deadly place to white men I know of, in all this habitable world. We arrived in the healthy season; I should like to ask what it can be in the sickly period. The slob which surrounds the village, and mangroves that grow upon it, seemed to fairly reek with fever.

CHAPTER II.

OUR ZULUS.

AFTER as much interference as petty Portuguese officials only know how to give, we shook the dust off our feet and departed, mind, on foot. This we should not have been able to do as expeditiously as we did, but for a piece of luck. We had scarcely landed when a Zulu accosted us with the extensive English vocabulary of "How do?" He brought another native of the reassuring name of "Sunday," who spoke our language intelligibly. From him we learned that he had been in the employ of Mr. Leslie, of Natal, and that he would undertake service; further, that he could bring with him some of his countrymen. Sunday was as good as his word; in half an hour he paraded before us eleven as likely recruits as ever took the Queen's shilling. There was not a word of haggling as to pay, &c.; all were ready to start there and then, for each man had his kit with him—rather a mysterious kit, for it was remarkable from its being invisible.

I learned afterwards that these poor fellows had got stuck down here and were literally starving; what was the reason of this I did not learn, but their misfortune was the luckiest thing imaginable for us, otherwise I do not believe we should ever have left Lorenzo Marquez by the land route. At that time no domestic animal of any description could come down from the Transvaal to Delgoa Bay, for the simple reason that the intervening country between the two swarmed with tetze fly, an insect whose bite is alike deadly to horse, ox, dog, or donkey, the wild game and man alone appearing impervious to its attacks. The country between the coast and the so-called South African Republic then swarmed with buffalo, in the dung of which, these pests of the explorer and hunter bred. The Portuguese call this insect the elephant fly, supposing it was produced in the ordure of the elephant; this is now well known to be a mistake.

The labour we encountered for the first ten days' tramp, with the exposure and scantiness of provisions we suffered from, was enough to break the hearts of any human beings but Zulus. They had their loads of about forty pounds each, led the way all day, made our night fires, ate with gratitude what food we could spare them, and slept with a single and very sieve-like blanket alone around them, but never a murmur escaped their lips. Truly they are a grand race, far, far superior to any indigenous people I ever met.

Hitherto we had been following native or wild beast paths through a tropical forest or intricate marshy river beds; now we struck the edges of spurs of hills, offshoots from the Bombo Mountains, where extensive open glades were encountered. Our course, then, was altered from north-west to due north, and four days after we reached a river, now called the Saabin. The country was simply lovely; above us and to the left hand rose range after range of hills, as attractive as those of Malvern, while in the other direction stretched what appeared one unbroken forest of tropical timber.

From the quantity of spoor and its variety, there was the most confirming evidence that we had arrived in a hunters' elysium; nor were we long in putting the place to the test, for meat we wanted, and that badly. Sunday was a good tracker; by his skill he soon recognised the evidence of the presence of buffalo, and that their sanctuary was a dense growth of reeds of several acres in extent that margined the stream.

Like an able general his plan of campaign was at once formed; he, with half a dozen of his followers, were to go up wind and return down it to start the game, while we, *perdu*, took our positions to leeward. The device answered to perfection, and two cows were killed. More buffalo could have been slaughtered if we had desired to add to the carnage, for there was not less than a hundred head of these magnificent game brutes turned out of their resting-place, where, doubtless, they had been enjoying their siesta, as the hour was mid-day.

I will pass over this hunt, as I want to get on to the elephants, with no further details than stating that one of the victims gave chase to a boy, and would doubtless have accomplished his death but for the agility he displayed in avoiding her charges. This exciting scene was continued for two or three minutes, when Selwin terminated it by a splendid shot at fifty yards, which sent the pursuer head over heels, as complete a somersault as ever a rabbit performed with a charge of No. 6 through its forequarters at short range.

How this exciting affair occurred is worthy of note, for its narration may be the means of saving others from putting themselves in such a dangerous predicament. Dillon knocked over this cow, and to all appearance killed her. The young Zulu, who was close at hand, rushed up to the prostrate animal to blood his assegai. The first prick seemed to imbue the prostrate beast with new life, for in a moment she was on her legs, and in full pursuit of her assailant.

The same thing happened to me in after years. On the Crocodile River, Cigar, my old henchman, shot a gemsbok. It fell only a short distance in front of me. It was a splendid animal, so I, without thought, went up to it and touched it. Whew! in a moment it was on its legs and charged. In the hurry and unexpectedness of the rush I fired both barrels, and missed with each, and I have ever since believed that it would have fared badly with me had not my attendant put in a lucky shot. *Moral.—* Never go up to big game unless you are certain that they are dead.

Here we remained two days making *biltong* of our meat, for we had at least fifty more miles to travel before we reached the country where Sunday expected elephants to be abundant, and not alarmed by hunters. So I will take this opportunity of describing my battery, both of which were muzzle-loaders and 12-bore. First, a shot gun, which threw a ball very well up to fifty yards, but was too light for heavy charges; secondly, a two-grooved rifle, weighing about ten pounds. With light charges, say three to three and a half drachms of powder, it was an accurate weapon, but when six were substituted, the less said about its precision the better. I soon discovered that light charges were absolutely useless against very large game, so, *nolens volens*, had to adopt the heavy.

There was one advantage about this weapon—it was bound to do execution somehow, for, if it did not knock the object over it was aimed at, it was likely to send the firer to grass, or at all events, badly wing him. I had no alternative but to use this beast of a "shooting iron," and, as may be well imagined, I always did so with fear and trembling. My companions' arms were identical in calibre, only Dillon had a smooth-bore rifle instead of a grooved, and the handiness and efficiency of this weapon up to one hundred yards caused me, I fear, often to break the commandment, " Thou shalt not covet, &c." There is no doubt that from my experience in this trip I formed the conclusion to which I have ever since steadfastly adhered, that for bush shooting, where the range seldom or never exceeds one hundred yards, the smooth-bore excels the grooved weapon.

CHAPTER III.

GREAT VARIETY OF GAME.

ON the second morning after our introduction to buffalo, a long string of elephants deployed past us at a distance of half a mile. They were travelling very rapidly, and Sunday assured us that there was no use going after them, as they would not stop till they reached the flats, near where an affluent river runs towards the Limpopo. His advice was willingly taken, for none of us were very anxious for more exercise than was absolutely necessary, the reason being that for three nights neither of us had had a wink of sleep from the number and audacity of the lions that surrounded our camp. We had no kraal for protection; only the most flimsy of grass huts to lie in, while the natives slept on the ground around the fires. Thus we were open to attack at any moment. Anyhow, we had abundance of fuel to help to keep things straight. The last night of our stay the anticipated crisis seemed to have arrived, for soon after midnight three or four of the natives rushed into our shanty, and the others took to the trees. The fire at the moment was burning brightly, and we all distinctly saw a lioness standing on her hind legs, with one fore foot extended upwards and leaning against a tree, endeavouring with her other paw to hook down the meat we had placed for safety in its forks. Selwin and I fired at her, but without effect. Our reception, however, caused her to depart; but in half-an-hour more the vixen was back at her old game. Dillon and I now gave her a salute. The fire had blazed up a little better at the moment, so our chance of shooting correctly was increased, the result being that her ladyship got both balls, where we could not say, but, much to our relief, she departed, not to return. Sunday vowed if we hit her she would charge into the hut. Why she did not do so goodness only knows. My later experience has taught me that such a course is usually to be expected from a wounded lion.

A tributary river here reaches the Saabin, in a succession of long, almost currentless reaches, flowing though rich alluvial soil, with generally deep precipitous banks. Where these do not exist the stream is margined by dense, lofty, interlaced reeds; along the edge of the water is a heavy growth of timber; outside that is as fine a *veldt*—here and there studded with a few trees and occasional patches of brush—as could be found for hunting purposes in any part of Africa. In my opinion this portion of the country does not get burnt up like the higher *veldt* of the Transvaal in summer, but remains green throughout the year—

hence, but for the tetze fly, it would be an inexhaustible grazing ground for horned cattle.

Our camping place was the *beau idéal* of what such an establishment should be, for we had our backs against a precipitous wall of rock, and abundance of water close at hand. As soon as the boys had finished their pipes and rested for a short time, they turned to with a will, and made a half-circular fence around our position, that was high enough and strong enough to keep at defiance any midnight marauders. Moreover, from the reeds they constructed a hut for us to sleep in that was not only fairly comfortable, but roomy. Game was in this vicinity very abundant, all the larger kinds, including giraffes, only excepting elephants, having been seen within the last hour's tramp. However, this grand animal's presence was made known soon after supper, by the passage of a troop to some water not over a quarter of a mile off. There must have been upwards of a hundred in this drove, for, as they generally travel on such occasions in single file, they took nearly twenty minutes to pass. Their drinking place was above us, or further up stream, fortunately, or otherwise they would have got our wind and departed for new pastures, so we anticipated grand sport on the morrow.

At sunrise Sunday informed us that he had been to the ford, for there is a *drift* over the river close by, and that the elephants were feeding across it, so, without water-bottles—no need of those troublesome things here—and plenty of biltong, biscuit, and tobacco in our pockets, we started in pursuit.

Our tactics were to spoor the herd from the drift; but, if after we found the game and got separated, Sunday was to remain with Selwin, Umpiqua—a cross-eyed, ugly little beggar, but a good hunter—go with Dillon, and a jovial, handsome savage, that I had christened Jim, for brevity, accompany me. From fear of disturbing the elephants, the greatest quiet prevailed when wading across; but all got over safely, as Dillon feelingly said, "without even a nibble, let alone a bite," crocodiles being numerous in these waters.

The trail was easy enough to follow, for it was as wide as a garden walk, although a little more irregular in surface. One of the Zulus kept about a hundred yards in front of the party to give us due warning of the proximity of game, which he did after half-an-hour's tramp. Then this wily savage stopped, and indicated with his hands for us to hurry up. Such a request did not require repetition. On reaching him, he simply pointed, with the air of an emperor, to the eastward, and, true enough, there were the objects of our search, and it only now remained for us to kill them. My companions I will now leave to pursue their own devices, so will confine myself to my experiences.

Dropping behind my friends, I passed silently

but rapidly to their right flank, hoping that a shot would not be fired till I had singled out my beast. First I came across a cow, but her duffing little tusks did not suit my cravings for big ivory, so I passed her unseen; then another cow, and, thirdly, a tuskless cow, generally accredited the most vicious and consequently dangerous of her race, presented themselves, but they were quite unaware of my presence, so I continued still taking ground to the right. But my forbearance was soon rewarded, for in front of me, and not over forty yards distant, stood a fine bull, with tusks of at least sixty pounds apiece, and such a lot of ivory meant a lump of money, so I determined to possess them. The poor beast was feeding daintily, that is, it appeared to be fastidious in its taste, for many of the boughs that it pulled down it afterwards rejected. Between me and the game was a fallen tree, the roots of which had torn up quite a wall of earth; could I but reach it, my shot would be fired within twenty yards of the object of my aim. I resolved to make a try for it. Jim, with my second gun, was at my heels, and everything promised well. From the shelter of one tree to that of another I successfully glided without being observed. Then there was a trifling gap; this I covered without being observed, and in front of me was the giant, but his position was such that not a single vulnerable point was exposed. For a couple of minutes at least I remained in this annoying predicament, puzzling my brain over to know what artifice I could employ to make the elephant change his position, but without coming to a satisfactory conclusion. During all this time the animal had not moved an inch, except to raise or lower his trunk, and exhibited no indication of doing so. Would a whistle, I thought, accomplish my purpose, and I was about to put this experiment in practice, when the report of one of my friend's guns echoed through the forest. In an instant my beast slewed himself round, as if to ascertain from where the strange noise had come, and he stood broadside to me, motionless, listening with the utmost intentness. Beween the eye and the base of the ear is a slightly hollowed space, always looking darker than the rest of the hide. For this I aimed and pressed the trigger, and the poor beast, swaying his trunk violently, simply sat down, like one of his Indian broken-in brethren kneeling to take on a load. The elephant was quite dead; in fact, the rapidity of his death, which I can only explain by supposing the bullet entered the brain, I think rather disappointed me.

CHAPTER IV.

A DANGEROUS SITUATION.

KNOWING that my late quarry was unquestionably dead, I started off in search of more ivory, and was not long in coming across another bull. He was on the move, evidently alarmed at the fusillade that was going on so close at hand, looked wicked, and evidently intended not to belie his looks. I ran through some brush, so as to head him, and got into a very fair piece of cover unobserved, within a few yards of where the brute would pass, but the report of a shot brought him to a halt, so that there was left nothing for me to do but aim at the animal's shoulder. I did so, and put in the two barrels as rapid as thought, within a few inches of one another, but the effect was only to stagger him.

I commenced to feel nervous for my security, for, although the shelter was not exactly bad, it was scarcely the place a person would select in which to secrete himself from a wounded elephant, but I was not long detained in uncertainty, for the beast trumpeted shrilly and started off at his best pace. I rose to see what was the cause of this new move, and for which I felt so grateful; nor was I long detained in ignorance; the tusker had seen Jim, now a hundred yards off, after whom he was in full pursuit. The Zulu appeared to take the matter very easily; first he dropped my gun in a bush, then ran a few paces further till he reached a tree, up which he mounted with the agility of a monkey.

Sportsmen who shoot large and dangerous game should truly bless the inventors of breech-loaders. I often wonder now, even feel amazed, when I recall to memory the many ticklish places, the old-fashioned arm placed me in.

Having loaded, I started in pursuit. I had no difficulty in getting near the bull, for Jim kept calling at him, and so attracting his attention. At about twenty-five yards I gave the animal a brace more bullets, but with no better results.

The elephant did not appear to be in a hurry to leave the tree that sheltered the boy, so without difficulty I got reloaded, and, taking what I considered must be a fatal aim, fired. No visible effect from either barrel was displayed, if I except that the poor stricken beast gave up watching Jim, and walked slowly and unsteadily off. Hurrying up my loading, I ran forward to head the beast. There was a fallen tree before me. This shelter I gained, and from it again fired, aiming eight inches or ten inches below the part I had formerly made my target. The effect was electrical, for with a crash the elephant fell, smashing to pieces a sapling upwards of ten inches in diameter. These were fair tusks also, about forty pounds weight each, sufficient reward for a day's work, which had neither been very exciting nor particularly dangerous.

From the recoil of my rifle, my shoulder had become so fearfully contused that I resolved to remain about camp, an example that was not slow in being followed by my chums. Gun cleaning and other home work occupied the forenoon, but when that was over it was determined unanimously to inspect a dead hippopotamus. What a scene there was around the remains of the carcass! On the land were hundreds of carrion-feeding birds, waiting for a chance to make a meal; in the water the heads of at least a dozen large crocodiles showed themselves, while one giant saurian, resting on his hind-legs, and clasping the dead body with his forepaws, was tearing off immense pieces of flesh, which appeared to find a difficult passage into its capacious maw. We were within fifteen paces of this disgusting, loathsome brute before it became aware of our presence, and then it only raised its head, as if to inquire who were the intruders. That movement was its death warrant, for Dillon placed a bullet from his smooth-bore into its brain through the eye. Death appeared to be instantaneous, for it rolled over into the water without a struggle, and doubtlessly afterwards became food for some of its own species. It is a pity we could not have measured this specimen; it looked to me fully twenty feet long.

After this initiation in crocodile shooting, my Irish friend went in for it in earnest. How many he killed that afternoon I could not say; only this I do know, that he kept up a very brisk fire till after sunset.

As some flesh I had left over a pool to be fly-blown and so attract fish was close at hand, I went to inspect it, but it was gone. How it had been taken I could not say, so I ordered a piece of the hippopotamus meat to be hung in its place; for I was determined to have some fishing, if only to learn what kinds and varieties of the finny tribe were contained in these waters.

All the wild beasts of the forest seemed to have selected this neighbourhood for a rendezvous, for such a row as they made throughout the night was quite unprecedented in the experience of our Zulus. Umpiqua, whom I deemed to be the most experienced, as well as the oldest, of our hunters, foretells that we will yet have trouble with the lions; for, says he, "there's an old woman among them that is always sniffing around the kraal, as if she were looking for a place to break into the camp." He seems to regard the females as the more dangerous sex.

However, I'll see if I can't stop her little game to-morrow night by setting a gun for her ladyship. There is no doubt but that the stranded carcass of the hippo has much influence in attracting the presence of these night prowlers.

CHAPTER V.

A GUN SET.

"Jim," who went off prospecting soon after daylight, reports having seen an enormous bull elephant cross the river above the ford and enter some thick jungle a few miles up the stream. The natives are such acute observers of animal life that they do not hesitate to pronounce what state of mind a beast may be in; if his suppositions are correct, then this old gentleman is in a most irascible temper, possibly caused by having come across the bodies of some of his dead companions. Selwin being lame, and my shoulder most painful, so quite unfit to shoot from, Dillon has resolved to go in pursuit of the grand old veteran, attended by Jim and a couple of his countrymen.

On inspecting the place where the meat, left to get fly-blown over the tributary rivulet, ought to be, I found it had again disappeared, so replaced it, elevating it on this occasion seven or eight feet above the level of the water. Crocodiles are doubtless the thieves, but I think it will puzzle these gentry now to reach their prey. I also set a gun in the outer edge of the kraal fence, in case the lioness should be troublesome at night.

Ant heaps of a conical form, from ten to twelve feet high, abound here in all such places as are safe from inundation by the overflow of the river. Anxious to discover some of the purposes to which these diminutive insects put such gigantic structures, I opened one of their sides. I found the interior swarmed with inhabitants, who were passing in one unbroken line into small holes, that apparently led into the centre of these hillocks. The entire building was most skilfully and scientifically laid out in diminutive cells, separated by passages, the partitions being constructed of the finest earth, vaulted and polished, and scarcely thicker than a sheet of paper. Certainly the rough exterior of the building did not give any promise of the masterly workmanship to be found inside. Independent of small apartments, there were found, as the exploration progressed inwards, what might be taken for large reception-rooms, while winding passages in tiers, often one above the other, threaded through the intricacies of the vaulted chambers. We are in the habit of admiring the result of the labour of bees; no doubt it is very beautiful and extraordinary, but monotonous, for one piece of comb is ever identical with another, unless it may vary in size; but the labour of these termites is far more original—in fact, it is impossible to examine the work of these small artizans and not be struck with amazement at the adaptability of the structure for the purposes for which it is designed, and the originality with which its construction is carried out. Some of these structures had a tree enclosed within its walls; could it be that this was with the intention of gaining shelter for their residence from the burning rays of the vertical tropical sun?

Snakes are also very abundant here, the most numerous being the beautiful water-viper, with bands around its body in alternate brown and copper-coloured rings; the green tree snake, not poisonous, whose principal food is small birds; two species of the repulsive puff adder, the cobra, and, last, the common green mamba of Natal. It is commonly believed that this last reptile will chase people; my experience of them leads me to believe this a fallacy, but if a human being happened to be between them and their retreat, most assuredly they will not turn aside to avoid him. Their bite is supposed to be deadly, but I have known persons cured of it by an immediate application, externally and internally, of "Croft's Mixture," the principal ingredient of which is ammonia. The mamba frequently grows to the length of ten or eleven feet; it is very active, so it behoves a person to get out of its way rapidly. There are two varieties, the green and the brown; in build they are slim, and taper to a very fine point at the termination of the tail.

An hour before sunset Dillon returned; he had

been successful, but to accomplish this end had experienced no end of dangerous adventures. But I had better tell his story as nearly as possible in his own words.

"We struck the spoor of the elephant about three miles from camp, on a sandbar by the edge of the river. The beast was evidently in no hurry, for its stride was short and regular. In places it had deviated from the sand into the forest, where it had fed for a short time, again returning to the margin of the stream. After an hour of this work, from the heat of the ordure, the freshness of the spoor, and the dampness of the sand that surrounded the tracks, we concluded that we were close to the game. Again the trail led into the forest, up a steep incline. Stealthily Jim ascended this; for some time he remained stationary, then beckoned with his hand for me to follow him. When I reached my attendant, he tried to point me out the elephant, but, although I craned my neck and looked from different levels, I could not see it. Nevertheless I was certain it was near, for I could hear, at briefly interrupted periods, the peculiar rumbling noise made by the water in its inside. After spending several minutes fruitlessly to find out the exact position of the beast, I determined, under shelter of the bank, to move a few yards further to my right. I judged that this would bring me closer to the animal and in sight of it. In this I was correct, for in front, and almost facing me, he stood. A tremendous brute, taller and more bulky than any we have killed, but his tusks, though massive, were not long. It was easy to see that he was not in an amiable frame of mind, for he was constantly shifting his weight from one foot to the other. His trunk also was everlastingly in motion, either to drive the flies off or rub his side or neck, where he had been bitten by the insects. Patiently and long I waited, hoping for a broadside shot, till I became tired of such inactivity, so resolved to see what a ball would do in the centre of the forehead, the distance between us being about twelve paces. There was a perfect opening in the underbush, thus no twig or bough could interfere with the course of the bullet, so I took a steady aim and fired. The moment I did so I ran several paces further to the right, to get out of the hang of the smoke and learn the result of my shot. It was scarcely what I expected, for, instead of a dead elephant, there was a very lively one indeed, rushing to and fro like a mad bull, shrieking with rage and searching for his foe in all possible places that an enemy could find shelter. At this time I would have taken to a tree, but could not find one large enough and with branches sufficiently low down to suit my purpose, so, taking Jim's advice, I hurried into the forest at his heels, going as nearly as possible down wind. After running about ten rods we came to a boabab tree (*Adansonia gigantica*), hollow, as they usually are, with a large aperture on one side, and a smaller one on the other. Into this most welcome sanctuary we bolted, for the infuriated beast could be heard breaking through the brush only a short distance behind. He must either have scented us through the irregularity of the currents of wind, or seen us cross some less densely covered ground we had traversed. I thought we were now safe, so took observations from our hiding-place. The elephant was roading us with as much certainty as a retriever would a wounded partridge. At length he came to the tree in which we were secreted, but supposing we had gone on, he would have passed it, when I gave him a bullet behind the eye and another in the neck. Neither of these shots appeared to do much more harm than increase his wrath, for, wheeling at right angles to his course, he charged the boabab through the centre of the smoke. The shock was not very great, for the animal had too little impetus to make it so. Still, the way that he made the bark fly, through slashing about with his tusks, told what a small chance a human being that fell into his power would have for life. By the time that I had got reloaded the elephant had backed several paces, when he again charged, this time to such effect as to make me fear that the shell of the tree would give way. The infuriated beast seemed to think that a repetition of his last manœuvre would accomplish his purpose, so commenced backing to repeat it, when I gave him both barrels in the forehead. The last brought him to his knees, but in an instant after, he was up, and charged with as much velocity as before. Fortunately, the tree stood this assault ; but it certainly did not look as if it would resist many more such attacks, so, while the irate beast backed to repeat his rush, Jim and I scuttled out of the back door and took shelter behind a meruli tree. This retrograde movement was accomplished without attracting observation, for the enemy still thought we were in our former sanctuary, so he charged it with as much vigour as previously.

"Twenty-five yards was about the distance that separated us from the elephant. I watched my chance when his head was down, slashing the boabab in his blind fury, and gave him two shots behind the shoulder. The first seemed to be well placed, but the second, in which I had not much confidence —for, being much excited, I had fired too rapidly— brought the huge animal down with a tremendous crash. His struggles to rise were terrible to witness, but each effort seemed less effective than its predecessor. The fact was that the beast's hind-quarters were paralysed, for he had been hit on the vertebræ.

"Although fired within a few yards, it took four more shots to kill the game. In fact, I thought it was bewitched, and would not die. As to head shots at African elephants, I have had enough of them to-day to last a lifetime, I am not tired of this world yet, and, such being the case, do not intend experimenting with them again."

CHAPTER VI.

A MANGY HYÆNA.

SUNDAY's report of the late affair, as learned from Jim, was out and out more exciting than Dillon's; but then a native, by the addition of his admirable pantomimic action, can always in effectiveness, beat a white man in narrating an adventure.

About an hour before turning in, the gun I had set went off. Result—a dead and very mangy hyæna, minus one of its hind feet. It is far from an uncommon occurrence to find hyænas, and even jackals, without one, or even two, of their feet. If steel traps were in use in this country, such a circumstance would not be marvelled at, but there is no such appliance known to the natives. The Bushmen's explanation is that, when these animals are detected by the lions interfering with their prey, it is thus (biting off one of their feet) they punish them for their presumption.

The first indication that we have had that we are in an inhabited country occurred to-day: about thirty natives, under the leadership of a giant, a fellow about 6 ft. 3 in., walked up to the kraal fence and there sat down. Nearly all had carosses, made from the skins of different animals, hanging from their shoulders, otherwise they were completely naked, if we except a few wild cat tails hanging from the waist, both before and behind, and feathers as head-dresses. Filthy is scarcely a name sufficiently strong for their condition, and they stank like skunks. Their arms were assegais of the lightest construction and heavy throwing sticks. Sunday did not know what people they belonged to, although he comprehended a good many words of their language. My belief then was that they were renegades from the Makalaca tribe, who had wandered thus far east to escape the control of the Matabeles. From their advent I had resolved that they should not be admitted into the camp. This they evidently did not like, nor did they hesitate to show their disapprobation of our want of hospitality. First they commenced by begging for food. This they received; then for tobacco, snuff—in fact, anything they could think of, not forgetting wire and beads. Our boys, at our request, explained to them that in return for ivory they would receive many presents; but this did not suit our visitors' views, and they became insolent. At length their chief attempted to make a passage into the kraal by dragging away some of the thorn bushes that composed the fence of the enclosure. Our remonstrances at his presumption he treated with contempt, so, if we did not assert ourselves, and that promptly, we would have the dirty wretches in our midst.

Sunday, Jim, and Umpiqua—in fact, our whole force—were standing at my elbow, and evidently wanted but little encouragement to have a go at the strangers, for each had armed himself with a stick. I cautioned our head man not to hurt the visitors too much, and then let them slip at the foe. There never was a doubt of the result, although the enemy were nearly three to one. They only stood their ground for a few moments, then broke and fled with the greatest haste into the jungle, but not before Master Jim, who had singled out the chief against whom to devote his own individual prowess, had sent that worthy representative of humanity spinning into the centre of our thick, prickly fence. Never was a victory so thoroughly successful and won with such ease. You may rely upon it, the Zulus are splendid fellows, and in fighting and hunting they cannot be equalled by any race on the African continent.

The hammering that our " boys " had given the natives did them a world of good. In a few hours they returned, first in ones and twos, then finally the whole party ; and so marked was the change in their demeanour that the alteration was perfectly marvellous. It is wonderful what a beneficial effect a judicious, wholesome chastisement has upon the people of some of these tribes ; but correction should only be administered when thoroughly deserved, and never be of unnecessary severity. But if the reader should chance to hunt in the countries where missionaries are located, he had better never take the law into his own hands, or these interesting, self-denying, self-sacrificing individuals will make it an excuse for mulcting the transgessor by a heavy fine in coin. To whom the specie ultimately finds its way we may well guess.

Now that our new acquaintances had become amenable to reason, if they had not been so fearfully dirty, their society could have been turned to many advantages, but oh! they were filthy—dirty is scarcely a strong enough term—and not improbably either the true unalloyed progenitors or descendants of the "great unwashed." The Zulus are not by any means forgetful of attending to their ablutions, but the otherwise sweetness of the smell of their bodies is somewhat nullified by the quantities of fresh animal fat with which, when obtainable, they are constantly anointing their bodies.

I have often spoken to the natives about their performing this objectionable habit; in answer they would invariably respond by saying, " Black man not smell as much as white man," and, in proof of this, inquire who could go nearest game down wind, black or white man. Of course they can; but the reason for this is that the wild animals do not dread the aborigines as they do the strangers, and it is quite natural that such should be the case, for the latter wounds and perhaps kills from distances so remote that he is almost imperceptible, while the former are only capable of doing injury when within a few yards.

But to return to the strangers who now were permitted to encamp without our gates ; of course we had to feed them, and in return for our food we resolved to utilise them. This idea was not original, but put into our heads by the sagacious Sunday and Umpiqua, and therefore is not a bad illustration of how the races treat each other.

An evening or two after our Zulus had whacked these visitors, while smoking our pipes round the camp fire, Sunday remarked in a stage whisper to his *fidus Achates*, " These Mantatees know where there is plenty of ivory ; suppose the Bass said, ' No ivory, no more meat,' you see how quick they fetch some." There was little escaped Dillon's sight, and just as little his ears, so in the quietest manner, as if the subject had not the slightest interest for us, he requested further information from Sunday. This worthy required no pumping, for he had made exactly the impression he desired, so it was resolved, as far as in our power lay, that the enjoyment of succulent hippopotami steaks, tender bits of cow buffalo, and gamey-flavoured strips of venison, was only to be obtained by purchase, and that ivory was to represent the coin. It was a day or two before our guests could comprehend our views, but they did ultimately, and did so very much to our satis-faction.

CHAPTER VII.

THE MANTATEES.

OUR visitors, whom I have called Mantatees, are doubtless an offshoot of the Bechuana race—who at one time inhabited all the north of the Transvaal— so are not Makalakas, as I had previously supposed. Now, among this tribe are to be found some splendid hunters—men imbued with all the acumen, patience, and perseverance of their neighbours, the dwarf Bushmen of the Kalihari desert, and, therefore, possess the making of just such a hunter as we found in the ranks of the new comers. He was a clean-limbed, slightly-built, wonderfully active youth, with the most accurate eye for a spoor, and, as we discovered afterwards, possessed of a knowledge of the habits of wild animals that must have made him in after years a most valuable acquisition to his kraal.

First one cause and afterwards another had confined us to the vicinity of our camp, but this inertness was suddenly brought to a close by the lad in question returning to camp soon after sunrise one morning with the information that a number of elephants had passed across the adjoining drift during the night, and were heading for the adjacent hills. Among the drove he confidently asserted that there were some big bulls, that the party were proceeding to fresh haunts, and that they assuredly were in a hurry, as they scarcely fed.

A council of war was held forthwith, and an immediate pursuit resolved upon ; but, as it was more than probable that the game would lead us a long chase, blankets and other necessaries for camping out were deemed indispensable adjuncts to our comfort.

The day was already warm and close, and threatened to be a scorcher before noon. Still, such trifles must not deter the elephant hunter from pursuing his avocation, if he desires to make his business remunerative.

The spoor was easily found ; it was so exactly what it had been represented that the skill of the young Mantatee received commendations both from Sunday and Umpiqua. Fearing that we might have to enter a country without water, canteens and gourds were filled to the bungs, a proceeding never to be neglected when entering a new country in Southern Africa.

The discoverer of the game led the way, and at such a pace that it seemed a marvel how he could so rapidly get over the ground and yet correctly follow the trail. For more than an hour our course led through heavily timbered land, then through openings, and later on into dense brush. Ultimately it required a practised hand to follow the spoor; still there was no abatement of pace, and God knows it looked to me like going on so for ever, so I insisted on a halt, not more for my own sake than for Selwin's and Dillon's.

Flesh and blood can stand a good deal when put up in the shape of a white man, but natives, when undergoing such an ordeal as the present, can endure a great deal more. Never shall I forget our respective appearances when we halted; each was dripping with perspiration, while the clothing on our backs looked as if it had been dragged through a river. Then the consumption of water that took place was marvellous. Satisfying our thirst seemed impossible, and how precious and delicious each mouthful tasted as it passed into our parched throats. The most precious wines of the most delicate vintages cannot possibly afford such delight to connoisseurs; if it does, well can I pardon them indulging to excess.

But our attendants were not idle while we were taking our rest; in fifteen minutes, or less, the spoorers returned with the information that the elephants were here and there feeding, and, consequently, not travelling so rapidly. On hearing the latter portion of this news how devoutly I uttered "Thank goodness" may be imagined.

After this halt I seemed to get second wind, which actually made me feel more fit than I did at starting ; this may have been partially caused by my hoping for an immediate introduction to the game, but that desired issue was still further off than anticipated.

The ground we had now to traverse was covered with dense bush, I should say of the average height of ten feet, and those who have shot in the colony know well what severity of labour it requires to get through such impediments. To the inexperienced it seems a hopeless task, for it looks interminable and resultless ; but perseverance, that valuable quality, will work wonders, and release you from your labours when, probably, least expected.

I have been through many, many pieces of African bush, both before and since the period I am writing of, but never in my experience traversed such a one as this. In it was to be found every variety of thorn I know of, the *wacht-embeche* predominating, which at times would so tie me up, that to regain my release, by compulsion I had to have recourse to my knife. It is not, however, so much being bound by this accursed climber, for then probably only your clothes suffer, but to have them go rasp, rasp, rasp across your face and hands, drawing blood plentifully in their progress, that is the agony.

The unclothed natives suffer from the thorns of these lacerating vines, there is no doubt ; for I have seen their limbs and bodies perfectly scored by coming in contact with them, but they seem to take it all as a matter of course, and never murmur. Is this not stoicism worthy of a Spartan?

I feel convinced we had an hour of this work, during which time we possibly covered two miles. But for the occasional assistance afforded by the late passage of elephants through this bush, our course inevitably would have been stopped.

No doubt elephants have for years been travelling this route, but if they neglect to use a passage for a short time, so rapid is the growth of vegetation in this part of the world, that it soon becomes as blind as if it had never been opened.

But, thank goodness, there is generally an end to such troubles, and we ultimately came to it, for through the bush in front sunshine became apparent in little patches, then in larger, till the country beyond opened to view, and a glorious country it was—a gradually, although rather steep hillside, covered with an abundance of dwarf vegetation, here and there interspersed with islands of diminutive trees. The beauty of the scene before us was almost a sufficient reward for all our labour, for it was charming Devonshire hills repeated in altitude and incline, only occasional clumps of trees usurped the place of grass and gorse.

CHAPTER VIII.

GAME IN SIGHT.

THOSE readers who are gluttons for slaughter are doubtless desirous of putting a cessation to what they may consider my twaddle, and wish to be brought *instanter* alongside the game. I will gratify their desire. Almost at the crest of the ridge was a string, in single file, of eight elephants. How many preceded these laggards we shall have to ascend quite a thousand feet, and get over considerably more than half a mile of ground, to learn. This task at first appeared very easy; but as we ascended huge boulders blocked the way, many apparently so loosely poised that they struck the beholder with fear, lest some rock-rabbit, clip-springer, or, more probable still, vindictive baboon set them in motion.

However, disregarding this and other dangers, *en avant* was the cry, and each and all put their best foot foremost, as it was most desirable that we should gain the ridge as soon as possible after the game had passed over it. This, the rear guard of the herd did not appear to regard as a very pressing matter, so a due amount of caution was necessary not to expose us to view. As for the wind, we did not fear any evil results from any fickleness it might choose to exercise, so great was the altitude of the elephants above us. Only those who have been accustomed to hunt this ponderous animal in a mountainous country have any idea what splendid climbers they are. The ascent that our game was now making would have been almost a stopper to an Iceland pony. Still it did not seem materially to retard their progress. At length the leader got over the crest and disappeared; in succession the others did likewise, until the turn of the last arrived. This beast was a veteran, a veritable grandfather, I should say, and was possessed of splendid ivories which fairly glinted in the declining sunlight. If I could get the consent of my companions, I resolved to become the possessor of those tusks, for they were fit trophies to adorn the palace of a king. I am able thus early to describe him so accurately, for when he reached the crest of the hill for some minutes he stood motionless, reflected against the sky and gazing into the valley beneath, as if he regretted leaving a country that possessed for him many cherished memories.

This was an anxious moment for us all, for we could not be over two hundred yards from the giant beast; however, all understood their work, both natives and white men, so in an instant each and every one was as perfectly out of sight as Rhoderick Dhu's henchmen. Slowly, and evidently with reluctance, the mammoth turned away, and by degrees the stony ridge shut him out from our view. Sunday, Jim, Umpiqua, and the Mantatee now made a rush; their start was a good one, but youth told in the race, so the last-mentioned first reached the crest, over which he peered with the caution of a professor in the art of stalking. In a few seconds the others were by his side, and did likewise, then all drew back and awaited our coming.

We wanted breath, and there was no occasion to hurry now, for the game was only a short distance below our hiding-place, and obviously ignorant of our proximity.

Our plan of attack was soon settled. I was to take the first large tusker I could find on my left, Selwin the next, and so on Dillon. Sincerely—I may say devoutly—I hoped that the patriarch would fall to my lot.

A last mouthful of water, a pull upon our belts, a passing down barrels of the ramrod to see that the bullets were home, a look at the nipples, and fresh caps placed upon them, all these necessary details performed, and over the ridge we stole. One look showed that there was a beautiful country below us; the next exposed the game, scattered through very rough ground, over which it was making a slow and obviously painful descent.

Almost under me, and not a hundred yards off, was the grand old man, and to his services I was to have the honour of devoting myself.

From this moment each attended to his allotted task, so knew nothing of the danger or successes his companions might be suffering or enjoying.

Possibly from a desire to fire the first shot, I did not approach as near my prey as I might have done; however, when I pressed the triggers I could not have been much over 25 yards from the object I aligned my sight upon.

My aim was taken for behind the shoulder, and both bullets told within an inch or two of the other. The elephant, from the position of the boulders that surrounded him, could neither hurriedly turn or hurriedly advance, and, although the wounds must have been both painful and severe, it was several moments before he could get upon more open ground. As to who or where was his foe, up to this time the poor brute seemed to be utterly unconscious, so stood dazed and utterly at a loss how to proceed. This was fortunate for me, as it gave me time to load, with the probability of giving the victim two more bullets at a very slight increase of range. Just as I was completing my capping, the elephant advanced a few paces with the intention of crossing my front; this course I had for some moments been earnestly hoping the beast would take, as it gave me a chance unseen to get behind a rock quite as high as my waist, and reduced my range several yards. As I fired the next two shots the old bull was moving slowly forward with his trunk in the air, and ears set out like studding sails on a ship—the shoulder was thus perfectly exposed.

Up to this time he said nothing, but certainly looked the incarnation of wickedness; so, hoping to bring matters to a climax, I fired both barrels. On reception of the balls he uttered a scream of pain, did not trumpet, but came hurriedly towards the smoke from my gun, which hung heavily on the ground from the want of wind. I had now to shift my quarters, and to do it very rapidly. This I managed again unobserved, and, moreover, was successful in gaining an excellent hiding-place—the lee of a very large stone, almost entirely buried in creepers. It may well be imagined how I hurried up my loading; but, just as I was completing it, the enraged brute scented me, trumpeted almost as loud as is the scream of a locomotive, and charged. Fortunately, I had placed my caps on the nipples, so was ready for the fray; so, when the infuriated beast was within ten or twelve paces, I emptied both barrels into his chest, dodged down under my stone shelter, and, watching my chance, with my figure bent double, ran for another hiding-place. The old bull on this occasion charged down hill, and had the greatest difficulty in stopping himself; but, as soon as he did so, he was round again in a minute, and returned to where I had fired my last shots, hunting behind every stone or plant that could possibly hide an enemy. At this time I began to think that I had undertaken a very hazardous task, to retire from which it was more than doubtful whether I should succeed in doing with a whole skin; but, as the situation was of my own choosing, and the enemy seemed to exhibit no intention of giving up the game, nothing remained for me to do, but to play out my hand.

Well, before I was capped I was chased out of cover. At length I succeeded in placing the troublesome things on the nipples; but so active was my pursuer, I could not obtain time to turn and fire with any prospect of seriously injuring the enraged beast; therefore I had to bolt down hill with my assailant at my heels, trumpeting with increased power. I veritably thought my days were numbered, for I felt instinctively that the foe was only a few feet off, when a thought struck me—I will practise the artifice pursued by the timid hare, viz., double, and I did so. The manœuvre was skilfully carried out; no wonder; it was the only chance I had of living to fight another day. But I had not done with the worthy old patriarch yet, for as he stumbled along in his efforts to stop himself he got both barrels in his stern, one of which shots disabled a hind leg and therefore placed the gallant foe entirely at my mercy.

CHAPTER IX.

A DISAGREEABLE EXPERIENCE.

I REACHED camp first, soon to be followed by my companions, whose success had been numerically equal to my own; but I bore the palm as to the weight of ivory taken. Each had his adventures to narrate, but Selwin's must have been more than exciting, for an elephant, after having received three shots, charged, and that so suddenly and rapidly that no chance of escape was left my companion but to throw himself into some brush and there remain until the infuriated beast left. Such means of escape are never adopted but upon the most pressing emergencies, and then the odds are that they are not successful, for an elephant has as keen scent for a man as a setter or pointer for a grouse or partridge. Sunday confided to me that Mr. Selwin would never do for elephant shooting, for " he altogether too foolish." And Sunday was right. Until his death my friend's carelessness, or rather recklessness, caused me an unceasing amount of anxiety.

My shoulder next day was in such a contused state that I was absolutely unfit to go in pursuit of big game, so I fear I not only anathematised the gun-maker who built the gun that had been the cause, but the person I bought it from as well. After all, it was the fault of neither of them, for I was shooting out of it double the charge for which it was intended.

Dillon, however, in the afternoon shot a three-quarter grown cow buffalo, as fine a piece of beef as ever I remember to have eaten. It was, moreover, as fat as a stall-fed heifer, the great desideratum in all meat obtained upon the African veldt. There one never tires of fat; in fact, you seem to have an insatiable craving for it, the result, I believe, of being almost entirely deprived of vegetable diet.

In my walk next day I selected the side of the river for my stroll. Francolins, guinea-fowl, bush-koran, and bush-pauw were very numerous. Of the two first-mentioned handsome birds there seemed to be no limit to their numbers. With the aid of a dog, a sportsman might have loaded a horse with his spoils. Spoor of all kinds of game, from the diminutive bush-bok, so common in Natal, to the towering giraffe, was to be seen wherever the river banks shelved and made access to the water easy. Up one reach of the stream that I had a clear view of for three or four hundred yards I saw at least six hippopotami. Doubtless there were many more belonging to this herd that were at the time submerged. Wild fowl were also in abundance, Egyptian geese, spur-winged geese, and Hottentot duck being possibly the most numerous, while darters sat upon every bare limb that overlooked the water, and surgeon birds ran over the floating lily leaves in eager pursuit of the water insects on which they feed. It was, in fact, a scene only to be witnessed in the tropics of South Africa, and one that, once seen, can never be forgotten.

To add to all this animal life, the river fairly swarmed with crocodiles; on one sand-bar, not over a hundred yards long, I counted thirteen of these hideous monsters, several of which must have measured over a dozen feet, while one veteran, I feel convinced, would have stretched the tape line to fifteen feet.

In Java I saw a crocodile almost seventeen feet long; it frequented the vicinity of a place where the village women were in the habit of assembling to wash their clothes, and, if report spoke truly, many were the Malay females it had carried off. At length it was captured by using a live dog for bait. After being transferred from its watery home to the commandant's garden, it was safely secured upon the lawn by innumerable moorings. Our assistant surgeon administered the saurian an immense dose of strychnine, enough, as he said, to poison a regiment, but it had not the slightest injurious effect upon the brute. Its skin, I believe, is still to be seen at the Dutch East Indian Museum, at Amsterdam. If there is one animal more than another detested by the human race, it is the crocodile, and, if possible, the hunter or sportsman hates it more than all others combined, for it is certain to carry off his dogs sooner or later. The alligator of the Mississippi has the same *penchant*. To both dog flesh is the *bonne bouche* which tickles most their far from fastidious palates.

I have forgotten to say that near camp was a tributary stream of the main river, about twenty-five yards across; in it were several fine pools, so I determined to bait one for a few days, and then try what fish it yielded. To accomplish this I procured some offal, and suspended it over the water at a deep and apparently currentless part, with the hope that it would get fly-blown, and, if so, that the larvæ would drop into the water and attract the giants of the finny race to the locality. Having sent Jim to camp for the necessary flesh, I soon constructed an outrigger, propped up by a forked stick, and when this labour was finished the darkie returned with the carrion, which was soon swung into its place, about four feet above the sullen pool. I mention this trifling matter, as a few days after it was the means of getting me into a scrape, which would have been intensely amusing to lookers-on, but was exactly the reverse to myself.

The fifth night in our camp was one of the most extraordinary manifestations of the quantity of game this neighbourhood afforded that possibly could be conceived. As soon as the sun went down troops of different species of antelope, mingled with zebras and wildebeests commenced filing past towards the ford; at dusk several parties of giraffes followed suit, mixed with buffalo, till darkness prevented our determining the varieties of game going to the water; but, in spite of night having set in, still the animals kept coming. It was a beautiful moonlight night after 10 p.m.—such a night as only to be witnessed in the tropics, so we sat late over the smouldering fire. Our boys, as usual when they have plenty of meat, made a night of it, and every now and again their monotonous but plaintive chant would rise and fall like the moaning of the autumnal wind through a forest glade. But above all the noise their singing made, there were other sounds that could distinctly be heard. These principally emanated from the river, and were doubtless produced by the hippos, assisted by the crocodiles (for they have a call like the snappish bark of an aggrieved dog), and numerous elephants enjoying their bath. From the high grounds, also, the voices of the lion, leopard, and baboon reverberated, mixed up with the plaintive wail of the hyæna and the merry, tittering yelp of the jackal. While noting all these novel sounds, and making our comments on each, there was a sudden outcry in the camp, and every native sprung to his legs and seized his assegai, then rushed from the fire into the shade of the fence, where they appeared to be engaged in an assault upon something, in which each was endeavouring to outdo his rival. No wonder was it that we were astonished and rushed forward into the crowd to learn an explanation. This we had not long to seek. An immense spotted hyæna—a most formidable brute, and almost as big as a donkey—attracted by the smell of cooking meat, had succeeded in penetrating the enclosure, but, in his hurry to escape after detection, evidently forgot the place of entrance, so got mobbed, and ultimately killed with numerous spear thrusts. This species, not to be confused with the striped, is much hated and dreaded by the natives, for it frequently carries off women and children, and has often been known to attack wounded or even footsore men.

CHAPTER X.

HIPPOPOTAMI.

As elephants had been heard to pass towards the ford in early morning, it was resolved to search for them in the woods across the river. The sun was just rising as we reached the drift, down which was passing a grand old hippo. The water was sufficiently shoal to show quite two feet of his back, so we opened fire upon him at once. I never saw an animal apparently in such a funk; but, in spite of his plunging, and the good speed he made through the shallow water, bullet after bullet hit him. At last he turned over, rolled like a log before the stream into deep water, and then disappeared. It is seldom that the sportsman gets such a chance at these animals, for they are exceedingly cunning, especially where they have been shot at, always rising to breathe, if possible, among the reeds; and when such cover is not available, then exhibiting above the surface of the water no more than the extremity of their nostrils and their two prominent, frog-like eyes. A hippopotamus always sinks when killed, but after the lapse of a few hours the carcass floats. If the stomach of the beast is only partially filled with food, this may occur in three or four hours; if, on the other hand, the paunch be full, seven or eight hours may transpire before it comes to the surface. I account for this by the supposition that in the former instance there is more room for the generation of gas.

However, we feared that our fusillade would disturb the elephants, and in this we were not mistaken. Once across the river we found spoor. The party was a small one and all bulls, two of which appeared to be giants. This the hunter learns from the size of the footprints and their shape, the indentation of the cow's trail being longer in proportion to its breadth than is that of the males.

As there was every probability that there was some heavy ivory among these gentlemen, we hurried up our pace with the hope of soon overtaking them, but that was not to be. In and out, through timber, then skirting it, afterwards along the river bed we trudged. Seldom were the trackers at fault, and when such was the case, I, for one, considered it a perfect relief. How I envied our boys! They stole over the ground as silently as spirits, and still kept up their long, swinging gait. True they were not hampered with clothes; but what could we have done in a state of *puris naturalibus?* Towards eleven o'clock the heat became stifling, and the mosquitoes perfectly dreadful. The perspiration seemed to make a watercourse down my back, and a lodging-place in each eye; but give up I would not, no, not so long as I could drag one leg after the other, and the chums held on. Fortunately, we had no difficulty in obtaining water, but time to drink it was not granted. In this dilemma I could only run forward to an available pool, scoop up two or three mouthfuls, and hurry on, or else Sunday and Jim would have been out of sight. At length Selwin, who at the moment was just in front of me, staggered, ultimately falling, when he protested he could go no further. He was almost black in the face from the rush of blood to his head, and I feard he was going to have an attack of apoplexy. A whistle recalled the spoorers, and Umpiqua darted off for water, with which he soon returned. It was marvellous what new life that draught instilled; but, for all that, our friend could go no farther, so Umpiqua was told off to guide him home.

A quarter of an hour had been lost, but that short time had given me fresh wind and renewed energy. The boys were anxious to go on, as they asserted the game was close in front of them, so once more we renewed the chase. Half-an-hour after we came on some ordure so warm that we knew that it had just been dropped, and soon after broken stems and detached leaves were found, indicating that the beasts were once more feeding, both of which signs prophesied that we might momentarily expect to see the elephants. Sunday was in front, Jim at his heels, each carrying a spare gun, while two of the other lads brought up the rear. Such was the line of march when the leader halted, bent his back, and ran for shelter behind a tree, his immediate attendant doing likewise. The game was now in sight, and our turn to complete the task had arrived. I was so blown that, to save my life, I could not then have held my rifle straight, so I sat down for a respite of a few minutes, and chewed a piece of biltong, an excellent plan in such emergencies.

At length we were ready for the fray, and joined our spoorers. They had kept their eyes on the beasts while we were refreshing, so had become conversant with each member of the herd. There were two large tuskers among them. I was to take the nearer one, Dillon the other. Jim followed close at my heels; Sunday going off in attendance upon my companion. After advancing about one hundred and fifty yards, carefully parting the bushes as I progressed, I came upon one of the elephants. He was a nice young bull, so, without disturbing him, keeping him to windward, I went on further, in search of the patriarch. A moment after my boy perceived him, and indicated his whereabouts; instantly I saw him, and he was a monster. As the beast was standing, he was almost a three-quarter turn from me, so I had to take ground to my right, in order to uncover a vulnerable place. This I succeeded in doing, but the animal appeared very uneasy and to suspect danger. However, I managed to crawl within twenty-five yards, and kneeling behind the spur of a giant anthill, aimed about a foot and a half behind the elbow, and fired. Instantly the beast charged headlong through the smoke and passed on a few paces and halted, while I slipped round to the other side of my shelter, from where I gave him the other barrel. This shot appeared to stagger the animal for a few instants ; then he seemed to recover, and again charged into the laggard smoke hanging on the ground. Jim now pushed the smooth-bore into my hand, but I refused it, preferring to take my time and reload the rifle.

The wounded beast continued to stand still, but his ears were out, while his trunk swayed to and fro, as if endeavouring to scent the nature of the hidden foe that he had to contend with. There is no doubt but that if he had made the discovery he would have charged, but I studiously kept the side of the anthill, and a quantity of bush between us. It appeared to me that I never was such an age in getting loaded ; the banded bullets would not get into the grooves without several efforts, and then they obstinately resisted being rammed home. Of course, this was the result of nervousness. At length, I was capped and again ready, so, clearing myself as much as possible from the scrub without betraying my whereabouts, I noticed that blood was coming both from the tusker's trunk and mouth; evidence, I thought, that my bullets were placed too far back, and had, in consequence, perforated the lungs. To obviate a repetition of this mistake, I resolved to shoot further forward. This I did, the result being that the poor brute tried to charge the anthill, but could not; then commenced to stagger, and finally fell with a crash that almost made the earth tremble. In the meantime I could hear a steady fire going on to the left, so hastened off in that direction. On my way Jim seized my arm and told me to look out. It was well he did so, for from the front was coming, straight in our direction, a most excited and savage elephant, judging from the manner in which he carried his trunk and had his ears set. I stepped behind a tree; the beast's trunk was in a moment after up in the air, the head was well raised and the mouth open. Into it I fired my first barrel, with the hope that the brain would be reached through the palate. For a moment the shot seemed to daze the beast, then on he came, screeching like a maniac. About five yards off he passed the tree I was standing behind, then clapping his eyes on the upturned root of a windfall, charged it full tilt, after which mad action, he stood still, as if satisfied with the revenge he had taken. Two more shots I gave the enraged beast. Afterwards he seemed more amenable to reason, but it was not till I had fired three more shots that the unfortunate yielded up his life. This elephant had evidently been wounded by Dillon before I met it, thus accounting for its temper. It was rather a small animal, with tusks of about 30 lbs. each. These were, however, beautifully matched, and unusually bent in the curve.

My comrade still kept firing, so I hurried off and joined him, as he was finishing a beast similar to the one I had just slain. He was in great glee; he had killed his patriarch, and the beast at his feet, as well as wounding another. Naturally we went to seek his mammoth. What may be imagined was the surprise of all when it could not be found. There was the crushed herbage on which it had fallen, also an abundance of blood, but no elephant. My friend cursed and swore a little, jumped around and stamped considerably; but this would not mend matters, so I tried to pacify him. This was no easy matter to accomplish, for he considered that the tusks of the missing beast weighed over seventy pounds each; their loss about as good as having forty sovereigns taken out of his pocket. If we intended returning to camp that night, it was time to start, and, although we cut across country instead of following the bends of the river, it was quite dark ere we reached home.

CHAPTER XI.

A BONNE BOUCHE.

To our surprise and alarm, Selwin had not returned. We knew that under the guidance of Umpiqua he could not lose himself; therefore there was no other way to account for his absence than that he had broken down, so it was resolved to send out a party in search of him as soon as supper had been discussed.

During our absence the hippo had floated; in consequence we were to have sea-cow steaks for our evening meal. Sunday, tired as he must have been, undertook the duties of cook, and anything more delicious I do not think I ever ate; it was like a cross between green turtle and pork, but better than either. We fortunately had with us some cayenne pepper, also some lime juice for medicinal purposes. A dash of both these relishes brought the flavour to perfection, and the quantity we both ate would have astonished anybody but elephant hunters. There was but one regret, viz., that our missing friend was not with us to enjoy the feast. However, much to our delight, he turned up just as the boys were going off in search of him. Through a badly fitting boot he had become lame : thus accounting for his delay. Of course there was fresh cooking for the new arrival, and, terrible to tell, I believe Dillon and self made a second meal. Neither the slaughter of the hippo, nor its flesh, however, laid heavy on our consciences or stomachs, for I do not believe any of us awoke from the time we turned in till the sun was high in the heavens on the succeeding morning.

Sunday started the boys soon after daylight to cut out the tusks and bring them to camp. To Dillon's joy, on their return they reported having found his missing elephant, in proof of which they brought back its ivory.

" Disabled, but not dead : " how many horrors do those four words imply to the sportsman ? for I suppose the sportsman to be a gentleman, and a gentleman to be a man of humanity. Moreover, strange and unaccountable as it may appear to some persons, the larger the animal the more barbarous appears the proceeding of taking its life, particularly in performing that part of the butchery that is denominated, administering the *coup de grâce*. It is most culpable, certainly, to permit such morbid feelings to delay you in executing this horrid task, when necessary, even a moment; for to spare pain to any created animated thing is the sacred duty of all men, and much more of the sect denominating themselves Christians, but I fear they are often the most unfeeling in this respect of any religious body in the world. The above remarks result from the following adventure with an old bull, which took place soon after the last hunt.

There stood my victim, grievously maimed, but not dead; yet I delayed the end. I had an excuse for this, viz., I was so terribly blown—"pumped," in popular parlance—that for many minutes I could not have moved from the spot on which I rested, even to save my life. Still, although in this temporarily helpless condition, I was able to witness the wonderful efforts that the victim made, either to ascend or descend the hill side, in both of which it utterly failed. Yet the poor brute showed the utmost pluck and gameness, evincing by its conduct that it was prepared to fight on to the bitter end. It was a grand picture of courage and resolution, chained as it was to the spot, and incapable of retaliation upon its destroyer. Its eyes still shot forth defiance; its ears stood at right angles from its body, while, almost interminably, it sounded forth from its trunk, now pouring with blood, a long trumpet blast of defiance. Loading my empty gun gave me time to recover my breathing, and, when that was accomplished, I was in a fit state to complete my work. No need now for caution, for the foe was, as it were, chained to the place it stood upon. Still, do as I would, exercise what chicanery I was cognisant of, the enemy, by extraordinary exertions, ever kept its front to me.

This, to say the least, was provoking, for I desired to obtain an aim at the most vital mark between the eye and the orifice of the ear. Again and again, by increased celerity of my movements, I thought I had succeeded, but, when I raised my rifle, the opportunity had slipped by. At length I hit upon a device; I lifted a stone, and hurled it almost to the foot of the wounded beast; it stooped its head to look at the novel weapon, and so exposed the vulnerable point. In an instant I pressed the triggers of both barrels, and the ponderous animal came to its knees. Now, I thought all was over, but, to my disgust, it was not so, for, with several terrible struggles and lurches, it regained its erect position; but, in these stupendous exertions to regain its legs, the injured hind limb broke above the hock, so that the persecuted wretch was in a worse strait than before. Even at this juncture it still recognised the necessity of keeping its front to the foe, and, in spite of pain and the manifold other difficulties it had to contend with, did so.

For some time I had heard heavy firing going on to my left, so I concluded that my friends were in the thick of it. Why or wherefore I cannot say, but all the natives had gone off with them. How devoutly I wished that at least one had remained by me. As the wish is father to the thought, so the desire produced Sunday. In a moment this invaluable servant comprehended my situation, for he made a rush as if to hit the elephant. To resist this unexpected charge the wounded beast turned its head from me, and in consequence received a bullet exactly where I desired to place it. A few tremulous movements of the gigantic carcass took place, then a stagger, and this tower of animal matter came down with a crash that seemed to make the hillside vibrate.

The head was a very fine one, even more so than I at first conceived, but for all this there was an alloy in my pleasure, viz., that Sunday's *beeker* was empty, so I could not obtain a mouthful of water. Now that the excitement was over I had time to consider my own state; it was most distressing, for a drink doled out even in dew drops I almost believe I would have parted with the finest trophy that hunter had ever risked his life for. The hardships that the sportsman endures who must shoot elephants are not fanciful, for they are the most severe trials of physical endurance that the human frame can be submitted to, and yet my countrymen, warned as they so constantly are, will do it, and so on till there are no elephants left to shoot.

Providence, however, was good to me that day; but this is stale news. When has she not been so? It seems more than ungrateful to give her credit for being so only on one occasion. So Umpiqua put in an appearance. Of all our people he was the one I most desired to see, for he was naturally so self-denying that if any one possessed a mouthful of water he was certain to be that individual; and he did possess it, about half-a-pint, every drop of which he willingly parted with. It was but a tumbler of water, very heated, and anything but attractive in appearance; but, never mind its looks, it tasted like half-a-pint of nectar.

The news I received of my chums was that Selwin had killed a big bull, and was in pursuit of another, while Dillon, with whom were Jim and the Mantatee, had been doing some heavy firing to the right. It was, therefore, proposed, as the shadows were beginning rapidly to lengthen, that we should descend into the valley, search for water, make camp, and light a fire, the last process having two benefits expected from it, viz., to assist in cooking and attract our comrades when their day's labour was terminated. But it will require another chapter to narrate the rest of that day's performance.

CHAPTER XII.

AN EXCITING NIGHT.

ALTHOUGH the sun looked quite half-an-hour high from the hill side, when we reached the bottom of the valley comparative darkness reigned around. Through its centre was very distinctly marked, where periodically flowed a river, and one that at certain seasons must be a formidable obstacle ; the precious fluid was, however, wanting. Umpiqua stated that he was certain there was water not far off, for there were fresh "*rhinoster*" tracks going along the dry bed westward, so if I would wait, he would go and prospect. Sunday also proposed the same plan, but started in the reverse direction. Thus I was alone in one of the most weird-like places I think that I have ever seen in my life. For amusement I will try to describe it. The channel of the watercourse was sunk about thirty feet below the banks, and these were margined with immense boulders and rocks of very fantastic appearances ; the sides of the river-bed also had an extraordinary and luxuriant drapery of many varieties and species of parasitic plants, all seeming to be incessantly on the move, thus constantly changing the face of the surroundings, and producing whispering sounds, sometimes loud, at others suppressed, that were really startling. On the upper banks of this dry course was a deep margin of trees, many of them species with which my eyes were far from familiar, and whose limbs and roots were twisted and twined in the most perfect representation of numerous pendant or gliding boa constrictors, or anacondas.

I had placed my back against a rock, and at first felt grateful for the rest, but as the final evidences of daylight died out, I unquestionably commenced to consider that I might have selected a place with more lively surroundings. However, it would not be worth changing my position now, I argued with myself, Umpiqua or Sunday will be back immediately, so hang the dismalness of the locality. This was all very well—a very proper resolution indeed—but when most unearthly noises reverberated, of whose origin I had not the most remote idea, I really commenced to feel—well, not to use too strong a term—uncomfortable. If I endeavour to describe the unknown voices that were being constantly forced upon my ear, then the reader may have a slight particle of sympathy for a matured—very much matured—man feeling just a wee bit nervous. First there was a whist! whist! whist! each whispering of caution becoming louder and more impressive, as if my silence was not only invoked but ordered; then would break in, "No you don't, no you don't," after which would come a wild hysterical laugh, such as a maniac would give vent to after he had done some atrocious action or made some most objectionable speech and thought the first clever and the other witty. Then suddenly there would appear to be two madmen, each trying to outcurse the other, when would slowly rise in the middle of their ravings, a low, plaintive, gasping call, as if it was the last earthly wail of a heart-broken woman; finally, at intervals, would come a yell, succeeded by sonorous guttural respirations, that spoke of a physique of power and an evil disposition. Added to the afore-mentioned objectionables are the notes of numerous nocturnal birds, whose voices vary from the deep hiss of the night-adder, to the solemn admonitory warnings of the most aged, irate, and objectionable of relations.

At length I heard a "cooey" to my left, soon after answered by a "cooey" to my right. I can assure my reader that I was glad, more particularly when I observed that the sky was illuminated in the direction of the first call—an indication that water had been found. Soon after Sunday joined me, and together we pushed up the river to Umpiqua, who had already formed the nucleus of a camp, with a roaring blaze close by, and a goodly pool of water in close proximity.

All that was wanting now to complete my comfort, and remove any anxiety that I might possess, was the arrival of my friends, and this, I had little doubt, would soon occur, as both had natives with them, and the reflection of the fire in the heavens would attract their attention.

The forethought of my "boys" had provided me with a meal, for they had brought with them, from my victim, the large, steak-like piece of meat to be obtained in the head of elephants, close to the eye, and is found between the skull and skin. It is considered by some a delicacy, and is certainly the tit-bit of all parts of these giant carcasses, but, in my humble opinion, to use a hackneyed expression, "bad is the best." I have tried both the foot and trunk baked; if you have no other food, it doubtlessly will satisfy hunger, but, using an Americanism, "I don't hanker after either." Possibly I may be fastidious, for I have heard many a hunter boast of them as fit to feast the gods upon. When such has been the case, I invariably concluded that his praise of elephant's flesh was made to tantalise the palates of those who had never tasted it, or had no prospect of doing so in the most remote future.

It must have been at least three hours after "gloamin" when Dillon came in; the "irrepressible one" appeared as fresh as paint, and was in excellent spirits, for he had killed two fine tuskers and seriously wounded a third, which he was most sanguine to obtain next morning. From his description of the day's operations, he had easy work throughout, no particularly dangerous animals to encounter, or no " die hards " to contend with. On his way to the camp he had picked up the bearers with our blankets and other paraphernalia, so that nothing remained wanting to complete our comfort but the return of Selwin. Some of the men surrounding me, I thought, were with our absent friend, but, on counting them over, my anxiety was much increased by learning that they were all present. Firing guns under similar circumstances is often adopted to recall an absentee, and would have been now; but what better beacon to indicate our position could be desired than the illumination the flames of our immense fire made in the heavens? The "boys," I will give them the credit to say, were all willing to go in search of the lost one; but I could not see what benefit was to result from such a course, and Dillon persisted that he would be all right and turn up immediately. " It is only a matter of time, you see; he has gone further than we have, but he is bound to see the light and come in, in no time, that is, if he does not prefer to camp out by himself."

Now, Selwin was just the person for whose safety one had reason to fear, because his courage often amounted to recklessness, and, without being particularly strong, he would undertake the most arduous and fatiguing ordeals that would conquer the most enduring. Again, if thrown upon his own resources, he was the last man to be capable of roughing, and turning to advantage for his comfort the numerous surroundings that Nature had placed at his disposal, In fact, to sum up his character, no better expression could be employed than that "he was a regular mother's boy."

CHAPTER XIII.

A DARK NIGHT.

A BLACKER night I seldom remember to have passed out of doors; in fact, it was so dense, so impenetrable, that you almost imagined you could feel it, but this was all in favour of the light of our fire being seen at a distance, so for the present the absence of our chum will be dismissed.

The earlier hours of night had been very quiet, nothing more to mark them than an occasional jackal's or hyæna's voice, and once the deep ugh! ugh! ugh! of a prowling leopard, but the passage of time was not destined to continue so monotonous. Just as I was coiling up in my blankets and had lit my pipe for the final smoke, Umpiqua said to Sunday, *sotto voce*, "rhinoster," which was responded to by a grunt of acquiescence. This was sufficient for Dillon's ever watchful ears. "Did you say rhinoster? Where is he? Where is he going?" And a thousand other queries. "To water, Bass, I think," said Sunday, with which Dillon seized his rifle, and went off into the darkness. The madness of some people is beyond explanation. Fancy going out of the camp to shoot an animal, however large, when you could not see a haystack five yards from you. However, any remonstrance against my friend's proceeding would have been perfectly vain, so I desisted, and satisfied myself by listening.

Distinctly I could hear the heavy laboured breathing of some ponderous brute, still distant a hundred yards or more. That it was advancing towards our position there could be no doubt, for momentarily the noise became more distinct. At length all appeared to be hushed. Soon, however, I noted a distinct tread close at hand which caused me to lay hold of my rifle, but, to my relief, it was the "irrepressible" who came in, vowing that "he could not see a house, although he had hold of it, so there was no use trying to shoot." Thereupon we both lit our pipes and listened. Again the heavy breathing was repeated, and, so far as could be judged, it was much closer at hand; then a pause, soon followed by some heavy footsteps, and instantly afterwards, distinctly became delineated within light of our fire the head and fore parts of a rhinoceros. This was too much for Dillon; he was up like a cricket, and fired as quick as those interesting insects can jump, and in an instant after there was a *sauve qui peut* in our camp. I ran because the natives ran, and my Irish friend followed my example. To an observer the whole affair would have been most ludicrous, for the rhinoceros was evidently as frightened of us, as we were of it, for we could hear for several moments its rapid footsteps dying away in the distance. When reassembled we both angrily enquired from Sunday what he meant by giving such a false alarm. That worthy's reply, and it was supported by all the others, even by the serious and taciturn Umpiqua, was that, he never knew a rhinoceros come up to a fire without charging into it. Fortunately for us, this one was a character apart in disposition from its race, for there was not within reach a bit of available shelter to take advantage of.

The events of that night were not yet finished, for soon after the rhinoceros had disappeared into the distance one of the big antelopes, supposed at the time to be a koodoo, took shelter in the water from the pursuit of a large party of wild dogs. The hounds, judging from their frequent complaining whimpers, seemed very loth indeed to give up the pursuit of their prey, yet did not have pluck enough to enter the pool and make an attack.* Patience, they seemed to think, would meet with its reward, so they apparently resolved to put that virtue to the test, and doubtless would have remained exercising it till daylight had not a number of buffalo arrived, who sent the *carnivora* flying; at least, so I imagined from the snorting and grunting of these formidable and irate members of the bovine family.

* When the water is just sufficiently deep to force the wild dogs to swim, the larger antelopes can beat off any number of them.

Dawn was exceedingly welcome when its advent was announced, for it is useless to deny that both were anxious about our companion; not that we anticipated anything serious happening to him, but in such a country as this, and following such an avocation as we were, who can tell when and where danger lurks? The spoor of our nocturnal visitor of last night, as soon as it became sufficiently light, attracted the attention of the people; with one accord they pronounced it to be that of the ordinary white rhinoceros (*R. simus*), which to some extent explains why it departed so hurriedly. If it had been a "keitloa" or "borèle," I should doubtless have had another tale to tell, as both these species are far more irascible and destructively inclined than the former. Not that either are to be played with at any time, particularly when wounded. Sunday says that he once saw a fight upon the Black Umphilosi between a "borèle" and several elephants, one or two of which were powerful bulls. The engagement occurred at an open water, where there was an abundance of room and drink for all. The rhinoceros was the aggressor, and soon put to flight his more peaceful and much taller neighbours. Andersson, the hardy explorer and able naturalist, mentions having witnessed a similar scene, with the same result. It is seldom a white man has an opportunity of being present at such a combat. It must, indeed, be a grand sight, and compensation for a deal of hardship and exposure. Like many other animals whose natural dwelling-place is the plains, the rhinoceros is a good climber, and will cross the most rugged hills and *kranzes*, when necessity or desire calls upon it to do so. The same is a characteristic of the Javanese species.

By sun up the whole party were under weigh, scattered in a long-extended line and facing towards the rising luminary. I kept the low ground. On my right hand was Sunday, the arrangement being that whoever discovered signs of the missing man was either to fire a shot or light a fire, making choice according to his means. It was a most glorious sunrise—a more beautiful I have seldom witnessed. The Indian Ocean always strikes me as the place to see these to perfection; and had not the gorgeous luminary just risen from her embrace? The temperature, moreover, was cool enough almost to feel bracing, while the country was simply charming.

> The wandering mariner, whose eye explores
> The wealthiest isles, the most enchanting shores,
> Views not a realm so bountiful and fair,
> Nor breathes the spirit of a purer air.

If this country could remain throughout the year as it is now it would be a perfect Paradise, for nowhere is there a greater wealth and variety of vegetation than in the bottom lands, while the hills, except on their summits, would doubtless produce the finest pasturage. As it is now, a wild beast population are almost its sole inhabitants, and for that reason I love it the more; certainly not the less. Dillon's remark to me showed that he thought very much the same. " Is it the apes you're speaking of? Shure they are perfect gentlemen, with genealogical trees as long as your arm, and are far pleasanter company than many folk you'd meet at home. One thing, I'll be bound, they never refuse to pay their rent or sleep with the pigs."

At the end of my moralising two splendid leopards crossed me on their way to some *kloof* among the hills; they were beautiful animals, and had evidently just fed most sumptuously. I thought I could intercept them in their course, but they were far too wide awake.

While trying to effect this futile attempt a solitary shot resounded from some distance off, so I hastened to discover what it told. It indicated what I hoped—the discovery of our lost companion, apparently not much the worse for his night's exposure. He, too, had killed an elephant yesterday, and severely wounded another, which he believed could not go far before it dropped. This is always the belief of those who wound big game, although they are nine times out of ten labouring under an error; so I left my friends to go in search of their missing beasts, while I returned with the majority of the natives to cut out the ivory that had fallen to my gun. This is always a disgusting job, for the carcasses become fearfully extended by the generation of gas in the stomachs, which, if pricked, emits the most fearful stench that it is possible to conceive. Of course, the actual labour of cutting out is the work of the attendants, but, for all that, it is far from a pleasant performance to superintend. We had thought the country deserted, but when we arrived at the body of the beast I had killed, we discovered our mistake, for round it was a crowd of natives of both sexes, all rejoicing in nudity, and fighting like fiends over every piece of meat that they could detach with their assegais. Their mode of operation in the art of butchering was simplicity itself. The men did the carving, and when the piece was detached, threw it to their better halves, who immediately bolted with their prize to hide it in such places as they deemed safe from the prying eyes of their sisters. All were therefore abundantly besmeared with blood and even more offensive matter, making the whole pack so disgusting to look at that, one could not help regretting that he belonged to the same genus. At first these people evinced great timidity at our approach, but the young Mantatee—of whose tribe they were—assured them of our good intentions, when shortly familiarity bred contempt, which it invariably does among savages. A climax was soon reached; a giant among his fellows, in spite of remonstrance, was resolved to carry off a tusk, but Master Jim stopped his little game by administering on his head a sharp application of *knob keerie*, which felled him like a bullock, and prevented further misunderstanding. The philanthropist may pronounce this rather a summary proceeding, but then he should remember that we were providing these half-starved gentry with tons of meat which they would not otherwise have obtained; again, that the correction was administered by a native, and without being instigated by me. That I approved of the step Jim had taken, it is unnecessary to state.

CHAPTER XIV.

GIRAFFES.

As I had anticipated, my friends, who had gone in search of their wounded game, returned unsuccessful, so we sought the camp where we had passed the previous adventurous night, and had a tolerably quiet time.

After an early breakfast I started for home, taking for several miles the dry bed of the river for my route. If you desire to learn how well your preserves are stocked in foreign wild lands, this is always an excellent plan. Before proceeding far I saw a pair of leopards, probably the same that I came across yesterday. The beautiful creatures were having a most wonderful game of romps, in which, at times, they seemed to deal rather roughly with each other. I would fain have shot one, but they were far too clever to let me get within range. Jim says they are man and wife; I should imagine sweethearts, or else the lady would scarcely be so coy, or the swain so patient. Further on I found a splendid pool, not more than forty feet square, very deep and clear as crystal. I imagine, it is fed from springs at the bottom. Whether or not, it abounded with fish of a pound or two in weight, and which are identical with the *mahseer* of India.* This is a regular drinking place for a large variety of game. During the full of the moon effective execution among the big animals might be done here from a *skerm*.

At length, with regret, we had to turn our faces to the southward, for I was anxious to get home (?) as early as possible, when Sunday, who was leading, turned and grasped my hand with an effort as if to press me down. Naturally, I obeyed this admonition, then followed him a few paces to the right, when he pointed out, through an opening in the trees, a family party of six giraffes. When these animals are not alarmed, and are feeding, they are very graceful, and as unlike your Zoological captives as is possible to imagine. Prison life, I am told, makes as wonderful an alteration in man's appearance. With great care and patience we stalked fifty yards closer, and I was about to rise and fire when my attendant gave a wonderful jump, which I hastened to follow; the cause of this was that my "boy" had almost placed his hand upon a black cobra that seemed more than disposed to give us battle. Of course, our apparently absurd conduct alarmed the giraffes, which went off at their best pace. This description of snake is, I believe, peculiar to South Africa. I never heard of it in India or elsewhere,

* This fish is called by Africanders the "big scale," but it is unquestionably the veritable *Barbus tor*.

and it has the reputation of being particularly venomous. The natives specially dread it, as they do all of its race, and no wonder, when we remember that they go about in *puris naturalibus*. However, the number of deaths resulting from the bites of noxious reptiles, cannot in Africa, in my belief, in any way compare with the fatality in Hindostan and Ceylon produced from similar causes. In crossing the upper spur of the range of hills I disturbed several koodoos and Harris-bok. Many sportsmen who have shot in South Africa are unacquainted with the last splendid animal, save by hearsay, and day by day it is rapidly becoming more scarce. In the time of Sir Cornwallis Harris—who first brought it to the attention of the British public, and after whom it is named—this grand beast was abundant within the confines of the Colony, but those who seek it now must go much further north. It stands about fourteen and a half hands high, and is of a clear black and creamy-white colour, with horns that make a clean sweep backwards, and ultimately downwards, similar in outline to those of the ibex. The base and more than half of these weapons are deeply corrugated, but the terminations are smooth and run to a graceful tapering point. When it has been much shot at it becomes naturally timid, but not so in localities where it is permitted to range free from danger, where it forms a most striking feature in the landscape from its bold, fearless look. All the antelopes of this part of the world are beautiful animals, but this one not only has this requisite, but is, moreover, a grand, noble beast. It lives in herds of from about six to ten, there only being one mature buck in the coterie. The description of this splendid creature, as given by the mighty Nimrod, Gordon Cumming, is here worthy of quoting.

"Cantering along through the forest, I came suddenly in full view of one of the loveliest animals which graces this fair creation; this was an old buck of the sable antelope species, the rarest and most beautiful animal in Africa. It is large and powerful, partaking considerably of the nature of the ibex. Its back and sides are of glossy black, beautifully contrasting with the belly, which is white as driven snow. The horns are upwards of three feet in length, and bend strongly back with a bold sweep reaching nearly to the haunches."

I should add that the Harris-bok, or sable antelope, possesses a very marked and erect mane with a tail that is strictly bovine. The specimen that I came across had evidently been alarmed by a sight of either of my companions or their native attendants, so I postponed a stalk with the hope that I should be able to undertake one at a future day with a better prospect of success.*

Early in the afternoon I reached camp; the heat

* The Boers call this animal *Swartz vits pense*, meaning the black buck with a white belly.

had been so oppressive that I was fairly done up, so welcomed a "pick me up" in the shape of some spirits and water with greater appreciation than ever I did previously that most useful of restoratives.

Many persons utterly condemn the use of stimulants. I do not at the proper time and place. Possibly this requires an explanation. When in the hunting-field—*id est*, when actually in pursuit of game—confine your libations to cold tea or coffee, but when your work is over, a stiff glass of brandy and water I consider almost an absolute necessity, especially in a malarious country. In fact, I have known more than one instance in which vertigo and fainting has been prevented by a judicious use of spirits.

Matters had gone on smoothly in camp during our absence. The Mantatees had learned to respect and fear our Zulus, so had not given any trouble, while a considerable reduction in their numbers had been made by several having departed, ostensibly for the purpose of bringing back ivory. If this should be true, it will probably make our venture remunerative.

Having had a good sponge bath, donned *pyjamas*, and lit my pipe, I contemplated with much pleasurable anticipation the ensuing rest of a couple of hours, when Sunday rushed into the enclosure with his countenance suffused with beams of delight, and such hurry in his progression that told distinctly that he had something important to communicate. So he had, for a short distance from camp he came across a black rhinoceros asleep in an open glade, and, without disturbing the beast, had come off to give me information. Although going in pursuit of this valuable prize entailed my once more dressing in my shooting clothes, and terminating my *dolce far niente*, such a chance was not to be lost, so, in a marvellously short time, I was once more *en grande tenue* for the chase. Our course led us directly from the river, through the heavy timber, till the more open lands were reached; these were skirted, through grass and brush almost up to my hips, for a distance of about two hundred yards, when my attendant enjoined upon me the strictest silence, and caution how I placed my feet down, so as not to break any of the withered boughs that occasionally occurred. From the expression of my guide's countenance, I felt convinced that the game was not far distant, so had a fear that the foolhardiness of my man might bring me closer to the dangerous animal than was desirable. In a short time we halted, and listened. All was silent to my ear, if I except the occasional utterance of an unknown bird, which had, at the same time, a most peculiar and plaintive note. A short further advance rewarded us with a view of the feathered stranger, which was about the size of our home-bred starling. In manner it was most peculiar, for every few seconds it would ascend about 20 ft., utter its call, and rapidly return from where it had previously started, incessantly chirping out its far from unpleasant notes. I was sufficiently close to remark that this bird was a dark brown colour, with black legs and feet, and light lines along the gape of the beak. Its configuration was that of the woodpecker. That it was aware of our presence there could be no doubt, for every time it made its ascent it kept its eyes persistently fixed upon our position.*

At this time I became aware that I could hear a sound that had not struck my ears before. It resembled the heavy, stertorous breathing of a very large animal when asleep. Sunday called my attention to it by placing his hand beside his ear; but this was unnecessary, for I knew of its existence minutes previously.

My guide again motioned to me to follow him. Silently as a panther stalking game we did so for several yards. Then another halt took place. My man was now all excitement; still he did not lose his self-possession and prudence, for by pantomimic action he expressed a wish that I should substitute new percussion caps for those that were already on the nipples of my rifle. This I at once did, so was ready for whatever adventure or danger was in store for us. That there was a considerable amount of

* *Pomerops niger*, Chapman; Namaqua, "Irrisor"; Rhinoceros Bird.

the latter to be apprehended I was thoroughly convinced, for there was neither tree, nor rock near, that could afford the slightest particle of shelter, if my aim was faulty, and the rhinoceros chose to attack us. However, it was a case of "in for a penny, in for a pound." I indicated to Sunday that I was ready for the fray. In a moment after he broke with a sharp, quick movement a branch of a bush, and almost at the same instant, stood before me the rhinoceros, certainly not fifteen yards distant.

CHAPTER XV.

WHO were the intruders and who disturbed the rhinoceros's slumbers the animal had not the slightest idea, but that there was danger in the vicinity the brute apparently was conscious of. The first action of the huge, unwieldy beast was to turn its head up to windward to learn if the tainted breeze could tell anything. This movement prevented me getting the shot I desired, for I had resolved to place my bullet as near to the butt of the ear as possible. After waiting a minute or two I was nearly giving up this intention, for the shoulder presented a most enticing shot, when the huge, ponderous head came slowly round, and ultimately remained motionless. As the creature's gaze was directed across our front, I pulled down my sleeve, a habit I have contracted when particularly desirous of taking an extra careful aim, raised my rifle, made due allowance for the shortness of the range, and pressed the trigger. The usual crushing sound announcing the striking of the bullet instantly followed the report, and then began a scene which beggars description, and would have been ridiculous even if a less powerful animal had been the principal actor in it.

From the moment the game was struck it commenced to spin round without altering materially its locality, at the same time squealing in the shrillest notes, alike indicating rage and a craving for revenge. This movement may have been the result of the concussion of the bullet on the brain, or it might have arisen from a desire to discover from what direction it had received its injury. I incline to the first supposition, for, if it had been otherwise, doubtlessly it would have charged into the smoke, which for many seconds hung to the ground owing to the absence of wind. All this time I had hoped to get a chance to put in the second barrel, but so wonderful was the agility that the stricken beast displayed that I really had not a chance to place a ball anywhere that I deemed to be vital. The rotatory performance now terminated; the shrill screams subsided into long-drawn, heavy breathing, and the wounded brute stood still almost exactly in the same position it had first occupied when I fired, but with this difference, that it was facing in the reverse direction.

Blood was flowing freely from the poor creature's mouth, and every respiration threw quantities of it out over the grass, so that I had little doubt but that the wound was fatal. Nevertheless, to prolong the termination of the drama would have been the grossest cruelty, and destitute of any compensating results, so I fired my left barrel, my aim being almost at the identical place of my first shot, but on the reverse side of the head. The result surprised me ; the rhinoceros, with a bound—no other words suit better—rushed forward exactly in the direction it was heading for ten or twelve strides ; the pace, for so cumbersome a brute, was astounding ; when suddenly the whole animal machinery failed in its action, and the *borèle* fell ; dead, I believe, before the carcass was thoroughly stretched upon the ground.

I got uncommonly well out of the fray, but there was just a sufficiency of danger in the whole affair to make me mentally resolve to leave, in future, black rhinoceros alone when out in the open, and no cover or shelter within reach. Throughout the whole *contretemps* Dame Fortune wonderfully favoured me, but if the fickle jade had played me any of her tricks I feel convinced I would not have lived to get out of the scrape. It is no proof of bravery to court death in the hunting-field, nor is it a mark of cowardice to use due precautions to ensure the protection of your life. Take my word for it, reader, a wounded black rhinoceros is a truly fearful opponent unless you are well mounted, and he who accomplishes its destruction on foot performs no ordinary deed of daring, unless luck should favour him, as it did me on this occasion.

There never was a less jealous triumvirate of sportsmen than our party, but for all that I had an intense desire to kill the first rhinoceros, or, in fact, the first specimen of any description of big game that fell to our lot. I knew that I was heavily handicapped in performing this feat, for both my companions were younger than myself, and Dillon assuredly much more active, so on my return journey I had quite a chuckle of satisfaction to myself over the victory I had obtained. The sun was setting when I reached camp, both my friends had returned, both assumed an air of mystery which I knew was indicative of some performance they had enacted, that would give them a crow over me. I naturally attempted to pump Jim and Umpiqua, but they had evidently received instructions to be silent, so my effort was unavailing. True, I noticed an extra pot upon the fire, but this did not strike me as strange, as it might contain a stew made from some bird or beast that our people had killed during our absence. At last dinner was served. The first course was excellent and satisfying. However, a second was produced. When the dish that covered it was removed, an odour greeted our nostrils that resembled the quintessence of musk *bouquet*. Summarily it was ordered to be removed.* Then naturally arose the question to my lips, What was it? I was not long detained in ignorance. The failure of the *pièce de résistance* to find favour set Dillon's tongue going with the information that, it was part of a splendid bull giraffe that he had killed on his way to camp. Although our palate had not

* The young giraffe cows are excellent eating.

been gratified by this addition to our larder, it in no way operated against my friend having a good crow over his success. So then my adventure with the *borèle* was told, which resulted in taking my irrepressible friend down a peg or two.

Over our nightcaps of brandy and water, which by universal consent were increased to a double allowance, our battles were fought over again, and we altogether had a most jovial night till " the wee small hours " had been reached.

Unanimously we had agreed to turn in without further delay, and were putting our resolve in practice, when a loud yell, followed by a babel of shouts, came from the Mantatees' camp outside our enclosure. In a moment all were on their feet, the Zulus grasped their assegais, we in turn seized our rifles, then demanded what was the cause of the disturbance. So many answers were made, and that in a language which at the best of times was far from being thoroughly understood, that for some time we were kept in ignorance. At length the Zulus, after a display of much patience, solved the enigma. A lioness, which had given no end of trouble during our absence, had walked deliberately into the Mantatees' camp, and had been discovered within a few feet of one of the natives, endeavouring to claw a piece of flesh out of a mimosa tree that grew in their midst. On detection, the intruder had retired a few paces, showed her teeth, and otherwise expressed hesitation whether she would depart or not. Such boldness, especially when a good fire was burning in close proximity, to say the least of it, augured for a renewal of the visit, and probable injury to some of the people.

Our approach had alone driven the lady back, but although out of sight she was not far distant, for at intervals we could both hear her breathe, and pass through the underbush. To prevent accidents similar to what now appeared to be threatened, I had strictly enjoined upon the Mantatees the necessity of constructing a high, impenetrable fence around their *kraal;* but, with the proverbial heedlessness of these people, they had procrastinated doing so from day to day. When one of them is carried off it is just possible that they will think it time to obey my orders.

A couple of days after that on which I killed the rhinoceros, just as breakfast was about to be served, the camp was put in a state of excitement by Umpiqua bringing the information that a party of giraffes were passing to the west of us, apparently with the intention of crossing the river at the ford. In a moment all were in a state of bustle—all I say, but should except Selwin, who was " laid by the heels" by a very severe attack of fever—otherwise our temporary home would soon have been comparatively speaking deserted from the desire to kill or to assist at the slaughter of some of these grand animals, the tallest and stateliest of any that dwell upon the earth. Dillon, headstrong as usual, and I, full of longing, would soon have been careering through the forest, with no greater thoughts in our heads, than that we had nought to do but to go forth and kill, however Umpiqua was of a different opinion and soon made us listen to his plans.

There is a wonderful amount of dignity in pure bred Zulus, of course they differ much in appearance, but there is the stamp of breeding upon all. It is this unquestionably that causes them to be listened to, and their counsel accepted, on such an occasion as the present. In spite of what our cousins across the Atlantic may say, there was a good deal of these very characteristics to be found among the American Indians that inhabited the western plains. The latter were, however, a much more taciturn people, possibly from their love of passing long periods of their lives in absolute solitude; the Zulu, on the other hand, is strictly gregarious and monarchical, causes that ever make him more sociable. I do not wish it for a moment to be supposed that I desire to desert my old love for the new—for in early life I spent a long period among the red-men and liked them well enough, but when I have said this I have said all—but the two races are diverse in character, for what the former lacks, is to an eminent degree developed in the child of Africa. Zulus can be and are elevated by association with the better classes of Anglo Saxons, the pure bred, unadulterated Indian degraded, and strange as it may appear, almost anomalous to what I have said, the former when properly treated will become a faithful, reliable, and happy servant, the red man never. The one willingly accepts the superiority of the European, the Indian never does so.

But to return to the giraffes. Umpiqua withstrained our impetuosity, for he had formed a plan of campaign, which in his belief was tolerably certain to lead to success and in which all his companions concurred. It should be known, however, by the reader that these animals when they go to water, unless they are travelling to new pastures and have to cross rivers in their route, invariably return after they have drunk by the path by which they have come. Trading on this knowledge, the old hunter desired us to accompany him, so as to cut off the game's retreat, while Jim and some others headed it, and so compelled it to run the gauntlet of a position on their trail, where we would be secreted. Time was an object in carrying out our *finesse*, so both parties at once started on their respective errands. Half an hour's rapid walking brought us to the fresh trail, to the leeward position of it we secured an admirable situation for shooting, distant about thirty yards from where the prey were expected to come. On the weather side we might have got much closer, but a giraffe's olfactory organs are as susceptible to the slightest taint in the atmosphere as a dogvane is to a breath of wind. This is surprising when we consider this animal's great altitude and leads one to believe that their powers of scent are superior to any beast's that wanders over these almost unknown and boundless wilds. This immense stature also gives them an enormous range of vision, while their ever restless largely developed ears, incessantly on the move, are susceptible of detecting the slightest sound.

From what I have said, it will be seen that to stalk the *camile* (Boer name) successfully requires in a pre-eminent degree all those gifts that compose the qualifications that constitute a first class hunter. There is one thing, nevertheless, that favours success in their pursuit, viz., that if possible they will invariably try to continue upon the path through the *veldt* that they have selected, but if by compulsion driven from it, then they will go up wind. This last peculiarity has its advantage to the sportsman, for it often affords him an opportunity to cut off the game and so obtain a second shot or even third.

We had not been a quarter of an hour secreted in our ambush when Umpiqua's quick ear detected the sound caused by the advancing drove. At the time that he announced his suspicions, the old hunter was lying upon the ground with his ear close to its surface. To my less sensitive organisation the forest appeared as still as death, if I except the occasional shrill and discordant cry of the crowned hornbill (*Buceros melanoleucus*) which every now and then broke the silence. For some minutes Dillon and self waited in the keenest state of expectation, still there was no indication of the approach of the quarry, and both would have considered Umpiqua's warning a false alarm had not our guide continued significantly to move his hand, invoking both patience and silence. The pantomimic actions of the Zulus are perfect, even when they do not understand a word of our language, for they convey by these means, even to the most obtuse, what they otherwise could not express. Umpiqua was a marvel, even among mighty hunters, for age had given him extraordinary experience in an avocation he loved, still had not in the slightest way impaired the acuteness of his senses or his power of enduring the most exhausting fatigue. Few Zulus of the middle or lower classes marry till they are forty, unless they have performed some wonderful act of prowess in battle or the hunting-field—for all are soldiers—and as a reward for which the king has presented them with a wife. To this lengthened celibacy I attribute these people so long retaining their activity, keenness of perception, and stamina to endure fatigue up into and even far beyond middle age.

But truce to my moralising, a faint sound strikes my

ear; it is indefinable and might result from the leaves having a suppressed conversation with each other, gradually it becomes more marked, and is sufficiently pronounced to be adjudged the answering cooing notes of numerous doves responding to each other, gradually this soothing sound dies away or gives place to the shuffling cadence that ever heralds the advent of a party of natives whose feet are protected by sandals. Umpiqua raises himself and points emphatically to the northward. Over the brush and bush appears what might well be mistaken for the masts of a wreck with any amount of hamper adhering to their tops, but this illusion vanishes when it is observed how those supposed spars sway to and fro, and then you are aware to a certainty that the ocean is not within a hundred miles of your position. At length the big eyes, well developed ears, and graceful neck with its numerous brilliant and regularly distributed spots become thoroughly defined, and I recognise that the tallest of all terrestrial animals are approaching rapidly towards our hiding place. Dillon's thin lips look set, and tell plainly that he is prepared for contingencies, in a minute—after having drawn a long respiration—I withhold my breath, and am ready for immediate work. The giraffes are in front of us, an old cow leads, then follow several matrons with babies close at their heels, finally, bringing up the rear is the *paterfamilias*, the lord of the *seraglio*. Into the second and third cows I fired; the object at which my first shot is directed drops upon her knees, but recovered and went on, while the thud answering the left barrel proclaims a second case of wounding. A material quickening of the pace of the creatures now ensued, their slow graceful walk being changed to the most rapid amble; for giraffes do not trot or gallop. I have seen them attempt the latter pace, but it is always adjudged by the sportsman when they do so, an indication that their course is nearly run. On such occasions their lengthy legs seem to go anywhere and be altogether out of their control. But at all times when in rapid motion their long tasselled tails incessantly keep moving from side to side or switch violently over their backs.

How fast a giraffe can amble is almost impossible to state correctly, for there must be of necessity some swifter than others, but I would say that I believe, on an average, they can get over the ground at a quicker rate than a mile in two and a-half minutes. Later experience has taught me that it takes a really good horse to overtake them, and then it can only be done by making the pace severe from the start. However the reader must remember that the country over which such a pursuit is conducted is never as smooth or level as a race-course, while frequently high and very stiff jumps will occur, over fallen trees and other obstacles, such as *dongas* and reefs of cropping out rock, and not the less to be remembered, the pursuer's mount is not a thoroughbred horse.

But it is time to follow the quarry. In a hundred and fifty yards one of the giraffes was found across the path dead. Both Dillon and self claimed the game, but it was discovered that it had received two bullets, each well placed, about fifteen inches behind the shoulder and a third of the way up from the brisket to the withers. Spooring the remainder of the *coterie* was child's play for Umpiqua, as the frightened beasts had still kept to the beaten game path, and over it their slipper-resembling tread was apparent. In a few moments more another victim was descried which had left the herd, and seemed to be objectlessly wandering about, while over a neighbouring swell in the *veldt* the remainder of the drove disappeared; all going strong and apparently uninjured. The death of the poor creature that was left behind was cruel work. It was apparently dazed, so there was no difficulty in approaching it, but for all this it took five shots before its towering head was lowered to the earth. At length a shudder and a heavy sigh told that life had departed; till that moment the victim had not even emitted a groan. The mute appealing eyes that gazed so steadfastly at its destroyers struck me with remorse; for several hours after its death I could not divest myself of its reproachful look. How different in this respect is the death of a buffalo, for, as long as strength remains to it, the beast grunts out defiance at its slayers, unquestionably expressing concentrated hatred and a desire for vengence. If sympathy can be produced in the sportsman's heart, and I am certain it frequently can when he is an Englishman, the death of a giraffe is always more certain to produce it than the death of a *bos kaffir*. This last is a very dangerous and always a vindictive beast to deal with, so one feels justified in killing it ; but the former is harmless, has no weapons of defence, except its hind feet, which of course cannot be used, unless the pursuer inadvertently or recklessly places himself within their reach. Four shots had at first been fired at these beasts ; three were accounted for, therefore who made the miss ? I don't think I did, neither did Dillon, *qu'en sabe ?*

CHAPTER XVI.

WEAPONS.

ON thinking over this episode, in fact, not only this one, but several other similar rencontres, I came to the conclusion that the weapons we used were not suitable for killing large game, for that they often caused protracted suffering, which could be avoided by the employment of larger bored guns and much heavier charges of powder. This theory I have since those days put into practice and have proved to be correct. At the date on which this is published, after many years of experience, I consider an 8-bore the most desirable weapon for shooting the mammoths of creation, but then everyone cannot use with comfort so heavy a weapon, for it must be massively constructed so as to admit of very strong charges being used out of it; next to it of course would come a 10-bore. It is questionable whether a smaller weapon should ever be used for slaying the *largest* game. In olden days the Boer shot them with a *roer*; they generally took bullets of four to the pound, but were always single-barrelled; however much of the recoil that might have been expected from so formidable a weapon was avoided by the indifference of the quality of the explosive power at that period obtainable. Game was not nearly as wild then as it is now, consequently by far the greater number of shots were made at comparatively speaking short range, so the result of employing bad powder was not felt; in fact, those pioneers of South African colonisation were entirely ignorant of a better material than was supplied by their traders. The *roer* now has entirely disappeared, a vast number of them having been burst by using the superior powders now common. The Boer in former days knew nothing of measuring a charge; as much as would lay in his hand was a load, and so he treated the manufactures of Curtis and Harvey and Messrs. Pigou and Wilks, when first they were obtainable; the consequences are easy to be surmised. I think an 8-bore double barrel should weigh—for this work— from fifteen to sixteen pounds, a 10-bore double about twelve, the load for the former is nearly twelve drachms of powder, for the latter from seven to eight, although I have been assured by the gunmaker who provided Commander Baker with his battery and by his near relative the late and much-regretted General Valentine Baker, that his cousin always shot elephants with eleven drachms of powder out of a gun of the last-mentioned calibre. My own experience is that from seven to eight drachms is a sufficiency, therefore I recommend it. For me, that quantity has satisfactorily performed its work; why then waste thirty per cent. of a commodity that is extremely valuable and difficult to get in those out-of the-way parts of the earth, where the giants of the animal creation are only obtainable. If not for their own safety, but through feelings of humanity, I should advise all to note well the instructions that I have given above regarding weapons.

Our tramp home was rapidly accomplished, and soon after the natives brought in piles of flesh—sufficient one would imagine to keep them for a week—till every adjoining tree was decorated with numerous joints, but these aborigines have such capacity for the stowage of food, that one night of feasting will make an obvious reduction in a large store. Many strangers from adjoining Mantatees' kraals also arrived, to whom we could not deny hospitality, particularly as the first comers of their countrymen had behaved themselves fairly well since our Zulus had giving them the drubbing recorded. From the difficulties of transport, the bugbear of sportsmen as well as of armies, the hides had to be left on the *veldts;* this was to be regretted, for it makes most valuable leather, soles of boots made from it are almost indestructible. An idea of its hardness may be imagined when I state that I have had washers made from it to go over my wagon axles and bearings on the interior of the hubs of the wheels, which, after trekking thousands of miles, showed little or no indications of wear.

About sunset, the Mantatees that had absented themselves returned; between them they brought quite 300 lbs. of superior ivory, worth at that time, close upon 100*l.* at Durban or Port Elizabeth. Since those days this valuable commodity finds easy sale at double this price.

I have neglected to mention—not from want of feeling let me assure my readers, but I wish to confine myself as much as possible to our shooting and my own personal adventures—poor Selwin is worse; he is so fractious also, that neither Dillon nor myself can control him. Of this we cannot complain, for we are ignorant of how much he suffers. I made him a large gourd full of cream of tartar water flavoured with the juice of some of the ripe fruit of the meruli tree—in colour and shape not unlike a ripe greengage, but similar to many wild fruits, by far the greater part of it is the stone—this evidently gave great comfort to the invalid.

Soon after dark the natives commenced singing; their noise, I thought, would disturb the patient, so I would have insisted on their silence, but no, he liked it! and when two or three notes of their wild music recalled the memory of an air he had known, his handsome, well-bred face would brighten up and his lips would feebly murmur out a continuance of the tune.

The music of the natives at a distance, I must say, sounds sympathetic. Night after night have I lain upon my bed and listened to it, when the distant song of twenty or thirty followers floated to my ears in rising and falling cadences of mournful music.

As the sigh of the cool night breezes wafted the sounds over the surrounding landscape, I could distinguish the voices, some deep and guttural, others shrill and youthful, and when the wind was hushed the sounds became indistinct, suddenly to burst forth again in its wild harmony, like the rising and falling intonations of an Æolian harp.

That night I did not attempt to turn in, for I knew full well that I could not sleep, so sat over the fire smoking more than was good for me, still when the first lines of light appeared in the eastern heavens, I was taken by surprise that daylight was so close at hand. Some of the natives were still eating and others still singing, when suddenly there was an outcry among them, and I jumped from my seat, and hurried to know the cause. I would have given more than a trifle to have had my rifle in my hands, for not fifteen paces from me passed a lioness —doubtless the lady I have alluded to before—at a slow measured walk, with a joint of meat close on 50 lbs. weight in her mouth. Although the fence of our *laar* was between us, she distinctly saw me, which neither disconcerted her movements nor hurried them. The brute certainly evinced displeasure at my proximity, but it was only denoted by the drawing up of her lips, and a fierce fixed stare. I hurried for my weapon, but when I returned it was too late, nor was there yet light enough to follow up the thief, so the marauder was permitted to escape unpunished. I learned afterwards that she had put in an appearance several times previously during the night, and that on one occasion she had been greeted with a shower of knobkerries, but an animal of her size and strength could well afford to laugh at such weapons.

CHAPTER XVII.

THE CYCLONE.

NEXT day, about three in the afternoon, we had a terrible tropical storm. It was what sailors dread so much and call a white squall. Our huts were in a moment levelled to the ground, and in one place even the fence of the "laager" was prostrated. It was accompanied almost uninterruptedly by heavy thunder and lightning ; the flash and report for some time so rapidly succeeded each other that the vortex of the gale could not have been far distant. It commenced with a sudden burst of wind. For some time before the clouds were in rapid motion, crossing and meeting each other, while along the face of the nimbus a heavy vapour fell. This is much lower than the rain cloud, and the closer it comes to the earth the more violent will be the gale indicated. The gathering darkness rapidly increased, the trees swayed to and fro, and when they came in contact produced shrieking, grating sounds, not unlike the groaning of the bulkheads in a sea-lashed vessel. The lack of light, the erratic and vivid lightning, the hoarse reverberating claps of thunder, with the screeching wind, everything combined to overpower the observer with awe. You gaze around you upon all that is terrible and threatening, all looks ghastly and unearthly against the ink-black background; the floodgates of heaven are truly open, for the rain descends like an avalanche. When at its height, the roar of the tempest drowns all other sounds, while rivers of water course over the formerly dry ground, undermining the drainage gutters you have made, and carrying away before its unrestrainable force everything that is movable. Although the tornado lasted little more than an hour, we were all drowned out, and looked most miserable. Poor Selwin; I could not help feeling for him, his exposure to the ruthless blasts and scourging rain made my heart bleed; but, strange as it may appear, it did not affect him as much as could have been anticipated. However, I feared the reaction; former experience told me that it had to be dreaded.

The termination of the hurricane was as rapid as its commencement, and, but for the ruin it had left behind, those even who had experienced its violence could scarcely believe that it had taken place. The river is now out in flood, possibly to-morrow it may have subsided sufficiently to be fishable; if so, I shall try my luck with rod and line. I love the gentle art, whipping a stream with fly for trout or salmon is the poety of recreations, but on the coming occasion I shall have to stoop to the use of bait. Bah! it is a sad come down from the other method of practising this graceful and entrancing form of the sport. But that a change of diet is desirable, I doubt much that I could be induced to demean myself by doing it.

The first thing to be done was to restore our camp to a habitable state. This was not a difficult task with able and skilled hands to work, so a new hut, more ample in space, and I might add more graceful and desirable in shape, soon occupied the space of our late residence. Next came the surface drainage to be reconstructed; although this is only a ditch a foot in width and nine inches in depth, still it is a most important factor to the comfort and sanitation of the residence. To Jim and two others I detailed this duty. In a minute after receiving their instructions they were in a state of nature, so no deception, no tailor's artifice, no actor's trickery of making up or padding figures were possible to exist. When they stripped off their clothes—to wit, their *karosses*—at their work they went, and I actually envied them their ease and comfort in their unfettered condition. They had better use of their limbs, were not impeded by tight clothing or corn-creating shoes, while in an economical point of view they far eclipsed all civilised working men I know of. Before me laboured these Apollos, as perfect in symmetry and development as the classical god himself. These men are the result of being the descendants of perfectly matured human beings—men of forty years of age and upwards, and women who had about reached the end of their teens. Truly the Zulu kings knew how to produce a stalwart race, whether for defence, invasion, or capacity to endure fatigue. Chaka and Dingan adopted exactly the same course in this respect as Cetchwayo in his time has followed. Truly these mighty potentates were wise in their generations, and set an example that might well be followed in our beloved home. It cannot be denied that the artizans and lower classes in England, taking the population of our manufacturing towns and capital as examples, are gradually decreasing in stature and stamina, and why is this the case may be well inquired? The answer is not far to seek, viz., the appalling frequency of marriages between immature representatives of our race. Finally, immorality scarcely exists among the Zulu people; can we say the same of Christian lands? For years I have thought, and the longer I ponder upon the subject the more convinced do I become, of the great benefit that might accrue to the Empire from enlisting five to ten thousand of the flower of the Zulu race for service in India. If such was done, we should then have in our own distant dependency a force that could ever be relied upon, whom Tartar, Cossack, or Muscovite would never be physically equal to, men who could love, honour, and obey those who were placed in superiority over them, and would be loyalty personified to the throne to which they had given their allegiance. We have done Zululand most terrible wrong; by the means I propose we could partially recompense this nation for what they had suffered. Moreover, those of this stalwart, grand people who returned to their homes, after completing their allotted term of service, would have their pensions to live upon, which would circulate money, the possession of which, with their former experience of life, would produce wants that could not fail to be a stimulus to trade, and an increase of revenue to our African Colonies.

I trust my readers will excuse my having laid the rifle aside for a few minutes. and departed from the description of the ways and habits of wild beasts for a few words upon the human family, for, after all that can be said and done, they are the most interesting animals in the Creation.

CHAPTER XVIII.

DILLON'S DEPARTURE.

THE day after the storm more Mantatees arrived at our camp; they not only brought several fine tusks, but information that elephants were exceedingly abundant about four days' journey to the north. Now our locality seemed to have become deserted by these mammoths, so it was resolved that either Dillon or myself should visit the new hunting grounds with an escort of several of our Zulus. Selwin's illness prevented both going, and my desire was to remain with the sick man, for I had more experience in such matters, and, I thought—excuse egotism—more patience than my companion. I dare not tell Dillon this, in case he should consider that I was casting a slur on his warmth of feeling, and attachment to his friend, so we resolved to decide who was to hunt, or was to remain at home, by the simplest of all means—" odd man out." Providence favoured me, so I won, and the " irrepressible " took his departure in the afternoon.

The details of a sick room are not interesting, and the reverse of lively reading, so I will not narrate them. However, I may state that I could not disguise from myself the fact that, my friend was seriously ill.

I had no time to be lonely, for there was lots to do about camp before the sun went down, not the least important of which was washing all our dirty clothes. These had accumulated from constant postponement of what is ever to me a most disagreeable job. A hunting trip to Africa will cease to make husbands wonder why the household is always upside down on washing days, and not unfrequently his wife fussy and out of temper. However, I will give an invaluable hint to those who choose to follow in my footsteps or do as I have done. After having thoroughly cleansed your dirty apparel, rinse them finally out in clean water, in which a dessert-spoonful of essence of pennyroyal has been mixed. Few insects can bear the smell of this extract, although it is far from objectionable to the human family. Moreover, it is an excellent disinfectant.

Over the camp fire that night, with Sunday's assistance, I manufactured a fishing rod that in strength would have pulled out a porpoise. On it I lashed rings, and a cross piece to the butt to serve as a reel. The whole being constructed of cane, it was remarkably light. For line I had about fifty yards of hard twisted hemp, almost as thick as an ordinary lead pencil, and much resembling whipcord in fabrication. My hooks were the largest and strongest salmon size, while the leaders were made of four ply of ductile brass wire, out of which the temper had been partially removed by heat. Of course I expected to find mammoths of the fish family in these unknown waters, so prepared for all contingencies. After an unusually quiet night, for the majority of the Mantatees, smelling an abundance of elephant flesh in prospective, had gone off with Dillon's party, I adjourned to the pool which I have earlier spoken of as being baited to attract fish to its neighbourhood. The water was exactly that colour which the plebeian worm fisherman would select to make a heavy basket of trout on one of Caledonia's streams. Moreover, the flood had subsided till the water was within its normal boundaries. For bait, I had fat of giraffes and grasshoppers, fine, lusty fellows, about three inches long. On plumbing the water, I found the depth about fourteen feet. While perfecting my arrangements, Sunday, under direction, distributed a quantity of ground bait, composed of finely-chopped flesh, mixed with clay. That fish were in the vicinity there was no doubt, for they came to the top and fought like savages for any fragments that remained near the surface. The sight was cheering, to say the least of it; so I contemplated with satisfaction the sport in store for me.

After these details, and by them it will be seen that I took every necessary step to insure success,

I will proceed to relate the result. Having cut a piece of fat about the dimensions of a mature tobacco worm—three inches in length by a quarter of an inch in breadth—I inserted the barb through one end, wound the remainder of the bait round the shank of the hook, then passed the bait again over it, leaving an attractive fag end. This glistened magnificently in the water as long as it could be seen; in fact, it showed as much as if it had been rubbed with phosphorus. All was now expectation; the float remained stationary, or circled round in abbreviated circles. At length it commenced to bob up and down, then disappeared suddenly, as if intent on diving to the other side of the river. I struck hard and sharp, had a few minutes' resistance, and landed a barber (*Silurus*) about ten pounds in weight. Again the same formula was repeated with the same result, only the prize was larger. At length I hooked and secured a thirty-pounder. In spite of the strength of my tackle, I had to exercise a certain amount of forbearance in its treatment. The struggle was a long one; in it was displayed none of the dash of the salmon, but it was characterised by a dogged resolution that deserved commendation. Several times the victim was brought to the surface, but it had a marked objection to dry land, so dashed off again for its favourite retreats. If there had been any submerged roots or trunks of trees, I must have lost my fish, but the place seemed to be tolerably free of such abominations, so I ultimately secured the mammoth. It was a well-fed, thick beast, of the same species as formerly secured, and apparently in the height of condition, and, but for the large flat head, was in no other respect objectionable in appearance. I now produced my hunting knife and split my trophies, removed the internals and vertebræ, which were thrown into the stream to act as ground bait, and Sunday started for camp with the proceeds of the expedition, previously having received instructions to place a sufficiency of the fish for the next meal in a stewpan, over some embers, and then return to me.

My servant having left, I recommenced angling, but, to my surprise, not a bite did I get, not even a nibble. This was remarkable, as formerly, scarcely had the bait descended to the vicinity of the bottom, when the cork indicated that there was a hungry claimant for terrestrial honours in its vicinity.

The day was pleasant, a soothing breeze agitated gently the surface of the water, the rushes, and tree leaves; thus the mosquitoes were not out on the prowl, so I got dozy. However, I was not too much asleep to discover that my cork had disappeared. Springing to my legs, I struck very hard, I fear savagely, and immediately afterwards I could feel that I was fast in something; what on earth it could be, I wondered, possibly a crocodile or hippo, for the weight and opposing power was tremendous.

Giving the unknown the butt, placing as much check on my line as I dared to, seemed to serve no good purpose; the fish, or whatever it was, went as it liked and came as it chose. "There was no 'darned' nonsense about it, it knew its rights and privileges, and was bound to have them, for it was a true republican fish, in spite of 'Johnny Bull' claiming one half of the river," as a "down Easter" once remarked to me, when fast in a large muscanonge, while fishing among the Thousand Islands of the St. Lawrence.

Now my present foe, though less active than the American, had a way of its own that was most confirmatory of its power and resolution. I could not help feeling a certain amount of timidity that my hook would break, and little could its maker have been to blame if such had occurred, for who on earth could contemplate the ordeal it was being put to; but this mischance did not take place, the metal proved itself well tempered, and quite equal to the emergency. I commenced to feel fatigued, for there was no excitement in my work, only a constant dead, heavy drag. The heat had now become oppressive, the breeze had exhausted itself, and the mosquitoes had forgotten their lethargy, so I hoped with no little impatience that Sunday would return, but that worthy seemed in no hurry to put in an appearance. An hour thus passed—an hour that appeared to have far more than sixty minutes in it—when I was hailed from above, and soon after my valiant henchman was by my side. The situation was explained, and a council of war held in regard to our future proceedings. Thus it was resolved to detach the line from the rod and drag the unknown ashore.

The first part of the proceeding took but a short time to accomplish. Then taking the line hand over hand, I tried to draw the captive on land, but this did not accomplish the results anticipated, so I turned myself into a draught animal, placed the line over my shoulder, and clambered up the bank. At first my effort was rewarded by a violent shaking of the tackle, then the steady strain told and I slid out upon the bank—what do you think? Well, give it up. Not a fish, but a river turtle, quite half a hundred pounds in weight. This was a prize, indeed. As soon as I beheld the beast it recalled to my memory feasts on succulent terrapins at Guy's Hotel, in Baltimore, Maryland, and feeds equally to be remembered on river turtles in South America. Thus terminated my first exploit with rod and line in this part of South Africa, and I would further add that the last capture made, proved quite as delicious as any of its *congeners* across the Atlantic.

Selwin much the same—possibly weaker, certainly not stronger; but his having fought the fever thus far so valiantly, gives me hopes that, he will ultimately shake it off. For him I made some turtle soup, which he retained on his stomach and apparently enjoyed. This was a blessing. However, I wish he would not at times wander so in his mind; but so it is ever with those that have African or Indian jungle fever.

CHAPTER XIX.

A CRAFTY OLD BUFFALO.

LIFE in camp being far from lively, I gladly availed myself of the excuse to leave it for a few hours, because meat was scarce and buffalo had been seen a mile or two distant. Of course we had fish, but Zulus will not touch it, and Mantatees showed no predilection for it as an article of food.

I had scarcely left home a quarter of an hour when I espied an old bull looking out of some reeds. His head was only visible; doubtless he had just risen from his mid-day siesta. The beast evidently took a lively interest in our progress, particularly as the course we were pursuing would have brought us in his close proximity; but as I neither desired tough beef, still less being tossed, I gave the gentleman a wide berth. This afforded my followers great satisfaction, for there was not within reach a tree, bush, or rock, behind which they could secrete themselves. That the old villain meditated mischief there could be no doubt; it was therefore fortunate that we had observed him in time. As often as not the aggressor, the Cape buffalo is certainly a most formidable animal, and as the heavy bases of his horns nearly unite over the forehead, it is almost impossible to kill him with a front shot.

On passing between two dense clumps of rushes, a three-year-old cow, fat as a stall-fed heifer, trotted into the open at a distance from us of fifty yards, where she stood broadside, in evident wonder at the unknown creature before her. The first shot knocked her over, and the second, at short range, terminated her career, but not before she had grunted out her displeasure, defiance, or summons for her comrades to come to the rescue. As the last it must have been taken, for inside the reeds we could distinctly hear the heavy tread of approaching animals, so deeming precaution necessary, we all took to our legs, till we gained the shelter of some giant water rushes. Considering myself safe, although I had not run over a hundred yards, I turned round to see if I was pursued, and so saw the performance of one of the most extraordinary exhibitions I ever witnessed. In it there were upwards of a dozen actors, each of whom apparently tried to do as much mischief as possible to his neighbour, or whoever came within reach. Then all would cease their violent exercise, smell the carcass, especially, it struck me, in the vicinity of the bullet holes, when, bellowing, bucking, and kicking, the same wildly enacted vicious battle would be repeated. This was not the result of grief for the loss of a companion, for frequently one or other of the combatants would endeavour to toss the carcass, or pierce it with his powerful horns. While the drama was at its height we left, not being at all solicitous of being discovered by such powerful, quarrelsome beasts, especially when they had worked themselves into a delirium of temper. I once witnessed on the prairies of the great West a similar scene—but far less effective—among some semi-wild cattle, thus showing that, the characteristics of the different species of the oxen family are somewhat similar, although they reside in portions of the earth so very far apart.

I have deprecated firing a front shot at the head of a buffalo; it may, therefore, well be asked, where would you aim when shooting the African species, with the best chance of immediately rendering it incapable of mischief or to produce instantaneous death? Through the heart, well down, below the shoulder, near the kidneys, or directly in front, about the junction of the windpipe with the body, provided the head be raised. These animals, when charging, do not put their heads down until they are within striking distance of their intended victims.

Between the eye and ear is so protected by the horns that there are few positions in which the game can stand that will expose it to be aimed at; but if such a chance should occur, let the sportsman avail himself of it, for a bullet placed there is immediately fatal. However, such shots can only be made at close range and when the animal is not in motion, for this is an extremely small mark to shoot at.

Having noticed immense numbers of aquatic birds flying south-west, I thought I would explore in that direction. The reward was to discover a large lagoon, or backwater, apparently very shoal and shut in on all sides by a deep fringe of lofty reeds. On bare banks of mud and sand rested numerous giant crocodiles, while even almost among them, far as the eye could reach in any direction, were thousands of waterfowl. It was a scene that once witnessed would ever after remain engraved upon the sportsman's or naturalist's memory. As long as I did not approach closer than five-and-twenty yards of the birds, they paid but little attention to me. Obviously they were quite unacquainted with the destruction firearms could deal among them. To see the result that a report from a discharge would produce, I emptied a barrel into a crocodile. The consequences were wonderful, for thousands of wings took flight at the same instant, producing a roar like thunder, and in a few moments after the air was filled with innumerable figures, sailing round and round on silent, wide-stretched pinions, the predominant clothing of all being the purest snow white. The poetically inclined might have compared them to angels, but their harsh, querulous voices soon dispelled such a figurative illusion. The *máhem*, or crowned crane (*Ardea pavonia*), the Stanley crane (*Crus paradisea*), the white stork (*Ciconia alba*), and African marabou stork (*Ciconia argala*) were most abundantly represented. The two first-mentioned are beautiful birds, but I award the palm in grace, beauty of colour, and *tout ensemble*, to the máhem (colonial and Boer name), which is easily tamed and makes a most interesting pet. When it has thus been domesticated, it can be suffered to go at large. During the day it will avail itself of this liberty, and take long flights into the *veldt*, mixing freely with its wild brethren, but always returning to its owner's domicile at sunset. It ever appears to me to have a great partiality for children, with whom it can safely be trusted. The marabou is not an attractive bird, but it gives good service to the human family as a scavenger about farms and kraals. All of the storks and cranes, with the exception of the last, are *piquant* food, a steak from their breast being particularly juicy and of excellent flavour. All who have travelled extensively in the Western States of America know with what justice a sand-hill crane steak is deemed a *bonne bouche;* but, in spite of this reason, I consider it a great pity to shoot them, except in cases of great emergency. The darter (*Plotus*) has always been regarded by me as a mysterious bird, uncanny and perplexing; the manner it swims, with its body entirely submerged, and nothing but its long and tortuous snake-like neck projecting from the water may cause these suppositions; however, whether it be afloat or ashore, it really has an unnatural look. As it was now nearly sunset, thousands of other birds of similar species to the above-mentioned continued to arrive. These doubtless had spent their day on the open terrain or river side, but made the bayou their resting place at night, from its shallowness and want of current. However, it must not for a moment be imagined that they pass the hours of darkness inert, standing on one leg; for such is not the case, all feeding at intervals during the night. Probably, in that portion of the twenty-four hours (night), the most active bird is the slender billed spoon-bill (*Platea tenuirostris*), a graceful slim-bodied creature, but looking strangely disfigured by its unsightly head appendage. However, the clouds are banking up in the east, and only a few lines of the most brilliant orange colour remain in the distant west, so home must be sought, for darkness in the tropics sets in with no laggard steps—a home around which many pleasures can be derived, but these are sadly marred just now by the illness of my companion, who has long endeared himself to me by his gentle yet manly ways.

We had scarcely commenced our return journey when there was an extraordinary amount of excitement and animation among my attendants

—for several Mantatees had joined me soon after I had shot at the crocodile. The cause was a large snake crossing our path. The reptile, I think, supposed itself mobbed, therefore showed fight, and looked very much as if it could and intended to do mischief, so I put a bullet through its head. Soon after it was hacked in pieces, the Mantatees taking home logs of it, doubtless to feed upon (I use the word logs, as the middle of the carcass was greater in circumference than the upper portion of my thigh, and looked very much like blocks of wood). I think the creature was over twenty feet long, and unquestionably belonged to the *constrictor* family. Its markings, shape of head, and general contour were exactly those of the rock-snake of India and China. [This estimated size is far from excessive in this species, for I remember one being killed at the back of the Murray Barracks, Hong Kong, nearly equal in dimensions to our late antagonist, and of encountering another at Kowloon, which my dear old friend Mr. Duus and self failed to stop, although each had fired into it a charge of No. 6. The provoking part of this adventure was that the brute took off with it a domestic fowl, that it had seized in the vicinity of some of the adjoining coolies' huts. I am under the impression, from this circumstance and the examination of the teeth of many others, that once this species takes hold of its prey it has a difficulty to release it, from the points of all the teeth being turned inwards towards the throat.]

That a reptile as large as the one I have just encountered could kill a man there can be no doubt; but that it would undertake to do so I very much question. Moreover, if a human being was armed with an assegai or knife—unless his arms were bound to the side of his body the moment the attack was made—he would have little difficulty in releasing himself. Their food unquestionably is the smaller mammals that frequent their habitat, chief among which I surmise to be the young of the grys-bok (*Calotragus melanotis*), ourebi (*Scopophorus ourebi*), and the mature yet dwarf species, the beautiful, graceful, and timid little bosch-bok. Larger and more powerful animals I feel convinced would break away from such an assailant at the first onset. I do not mean to say, however, that an occasional victim is not made of mature beasts as large as the springbok.

Their usual manner of taking their prey is to keep watch from the bough of a tree over the paths frequented by the game when going to water, but I am far from certain that they do not also make captures by their powers of scent. This surmise, if such it should be considered, I have formed from the following incident. When shooting one day along the Indian Ocean washed shores of South Africa, a half-grown *inchalla*, familiarly called a reed-buck, crossed me. I did not fire at it, as its manner was most peculiar; in fact, it looked dazed and quite uncertain in which way it was to go, at the same time uttering a peculiarly plaintive call. Soon after it was followed by a large snake, pursuing its course with unusual velocity. I regretted afterwards that I did not wait to see the *finale*. My dislike to reptiles caused me to give this one a couple of charges of buck-shot, which effectually finished its supposed bloodthirsty intentions. Now, if this serpent was in pursuit of the buck, which I strongly suspect it was, it could only have been caried on by scent, for its head was close to the ground, and the surface it traversed was covered with grass and brush many inches high. The whole features of the incident struck me at the time as exactly resembling what I have often witnessed at home, a weazel or stoat pursuing a rabbit or hare, and there is no question that the first-mentioned animals do so by nose.

CHAPTER XX.

NOT UNATTRACTIVE HARMONY.

It was dark when I reached the camp, and the night threatened to be both stormy and wet. The nocturnal prowlers were out in force—which they always are when a change of weather is threatened—for their voices constantly kept breaking the silence, to be reverberated back from *kloofs, copjes*, and rocks. There is a wonderful amount of mysteriousness about these sounds; familiarity informs you that animals produce them, but where the brutes are, their numbers, and their intentions, you are perfectly ignorant of. There is also a far from unattractive harmony in the blending of their voices, and a listener might almost suppose that this was studied.

For instance, the jackals will strike up their merry, tittering *alto* bark, then the hyænas join in as *tenors*, while the *basso profundo* of the lion, in fitful gusts, is added. The hyæna's notes at such times are not disagreeable, being a protracted call, almost verging on a deep whistle; but when they are fighting or wrangling over their prey they can make as diabolical a row as it is possible to imagine.

CHRISTIANISING THE NATIVES.

In the wilds of Canada and the Maritime Provinces there is a little rodent that makes a noise similar to the clanking of a chain. Hence it is called the "chain mouse." While camped out on the great and grand Western Continent, when in pursuit of moose and caribou, I had often heard it, but long was ignorant of what produced the strange sound. At length I discovered it to be an insignificant—as far as size is concerned—rodent. Here I frequently hear an identical metallic clink. I have not yet succeeded in capturing the producer, but have little doubt but that it is a relative of the family across the Atlantic. For the study of natural history I think there is no land existing, to be compared to tropical Africa, yet, strange to say, how few persons, thoroughly conversant with this fascinating science, visit it. It cannot be the distance that prevents their going there; probably it is the danger that is supposed to beset the European as soon as he passes beyond the boundaries of civilisation. For my part I think these dangers overrated, for I would far sooner trust myself among the African heathen than I would place myself in the power of home-bred roughs.

Making Christians of these aborigines certainly has the immediate effect of spoiling and injuring them, for it causes them to become dishonest, ape the vices of the white man, and eventually unhappy and discontented with their lot. Whatever the

K

result may be in the very far future, when very many generations have, so to say, been educated up to a knowledge of the benefits derived from our religion, of course it is impossible to say. Again, the class of men who are generally sent out to convert them are those who are most unfit for the calling; persons ambitious of authority, and power, to gain which they cater to the ambitions and avarice of the chiefs, and, sooner or later, succeed in bringing about a hatred of one race for the other, as well as placing impediments on trade, and not unfrequently closing the routes of travel through the country. These people ultimately return to their native land rich, and abundantly supplied with mock modesty and sham enthusiasm for their calling. Two exceptions only have I met to this severe stricture on the missionaries: the one came to the country, comparatively speaking, in independent circumstances; the other was a Lutheran, and of Danish birth. Whitechapel, Seven Dials, and the slums of Westminster are the scenes adapted to the labours of those who wish to make converts, and there is plenty of scope at home, God knows, in which to exercise their 'prentice calling. I am aware that these sentiments are different from those I entertained a dozen or more years ago; but should not a man profit by experience? and experience is answerable for this change. Let the money that now, in such vast quantities, is being sent abroad to christianise the heathen be retained at home for the benefit of our own infidels and criminals. Till our gaols and penitentiaries are empty, our foreign missions are nothing more or less than a mockery and a flaunting presumption. I know men that annually give immense sums to foreign missions, and would sternly refuse a dollar, yes, even a cent, to forward home work; charity truly, in such cases, does not commence at home.

I regret to say that Selwin is worse, much worse; I cannot disguise from myself, try as I will, that he is dangerously ill. What would I not give to have Dillon here; it would have much reduced the great responsibility of my position. Before I left Selwin to-day, he professed to be much better, and insisted on my going out; now, on my return, he is *in extremis*. Pain he appears to have none, but incessantly he keeps talking unintelligibly; I imagine of his home life, or scenes of his boyhood. About four in the morning he passed away so gently that at first I thought he had gone to sleep. It was a long time before I could convince myself that I was alone with the dead, for his features wore their old, familiar, intelligent smile. Without agony he died, and I fervently thanked the Almighty for this blessing.

Up till then the night had been stormy and wet, dark as Erebus; then the tempest howled. The interior of the hut was lighted by only the faintest flicker from a lamp, the surroundings were fearfully depressing; still I could not tear myself away from them.

> By many a deathbed I have been,
> And many a sinner's parting scene,
> But never aught like this.

I do not mind confessing it, I shed tears. Talk not of grief till thou hast seen the tears of warlike men. It appeared that I was not to be left alone in my sorrow, for, scarcely had death closed poor Selwin's eyes, when a shriek so wild and despairing rent the air, that I sprang to my feet, seized my rifle, and rushed forth into the darkness. The fires were all out, the rain had extinguished them, but the voices of my Zulus soon led me to where they were. As I suspected, so it turned out to be. A lion had carried off one of the Mantatees. A rescue could not be attempted without fire, and what an age it seemed to take to produce it. That the victim was dead I could not doubt, for his voice was silent, and silence proclaimed death. We all know the truth of the adage "the more hurry the worse speed," and here it was most provokingly verified. For what appeared quite an age, nothing could be induced to burn, so saturated was all inflammable material by the heavy rains. At length I had to return to the hut where the corpse lay, to procure some of the dry grass and brush that formed the groundwork of my couch. The feeble lamp glimmered in its resting-place, but threw sufficient light upon the face of my friend, so as to distinctly reveal his features. On them still rested the same sweet smile. It seemed to me to rob death of half its victory. However, I could not delay, the dead must be forsaken for a time, there still being a possibility of saving a human life. At length a blaze was obtained, which was transferred to sticks and boughs, and we were ready to proceed on our search.

To those unaccustomed to savage life let me say that without the assistance of torches we could not have gone fifty yards into the jungle, from fallen trees and intertwined creepers impeding our progress. Moreover, I should have been placing my own and followers' lives in jeopardy by so proceeding, and felt that such a course could not be justified, for it must be remembered that the homicide could see our position, although we were in unfathomable darkness.

CHAPTER XXI.

A TRYING SEARCH.

A PATIENT search rewarded us with the discovery of the spoor, but after following it for a hundred paces or more, it became entirely lost. However, we were confirmed in our belief that, so far, we had followed the right course, for on it we picked up the poor lad's girdle of cats'-tails, evidently dragged from his body by the thorn bushes. A little further we discovered drops of blood upon some prostrated herbage, a clear indication that the murderer had here rested with the victim. Another compulsory halt was a great source of disappointment to my followers. They, as well as myself, knew the urgency of haste, but that haste could only be productive of good if made in the right direction, and which now was the right direction no one could tell. To the front, right, and left we made repeated casts to recover the spoor, but neither a broken twig, crushed blade of grass, nor tell-tale "pug" could be discovered. That our work was dangerous, all knew, for my followers were only armed with assegais, scarcely the weapons to be selected for meeting the onslaught of a lion about to be deprived of its prey. But they never faltered in their ardour, and far too heedlessly, to my thinking, exposed themselves to be attacked at great disadvantage.

Disgusted at our want of success, we were about giving up the prosecution of our search till daylight, when the angry voices of several hyænas broke upon our ears. These carrion feeders were not now calling to each other, but uttering, with repeated yells, their disapprobation that they were not permitted to join in the banquet on human flesh. Intuitively my men knew what these bloodthirsty notes indicated, so, with one accord, they rushed in the direction from whence they emanated. The distance was not very great—300 yards at the most —but the surface of the ground was fearfully rough to traverse, from the innumerable boulders and fallen trees that rested upon it. Our course, too, was a steep ascent, well calculated to knock the wind out of any one not in the most perfect training. Several times I had to call my people back and explain that upon me and my rifle they must depend ; but even this obvious fact did not produce the effect I wished to instil into them. I thoroughly believe that these brave fellows—there were only my Zulus with me—regardless of consequences, would have attacked the adversary, although so inadequately fit for such a contest.

At length we reached the vicinity of the place indicated by the hyænas ; the torches were replenished, and so burned up into a brighter flame. Occasionally I got a glimpse of an animal, but discovered, in time to prevent my firing, that it was only one of the satellites waiting for his turn to participate in the feast. At intervals I could distinctly hear the breaking of something, I surmised it to be the bones of the victim; my followers were of the same opinion. These ominous sounds proceeded from the back of a large rock, encased in creeping plants. To get the utmost advantage to be derived from the light, we approached it from the lower side. For a second or two I saw a yellow moving mass; the next instant it was out of sight. It was, unquestionably, the lioness that had so persistently haunted our camp. So brief was the view I obtained of her, that I had not even time to fire a snap shot if I had desired to do so, but I resolved from the outset, not to press a trigger until I had reason to feel satisfied, that my aim would either kill the brute outright, or so maim it as to render it incapable of further mischief. No, the enemy had escaped, but the remains of the victim were left, a fearfully lacerated, mutilated, and unsightly corpse. To have told that the mass before us had been a living human being, in all the enjoyment of health and strength, scarcely an hour before, would have defied anyone not skilled in anatomy. I ordered it to be carried to camp. The hyænas followed close on our heels, expressing their disapproval of our proceedings by the most melancholy howls. Never, I venture to say, a more dismal *cortège* wended its course through forest or over *veldt*.

Something, I knew, must now be done to get rid of this daring brute, for, as she had tasted human flesh, her visits would be repeated whenever she wanted a change of diet, or had failed in her excursions in pursuit of game.

I handed the remains of the poor lad over to his people for interment. Next morning I saw them depart, obviously for that purpose. Where the grave was I did not ask, neither did I enquire the method of their burial. This may appear heartless, but I had to attend to the obsequies of my dear friend and fellow countryman—a duty more painful than any I had ever previously performed, and sincerely do I trust that I shall never be required to go through such an ordeal again.

Under a cliff of ten or twelve feet in height, a bright green stretch of sward existed, on which the sun appeared ever to shine when he was above the horizon; my Zulus dug a grave; the corpse of Selwin, enveloped in his scarlet blanket, was lowered gently into it. I read the "funeral service," with my followers sorrowfully standing around me. Then, at my request, each went and brought me arms full of green leaves and brilliant tropical flowers—purest white water lilies and dazzling scarlet orchids were numerous among them. The idea that the cold, dank earth should lie upon his form was repulsive to me, so many a stratum of these beauteous ornaments of the world were gently laid over the body, till a foot or more in depth they rested upon it. Now followed the mould till the grave was covered in, and the last connecting link with his race severed. That no wild beast or savage human should disturb my companion's last resting-place, my attendants and self built a cairn over the grave, many of the rocks composing it weighing a hundred or more pounds. Possibly before the date on which this is written, some stealthy hunter or half starved seeker for gold has viewed this pile of stones obviously placed together by man's hands—with what object, or for what intention? well may he ask himself. Alas! there will be no friend near to tell that it is the last resting-place of the mortal remains of one of the noblest-hearted gentlemen that ever lived.

> We are all changed. God judges for us best.
> God help us do our duty and not shrink,
> And trust in heaven humbly for the rest.

I felt now that I had done my duty, whatever my readers may say of the disposal that I have made of several pages in narrating a scene of life, or a termination to it, in which all will have some day to play a principal part. But I believe it has a wholesome and beneficial effect occasionally to look on death, as it certainly has now and then to visit a cemetery, and those who would go exploring and hunting in far distant savage lands ought by right to learn some of the trials that are almost certain to occur even in the most profitable and successful ventures. But there are persons such veritable gluttons for what they deem sport, and which I designate slaughter, that the reading of a paragraph that is not a record of long and short, difficult and easy shots, is simply to them a waste of time and an imposition on their good nature.

But let me bury my sorrows, and cease from moralising. So return to work, for there is nothing like labour to bring the mind back to a healthy tone.

CHAPTER XXII.

TROPICAL FLORA.

Dillon I cannot expect for several days; one of my Zulus has cast the "bones" to learn what luck he has had, and these say that he has already killed four big elephants, and that one of his followers has met with an accident. We shall see what truth there is in these prophecies; I know many white men who put absolute faith in them; I, for one, do not.

A day or two after Selwin's interment I started with Sunday for the uplands in search of buck. In passing along the edge of the forest, my attention was attracted by a detached yellow-wood tree of unusually large circumference and altitude. The stem was thickly clothed with a parasitic plant, of such healthy growth as to shut in and completely envelop the trunk to a height of thirty or forty feet. This creeper was densely covered with scarlet blossoms, not unlike in shape large anemones, but of a less evanescent construction. The perfume this flower emitted was so powerful, that to remain close and to leeward of it for even a few minutes produced headache. However, this did not prevent the feathered beauties of the forest frequenting it, principally those gems of creation—regular living jewels—different species of sun-birds. The humming birds of America are the only rivals they have in beauty of plumage, in my opinion. The double-collared sun-bird *(Nectarina afra)* was most numerously represented, but, as it is common in Natal, it does not require a description. There is one thing about it that may not generally be known, viz., that it can be partially domesticated. A young lady, resident in Petermaritzburg, had several pairs of these interesting pets. For their accommodation a small attic-room was set apart, the window of which was always left open. Here they nested. If at any time during the day their mistress entered their apartment with such flowers in her arms as they were partial to, the little pets would fearlessly fly around her, even presuming to insert their bills into the flowers in search of nectar before the stems and twigs were deposited on the floor. At Pynetown I knew a similar instance. This species does not, I think, occur in the Old Colony.

The other sun-bird I noticed is comparatively new to ornithologists. Its habitat does not extend much south of the Tropic of Capricorn, although it is migratory. The vicinity of rivers and mountain streams seems to have a peculiar attraction for it.

The late and much-to-be-lamented Charles John Andersson, the chief of South African naturalists and most intrepid of explorers, was the first to call the attention of the scientific world to it; hence it has been called Andersson's sun-bird *(Cinnyris Anderssonii)*. Its discoverer writes most enthusiastically of this attractive little creature :—" At the approach of the pairing season," he says, " it becomes inspired with the most lovely and exquisite melodies ; in fact, its voice is then enchanting beyond description, being a concentration of the softest, thrilling, and melodious notes." The late Mr. Strickland's description of this rare and gorgeously-plumaged gem, taken from a mature male bird, is well worthy of transcribing :—" Head, back, and lesser wing-covers metallic green, the crown with a coppery gloss, upper tail covers bluish green, greater wing covers and remiges, deep fuscous, margined externally with greyish brown, chin bluish green, cheeks and throat bright coppery green, a broad zone on the breast of violet-purple, followed by a narrow one dull greyish brown, axillary tufts gamboge-yellow, abdomen, sides, and lower tail covers dirty white, beak and legs black." In this there is an extraordinary combination of shades and colours, but they harmonise and blend so beautifully that the *tout ensemble* of the costume is simply perfect. But while I have been giving the above description, let the reader suppose that Sunday and self have reached the rising ground that forms the foot hills of the range beyond my residence. The walking is rough, but not more so than would be found in Scotland in similar situations; however, as we gain greater elevation, boulders and rocks become more numerous, rendering progression slower. On traversing a little valley, the bottom of which had a thick covering of reeds, an ourebi jumped up at my feet and made for the hill sides. This animal's erratic doubling course, every few seconds broken by an extraordinary leap, is very amusing. This last habit must be performed for the purpose of examining the country before it to learn whether it is free of obstacles or enemies; in spite of this it can scarcely be deemed wary, for it will invariably, when it considers itself out of sight of the alarmer, turn up wind, and squat under the nearest grass, or reeds that will secrete it. Scarcely had the ourebi passed out of sight when a duyker bok jumped from under a bush, and, with this species' usual artfulness, availed itself of every piece of cover that could hide it, if only momentarily, from the human eye. At neither of these did I fire, for my ambition soared to larger game.

Soon after I was rewarded with a sight, although not with a shot, at some pallahs on the opposite hillside. They were certainly aware of our presence; still they appeared to be in no hurry. To head them would have taken too much trouble, although this is the best way to get a shot at this species, for once they have selected their path they will not, except under most urgent circumstances, deviate from it. They stand nearly forty inches at the shoulder, and possess magnificent lyre-shaped horns, well deserving a place among valuable trophies of the chase. At one time they were very common in the Colony; now I doubt if they can be found within its limits.

I had come out in search of Harris-bok or sable antelope. This Sunday knew, and, with the sharpness of vision peculiar to the black races inhabiting the southern part of the great African continent, he soon discovered a troop of the noble animals I was looking for. With the aid of my glass I found that they were six in number; but, from their commanding position, impossible to stalk. After debating how I could best get a shot at them, my follower, ever willing, proposed that he should go round and drive them gently towards me, down a hollow that lay at my feet. "But they will have my wind," I said. "No," he replied; "not if you get well above them, and with a big rock intervening."

So, taking up the position I was desired to occupy, my factotum departed. I knew well that he could not get round to the place he wished, under half-an-hour, so I had time to admire the terrain, without losing sight of the game for over a few minutes at a time.

A splendid view was before me, hills as green as emeralds—the result of the late rains—and most picturesquely charming from their irregularity of outline.

Within a quarter of a mile was a tiny waterfall, descending about fifty feet into a dark, sombre pool, the surface of which was, in many places, touched with the boughs of water-loving trees. Those limbs that did not descend so far had, at their terminations, the nests of numerous weaver birds, that swayed to and fro with every movement of the atmosphere. At present this is a well-conducted burn, but after a tropical downfall of rain, or during the wet season, I could imagine it one of the most turbulent of watercourses. Beyond this channel stretched many an undulating swell of verdant green, gradually decreasing in height till it reached the woodland, which, in many a varied hue and colour, was lost to sight in the far, far distance, only to be terminated by the sand doones or mangrove-fringed, fever-exhaling swamps that border the Indian Ocean. I was alone, but not lonely; still I could imagine what a pleasure it would be, if it were possible, to take a flight due eastward and light on some well-found steamboat, bound for the Mauritius or India, round the Cape of Good Hope.

Rousing myself from this dream of imagination and impossibilities, I took my glass and brought it to bear upon the game. They were already moving towards me, heedlessly and carelessly, it is true, still there was an indication in their manner as if they smelt danger in the far distance. I could scarcely believe that Sunday had so rapidly got beyond the quarry, and, therefore, thought at first that they were only feeding up wind, as is their natural habit; but, no, this could not be the case, as they seldom stopped to pluck the attractive herbage that so luxuriously grew around them. But soon the Harris-bok commenced to hasten their pace, and that in the right direction, so I changed my caps, after seeing that the powder was well up in the nipples. On they came till a rise in the ground interfered with the object they dreaded, when all reduced their gait to a walk. As usual, the females came first, the position of honour, in the rear, being occupied by the buck. These animals were truly a grand sight as they threaded their way, for they followed each other in single file, appearing each to tread in the track made by its predecessor. At length they were within shooting distance; no air contaminated by my presence had, so far, reached them, for their walk was now indolence personified. I would sooner not have injured them (for trophies of the chase I could not take, from lack of porters, as evidence of my success); but, on the other hand, meat was wanted in our camp, although I had killed a cow buffalo only a few days previously. So I fired at the queen of the herd, the leader, a beautiful beast, sleek as a thoroughbred horse and plump as an old gentleman's cob. My aim was true, for although the distance was a good hundred yards, she fell dead without a struggle. The survivors seemed alarmed, but ignorant from where the danger threatened, so stood still. The noble-looking buck was nearest me. The report of my left-hand barrel answered to the pressure of the trigger, the stricken beast sprung into the air, then blindly rushed forward, cannoned off a rock, fell, attempted to regain its legs, and soon after ceased to struggle. But where were their comrades now? the description I have given asks that I should state. From whence the danger came had been discovered by the remainder of the *coterie*, and they are flying up the hillsides at a pace that would defy any horseman in the world to follow from the break-neck nature of the country. For more than a mile I watched them with my glass; still there was no diminution of their speed. Then a crest of a hill shut them out of view. Will the survivors ever visit that valley again? I doubt it; for within its picturesque embrace, friends and relatives dear to them had been ruthlessly slain, and I attribute an amount of intelligence to the brute creation, that I would withhold from many representatives of my own race.

Sunday had seen me shoot, and he was in ecstasies at the result. My skill by him was weighed by my success, but there was no credit due to me as a marksman. Anyone, unless partially blind or cross-eyed, could have done the same. It is marvellous where the people turn up from. Scarce had I finished smoking a pipe of tobacco, and

Sunday skinning one of the victims, when half of the Mantatees from the camp put in an appearance. They must have followed me from a distance—an objectionable habit that they are addicted to oftener than I am aware of. One thing I will give them credit for, viz., that they take care not to alarm the game I am in pursuit of. Selfishness probably dictates this, as well they know that they always come in for the lion's share of the spoils obtained.

Leaving Sunday to see these gentry loaded with the meat, I started homewards, and got into a drove of baboons—forty or fifty in number—who made a most threatening demonstration against me. If I had not presented a bold front, I almost think they would have attempted an attack. Women and children, if placed in such a position, would get frightened; then attempt to run away, so get maltreated by these otherwise harmless beasts. It is, moreover, a well-known fact that baboons have not the same fear or, may I add, respect for a coloured man that they have for a white one.

CHAPTER XXIII.

A NARROW ESCAPE.

NEXT day I went to renew my fishing experiences. The water was clearer than on my previous attempt, so I confined myself to grasshoppers for bait. With a short line I had no success, but when the current took out the float thirty or forty feet from the tip of my rod, down it went, and immediately I was fast in a fish that gave me splendid play. On being hooked it exhibited any amount of dash, like the majority of coarse freshwater fish, but soon the bad-plucked one gave in, and I landed it unresistingly at my feet. It was identical with the mahseer (*Barbus tor*) of India, and weighed about 8 lbs. A salmon or trout of that weight would have given double or treble the play, but then they are residents of rapid streams with a temperature ever low, instead of waters partially stagnant, and always heated by the all-powerful rays of a tropical sun. So it may be said that they live in a relaxing climate. This fish is a very handsome animal, and much resembles a chub, but for the different shape and position of the mouth. Again a grasshopper was impaled upon my hook, and the eddy carried out my cork far from me; down it dipped, then rose nearly to the surface, when off it went up river, directly against the current. A sharp strike informed me that I had sent the barb home, and I had an exciting five or six minutes. Ultimately I got my prey ashore, and it would have weighed—unless my skill in such matters has lost its cunning—close on 12 lbs. Three more fish were taken of less dimensions than the last-mentioned, when Sunday, wearying with watching the work in which he took no interest, asked permission to go in search of honey, as he knew from certain indications that there was an abundance of that luxury to be found in the neighbourhood. After my henchman's departure, I captured the largest fish I had yet taken—I should think it scaled good 15 lbs., and was of the same species formerly landed; then all ceased biting, and not a nibble could I get. This slow work made me drowsy. The situation was well suited for a nap, as it was protected from the sun, so I stuck the butt of my rod in the ground, the point stretching out well over the pool, with a fresh bait upon the hook. I thought I would just take forty winks—not a moment more—so cuddling up my rifle between my legs and arms, I dozed off. How long I slept I know not—probably, from the difference of the sun's altitude, a couple of hours—when I was brought to the consciousness of my position by a shriek—I could not call it otherwise—from Sunday. In a moment I was myself. In front of me, in the pool, were several large crocodiles, while within almost touching distance of my rod was a perfect mammoth. Their eyes were all fixed upon your humble servant. Intuitively I grasped my rifle without making more movement than was necessary to take aim at the brute's eye. The distance was short pistol range, and neither my sight nor finger failed me. Consequently it gave a spring, that nearly landed the repulsive brute on shore. The others started down stream on hearing the report; some submerged, the remainder on the surface. With my left barrel I hit the last of the crew, which was rapidly sculling in pursuit of its comrades. For a moment it lashed the water's surface, then disappeared.

There is no doubt but that I had had a narrow escape for my life, for if the leader, the first crocodile I had fired at, had gained sufficient confidence to come into shoal waters, where it could have touched bottom with its feet, it would have struck me with its tail a blow that would have sent me insensible, probably broken-limbed, into the river, where I would have been seized and carried off to a favourite haunt, there to remain till my body become decomposed, for these repulsive creatures do not eat their prey until it is corrupt. A person has but to experience the danger I was in, to know how thankful I was for my escape. Sunday knew the difficulties that surrounded my position, hence his shout, but that warning of his proximity would not have sent the blood-thirsty *saurians* off, if it had not been backed up with the assistance of my rifle.

As may be imagined, I had enough of fishing for that day. Further, it is doubtless the case that, the arrival of one of these loathsome beasts on the scene of my sport, was the cause why the mahseer had discontinued to take my bait.

As a question might arise whether the fish I am speaking of is properly named, I have only to say that the positions of their fins are identical with those of the fish I have captured in India, and which is called mahseer. Whether they have respectively the same number of spines in each fin I cannot assert; but this I know, the mouth and eyes are alike in both, while the scales are almost identical in their situation and consistency.*

The lioness again came into camp, and carried off a hind-quarter of one of the Harris buck I had shot earlier in the day. As lately I have been so worried and upset, I cannot sit up for her, for the reason that I desire as much sleep as I can obtain. Under ordinary circumstances I should hesitate to adopt the plan I am about to pursue for her destruction. It is not a sportsman-like proceeding, I am well aware of; but the provocation must be remembered.

---

* Since then I have captured numbers of these fish in the upper waters of the Limpopo. They are called by the Boers and traders "big scales."

Moreover, the camp of the Mantatees is quite unsafe while her ladyship is frequenting the neighbourhood. So I placed strychnine in a hind-quarter of a buffalo calf, hung it in a conspicuous place and one easy of access, in fact where she had committed her numerous depredations on our larder. In the morning the bait was gone; soon after sunrise the man-eater was found near the river, dead, her carcass blown out to an extraordinary size. On inspection of the body, I discovered from her teeth that she was very old, further in very poor condition; moreover her claws were broken and split, with a large lodgment of earth and hair underneath each. From this I surmise that she had, from decrepitude, the result of having lived to a very great age, been compelled to become the terror of my people—as men are taken with greater facility than game—and an outcast from her own race.

Any person would suppose that after the frightful tragedy that had been enacted in their camp, the Mantatees would have devoted a little of their spare time to render the place impervious to the ingress of wild animals; not a bit of it, not a stake or a thorn bush did they add to their enclosure since their companion was carried off. The wretches did not seem to care; their indifference or apathy to danger is extraordinary. "Live to-day, if we die to-morrow," ought to be their motto.

But it is far from agreeable to me to have

another episode—such as a man being carried off—enacted near my camp, so I ordered them, on pain of instant dismissal, to make their camp secure. No! commands were equally useless; each of them considered that it was the other's duty to obey them, so nothing was done. These people were useful in their way, more, they were remunerative companions, so I did not wish to drive them off; thus I called Sunday into consultation on the subject. Did he think that I should make his companions strengthen the outworks of the Mantatees' camp? I asked. "No," most emphatically, "no, "make them do it themselves." "But I have ordered them to do it, and they have not obeyed my instructions!" I exclaimed. "Well, Bass, let them be eaten." But I did not like this alternative, and remonstrated with my henchman. After a moment he said, "Suppose you do not say no; we put it all straight." "How?" I enquire. "*Slaught* them." So two of the Zulus went into the woods, and returned with armfuls of good supple vines. Each of my followers took possession of the most formidable rod he could find; then Sunday made a speech to the Mantatees. At first they grinned, but when they saw he was in earnest, and several had received an instalment of the chastisement in store for them, they went to work with most praiseworthy energy, and soon had a *laager* as impervious as my own. The apparent chief among these extraordinary people wanted to know, after their work was completed, why I was so anxious about their lives. To enter into an explanation with such wretches was utterly impossible, so I refused information. The indifference to death of some of these tribes, particularly those in the lowest grades in the scale of the human family, is marvellous. I am inclined to believe that they dread a few cuts of of the shambok more than they do to die; but in spite all this they are a happy-go-lucky lot when they have sufficient to fill their stomachs. At first, when the Mantatees camped alongside of our *laar*, their residence was a perfect eyesore, and nose offender, from the filth and *débris* of animal matter collected around it. A military love of order, backed up by sanitary precautions, made me insist that this should not be. For a time little attention was paid to my orders; so, to command obedience, I stopped their rations. Deprivation of food touched them on a most sensitive point. They were clamorous, almost defiant for a time; but I was resolute. The Zulus counselled their submission. Ultimately they took the advice tendered them. Since then I have never had occasion to find fault with the strangers encamped by me, in this respect. I believe that latterly they have learned the advantages of order and cleanliness, thus proving that they are capable of instruction in some matters. From the first day that our Zulus joined us at Lorenzo Marques, I had no such difficulty with them, affording good evidence that they are a superior race. Kaffirs and Hottentots are quite as filthy as Mantatees, so I place the Zulu race on a pinnacle far above them all. "Cleanliness is next to godliness" is an accepted axiom among us; it should be equally so with the heathen. For my part, and I doubt not but that many will agree with me, in spite of what philanthropists and sentimentalists may say, a clean heathen savage is infinitely to be preferred to a dirty Christian one.

CHAPTER XXIV.

TRIP TO THE LAGOON.

ANOTHER trip to the lagoon afforded me as much pleasure as on the day of its discovery. The same amount of bird life was visible, but four species that I had not formerly seen were now conspicuous. The first, the scissor-bill (*Rhynchops flavirostris*), remarkable for its graceful flight, but awkward, unfinished, or broken-looking beak; the white-winged black tern (*Sterna leucoptera*), heavy and slow upon the wing, and, therefore, as great a contrast as can be imagined to its near relative, our well-known British bird the "sea swallow. Pelicans and boatbills were also numerous, the first rotund and comfortable-looking at a distance, like a well fed but overgrown goose, but gifted with a far greater air of importance than the familiar fowl of our village greens; while the last, the boatbills, resemble cranes with the mumps, and human beings suffering from polypus. Their bills are certainly a novel-looking arrangement to the human eye, but they doubtless answer the purpose for which they were intended, and the owners, knowing no other, are perfectly satisfied with the want of grace of their boat-like appendage. As transport on our return journey is the great difficulty that we shall have to contend with, and we have now more *impedimenta* than we at present exactly know how to deal with, it would have been barbarous to make a collection of skins, taken from the innumerable rare swimming and wading birds that surrounded me, as inevitably I should have to leave it behind, so I turned away with a sigh of regret, from the most extraordinary aquatic aviary that I am ever again likely to visit.

On leaving the lagoon we struck a rhinoceros trail leading to the southward; it had lately been traversed by two of these animals—an old and a young one. It soon took us into the open veldt country; but, although the spoor was fresh, not a sight could be obtained of the game, and this when the human eye could well have distinguished such large objects quite a mile distant. It was quite possible that the beasts had lain down in some indentation or hollow in the surface of the plain, so it behoved us to be careful that we did not, too suddenly and unprepared, come upon such irascible animals. Our tramp in pursuit was not very far. One of the Zulus led the way upon the spoor, next followed Sunday carrying my rifle, close on whose heels I trod, when our foremost man stopped, squatted, mumbled something in his own language, which my henchman translated into the information that the game consisted of a cow and a calf, and that they were just over the swell of the land in front, drinking in a *vley*. I placed some grass around my cap, raised my head, and had a survey. The view was very attractive and uncommon from the brute life that figured so prominently in it. The old lady, who belonged to the species familiarly known as Sloane's rhinoceros (*Rhinocerus keitloa*), was standing in the water more than belly deep ; consequently her udder was submerged, which the youngster, desirous of obtaining sustenance, much resented, showing his indignation by giving his parent many a butt in the flank, which, but for her size and power, would have been deemed dangerous blows. At length the matron got angry and hit her progeny no gentle knock, which nearly sent it over, causing the youngster to retire to the margin of the water in high dudgeon. However, this humour did not long continue, for, soon after, the youth was wallowing in the mire, and giving itself a coat of mail, more than impervious to any blood-sucking flies that thought fit to attack it. This baby rhinoceros was nearly ten hands high and had simply excrescences along the front of its head indicating the position of the future horns.

Of all the African rhinoceri, Sloane's, or the keitloa, is considered to be the most dangerous, not that it is possessed of a more daring and vindictive spirit than the borèle, but from its superior weight, size, and I think speed, it is capable of perpetrating more injury. Moreover, although all this family are comparatively easily killed, I believe the animal of which I am now writing has more vitality than any of the others. This being the case, it behoved me to be extremely careful how I approached it. The wind suited admirably from my present situation, but I deemed the range—quite a hundred yards—much too far for my two-grooved rifle to produce instantaneous death, so looked about to see how I could better my position. The *vley* was about sixty yards wide, and evidently deep, but from where I lay, there was not a bush or stone to hide behind, right up to the margin of the water.

To my left, however, there was a tall ant-hill, a straggling structure with several peaks, which, if gained, would reduce the range one third. This flank movement was easy of accomplishment, for I had but to withdraw behind the knoll, compute the correct distance, and keep it between me and the game till I reached it. The plan of campaign being decided upon, it was rapidly executed, all except Sunday being left in the original position, with imperative instructions to remain as silent as the proverbial mouse. When I had selected the best situation for making correct shooting, I aimed a few inches above the waterline on the game's flanks, and fired about a foot behind the shoulder. The response to my shot was that the rhinoceros came down upon her knees—a frequent occurrence with these animals, even when the wound is not deadly—but soon after recovering herself, when

I gave her the second barrel. It took effect, for I distinctly heard the "thud" caused by the striking of the bullet. The cow now left the water, slowly at first, for the bottom was apparently very sticky, but as she gained the margin she hastened her speed. The youngster, who had not shown the slightest alarm at the reports, hastened to meet its dam, evidently thinking the mother had come ashore for the purpose of nursing it. However, these surmises were incorrect, for no sooner did young hopeful get its head under her flank than she gave her infant such a blow as sent it reeling off several paces. The child now became rebellious and revengeful for such cruel treatment, so charged full tilt at its unnatural parent, but was repulsed so effectually that for some moments it stood still, gazing with astonishment at the cause of its discomfiture. This scene took far less time to perform than it does to describe, for, although I hurried up my loading, I had not finished this necessary operation before both rapidly took their departure, the baby trotting along, so close to the dam's side, frequently almost under her chest, that it appeared marvellous how it avoided being trod upon. From the moment the rhinoceros received the first shot till she left the *vley* she had not uttered a note, but the instant she commenced to move off she gave utterance to a shrill, plaintive note, not unlike a wail; it might have been a summons for her offspring to accompany her, or it might have been a lament forced from her by the intense pain she suffered. *Quien sabe ?*

Rapidly we followed ; not a drop of blood was to be seen on the trail ; this was not surprising, for the skin of these animals frequently closes up over the bullet hole ; however, we did not want such tell-tale evidence to enable us to follow the *spoor*, for both beasts were in sight and less than half-a-mile in advance. After a time the pair turned off to the left, and entered a quantity of high reeds, such as denote the presence of water. Here spooring became difficult, if not impossible ; moreover it was exceedingly dangerous, as we had to proceed down wind, so I called my people off, being desirous of risking neither their lives nor my own.

By this time the day was pretty well spent ; in half-an-hour more the sun would dip the horizon, and we had quite five miles to traverse before we reached camp, so the last mile or two would have to be performed in darkness. For all this I could not hurry, so beautiful appeared the landscape and its surroundings, wrapt, as it were, in a celestial repose.

CHAPTER XXV.

AN ENCHANTING SCENE.

IN no other country in the world are such evenings and and mornings to be seen, while innumerable brilliantly coloured birds, and various species of doves, make the air musical with their joyous hymns of praise to the setting and rising sun. The air at those hours is so clear, bright, and sparkling, as to form a wonderful contrast to the mid-day stillness and heat. Moreover, the scene was so rich and glowing in atmospheric tints, so teeming with unbounded opulence in all that gives vigour, health, and beauty to animated nature, and inspiration to the higher faculties of man as to make it entrancing.

When the sun descended and spread over mountain top draperies of its glowing light, the valleys became more and more sombre, and the notes of rejoicing that issued from the warblers' throats ceased, as if they had sung their vesper hymn, and were now prepared to seek for rest with the disappearance of " the Sun God."

More lonesome and still became the country as we progressed, our course being frequently through wooded ravines and along watercourses. Innumerable stars glittered in the sky overhead. Their refulgence was sufficiently strong to cast many a fantastic shadow from rocks and trees, while there was a delightful balminess in the atmosphere.

I could not help thinking that the present surroundings and mysterious light must give to the eye and brain a strong imaginary resemblance of that spirit world, many of us so often paint in our night dreams. To give strength to these suppositions, long shadows would sweep across the trail, giving evidence of the presence of some nocturnal bird of prey, while mystic forms seemed to flit through the dim distance, or stand silent and still like ghostly sentinels. Again, some stump of a tree, riven asunder by a fierce tropical storm, loomed up like a grim spectre; and even the bushes assumed curious outlines, often those of weird figures, that waved back our advance with their hands, as if indicating a wish to keep out humanity from intrusion on their own spectral world. My companions, known to the world as heathens, and savages, felt the impressiveness of their surroundings as much as I did, possibly more. This I surmise from all conversation between them having ceased, while every now and then fell from their lips a mournful cadence that might have been taken for a dirge.

I cannot help thinking that if I understood the beautiful mellifluous language of the Zulus, or they had the power to express it in writing, that it would far exceed in describing their sensations the poetry of words expressed in our tongue.

However, the yelp of some jackals and the howl of a hyæna broke the charm, and from dreams of spirit land, and surmises of what its inhabitants resembled, I was brought abruptly back to my position and surroundings. In a few minutes after the light emanating from the camp fires was visible; soon we gained its vicinity, and so terminated the labour of the day.

Camp is very lonely now for me, although my people do their utmost to make it otherwise. The numerous little delicate attentions that they often pay cause me frequently to compare them more than favourably with my own race, and as for selfishness, they appear to be entirely without it. One day Sunday brought me some of a delicious plum-like fruit; it had the taste of a raisin, yet was acid. I asked him why he did not bring more. "It was all," he said; "three or four days have more." And he brought the "more"—about a dozen—at the termination of the period mentioned.

Again, we came across some wonderful mushrooms—quite as large in circumference as fashionable ladies' parasols—my henchman fetched them all home and deposited them in my hut, although there were far more than I could possibly consume, and his people were as partial to them as myself, A dozen of these little attentions I could enumerate.

but the instances above will suffice. To exaggeration they will sometimes stoop. I believe British sportsmen, whether adepts with the rod or gun, have been known to do the same—but to tell a deliberate lie these African aristocrats never condescend. These men were essentially soldiers and hunters, and their parts as such they performed to perfection. No more would they stoop to the chicanery, artifice, and prevarication in daily use by many of our purse-proud, blatant, self-righteous citizens, than they would be false in their allegiance to their king and country. Nevertheless they are keen traders, and will lose many an hour in bartering, so that they may obtain the highest price for their wares, but once the bargain is struck they will neither deviate from it nor permit another to do so.

CHAPTER XXVI.

AN UNCOMMON PET.

But to return to the game. I left the cow rhinoceros and her calf in a jungle of reeds, through which we could not "spoor," and exceedingly dangerous to traverse. At that time I thought that I had done with this couple. Not so! as the reader will learn. Soon after breakfast a Mantatee reached camp. He was very much excited, fatigued, and out of breath. On his way from a distant and unknown kraal, his course took him near my hunting range of yesterday afternoon, where he was pursued by a rhinoceros and her calf for a considerable distance, and only escaped by gaining a tree, after having some very close chances of losing his life. All was now bustle and excitement in the laager. Assegais were sharpened and belts tightened by the people, while I lost not the opportunity to sponge out my rifle and reload it with an extra drachm of powder to each charge. Half-an-hour's sharp walk took us to where the Mantatee had parted company with the irate beasts. I expect that here my informant had had a very narrow escape, for one of the branches of the mimosa tree in which he took shelter, about five feet from the ground, was broken short off by the trunk, while the earth around its stem was ploughed up in many instances to the depth of over a foot. The trail here was very distinct, the country comparatively speaking level, and covered with short, crisp grass, such as is only to be found on the uplands that reach to the base of foothills. Although our view was uninterrupted for nearly a mile, nothing was to be seen of the game, so the pursuit was commenced at a swinging trot, so much too fast for me that I had to insist on a more moderate gait, as I was rapidly getting into the state so familiarly known as "bellows to mend." In encountering so dangerous a foe it was absolutely necessary for me to shoot straight, and how could I do so if blown? so I ordered a halt. Having reorganised our advance, and strictly insisted upon a more moderate pace, we soon after entered a brush-covered country. Our leader, the same man who led the race yesterday, suddenly stopped, shaded his eyes with his hand from the sun, then pointed out the game. The wind being unsuitable, a considerable detour had to be made to avoid the disadvantages that might accrue from it. Sunday then handed me my rifle, I raised my head, and in front of me, at a distance of one hundred and fifty yards, were our old acquaintances. The youngster was almost between the mother's legs, while she kept restlessly turning round as if to repel an attack of some persistent foe; what it was, at the time, I could not distinguish. That the keitloa had got our wind, and thus become uneasy, was impossible, so I put down the beast's restiveness to her suspicious nature. Being desirous of making sure work, I resolved to reduce the distance as much as possible before shooting, so crawled in considerably over fifty yards, accompanied alone by Sunday. An observation here informed me that the game had not changed their ground, although still turning from side to side as if to offer a front to an enemy. Over twenty yards closer I crawled; now or never, I thought to myself, so raised myself to shoot. To my surprise, in front of the rhinoceros I saw a lioness; ten paces scarcely separated the belligerents, while at a short distance behind her ladyship sat a very large mature lion watching the proceedings of his wife, evidently prepared to assist her if any emergency should arise to demand his aid.

This was not a moment for deliberation; prompt action was demanded. The wounded animal was far the most dangerous to us, so I resolved to kill her first. Just as I was going to press the trigger, the rhinoceros changed her position from broadside to me, half-face to the right; I consequently aimed low down, and immediately behind the ribs; with the report my victim fell upon her knees, and immediately afterwards rolled over on her side. The lioness then joined her mate; both looked surprised, but did not evince any inclination to leave. I much doubt that they knew what had produced the noise and demise of their late antagonist, for it was evident from the way that they looked about that they had not seen the cause of the disturbance. I whispered to Sunday to keep watch upon the movements of the interesting couple, and while he did so I hurriedly reloaded. When I had capped, the pair still retained their position, although it struck me forcibly that their manner evinced uneasiness, possibly only curiosity, so I "drew a bead" upon the old gentleman's chest; as I rose to do so he saw me, his earnest gaze attracted his wife's eyes in the same direction, and she also became aware of my presence. They certainly looked a most formidable and dangerous couple. But no time was to be lost, so I fired. The old gentleman sprang head foremost into the air, with his limbs extended to their utmost limits, grasping about with them as if to clutch some invisible foe. I knew this action was indicative of death, so I gave the lady the second barrel. I shot rather too quickly, but she got its contents, for I heard the ball strike; then off she went at her very best pace, every third, or fourth stride, uttering a deep wah! wah! a guttural note alike common to tigers and leopards when alarmed.

Now my followers rushed up, joy was in their faces, but each appeared to think that there was further work or fun in store for them, for all fingered with delicacy the points and edges of their assegais, as if to ascertain their condition for immediate service. In a moment I comprehended their intention. It was the baby rhinoceros they contemplated sacrificing with such gusto. Now this was exactly what I had resolved that they should not do, for already I had formed a decision that it should be captured alive, and, if possible, domesticated, and ultimately taken out of the country. My attendants evidently did not at first appreciate my humanity, but I gave them to understand that I must be obeyed. As we approached the carcass of the mother we soon became convinced that the youngster would give us no end of trouble, and that he was determined, cost what it might, to defend his parent's carcass from the pollution of human touch. Certainly our new antagonist was not formidable from his height, about ten hands, but he was very heavy in proportion, and possessed of an amount of speed and dexterity that was wonderful. My people evidently knew that they had their work cut out for them to secure this creature, and so approached it with considerable caution. Not so with myself; ignorance of danger, as it often does, made me too self-confident, so when the little beast charged, the Zulus dodged on one side or ran away, for the poor little thing would not go any distance from its mother's body. I was admiring one of these chevies and thinking to myself if the "boys" would only stand their ground they would intimidate the cantankerous youngster, when, like a shot, it wheeled to the left, made an opening for its broad carcass between my legs—which, let me tell the reader, are rather long ones—and sent me spread-eagle fashion into a bush. I have had many a fall in the hunting field and in riding steeplechases, but never before got such a severe one. Of a fact, an irate young rhinoceros is a small devil incarnate, with power enough in his body to serve all the purposes of an ordinary ship's donkey engine.

We had not with us anything to tie the little beast up with, and, without making him captive, nothing further could we do, not even approach the dead mother; so I despatched one of the Zulus to camp for a buffalo hide which I used as a ground rug, intending to cut it into *rheims*, out of which to form a couple of lassoes, with which I had no doubt we would soon bring the headstrong juvenile to reason.

While my messenger was gone we inspected the lion; he was a splendid beast, and in the perfection of health, condition, and coat. My bullet had entered his body just over the apex of the breastbone, and must have caused instantaneous death. I asked Sunday if it was a common occurrence for lions to attack rhinoceri; he assured me that he had never known an instance before, but supposed that from the smell of blood, or indications of weakness, they thought that the mother was incapable of defending her young, so intended, as the Colonists say, "jumping it." I am convinced that the marauders would have had a more difficult task on hand than they contemplated, for the little beggar was, as our cousins across the Atlantic say, "true grit," and would have, as worthily, as any Orangeman that ever stepped over the ground of Ulster, adopted and practised the motto of "No surrender."

CHAPTER XXVII,

AN UNWILLING CAPTIVE.

At length the hide arrived, and was promptly cut into *rheims*, and looped at each end, but place the lasso over the fractious, pugnacious beast's head we could not. At length one of the " boys " succeeded in getting a foot fast ; in an instant after he was on his back, and a dozen others on the top of the fallen man. Such a *mêlée* might have been witnessed in the palmy days of Donnybrook Fair, but certainly never excelled ; and more than that, there seemed no end to the farce, for the mobbed animal appeared to be gifted with interminable endurance. At length two nooses were got over the muzzle just behind the rudimentary rear horn, and the young rhino' was a captive, but far, very far, from being subdued.

For the farce was not here finished ; the young rebel hauled first one way, then another, now dashed forward, then retreated, and so great was its strength that, although handicapped with the resistance of eight powerful men, it seemed at times as if it must get loose ; and how the young villain screamed, a pig's squeal after being stabbed by the butcher being nothing in comparison. Possibly all these demonstrations resulted from it being led from its mother's body. In my belief, it was nothing more or less than "pure cussedness." For a long time after being brought into camp it would not feed, and indignantly rejected the most enticing twigs and boughs, casting them scornfully aside; but I looked forward to hunger effecting two radical cures in the juvenile's disposition—an appetite, and after that submission to captivity.

Inside the *laager* its movements were somewhat restricted, but at night it was the only place of safety we possessed. However, during the day it was led forth for water and an airing, and afterwards picketed to a tree in our immediate vicinity. In a few days the little beast commenced to recognise me as a friend, but still showed great antipathy to the darkies; this possibly resulted from their having to do all the hauling about that was requisite in removing the captive from place to place. Now that my people knew that I wanted to preserve the animal's life, they showed it great kindness, and put up good-naturedly with the numerous knocks they received. Our novel pet was a constant source of amusement to every one, its ways being so eccentric and petulant that it constantly reminded me of a spoilt child, although I am convinced it was not possessed of half the destructive propensities of the majority of the children of our race. In particularising white children, I mean what I express, for the immature Kaffirs, or Zulus, are paragons in comparison with those of our colour. Fighting with each other, and coveting and purloining their playmates' toys, are species of cupidity and selfishness they are not possessed of. I am inclined to think that a high standard of education through successive generations is to a great extent answerable for our brats being so objectionable.

Being naturally of a confiding disposition, and not impossibly with a desire to show to the natives that even brutes recognise the superiority of the white man over their race, I one day intentionally trusted myself within the restricted range afforded the young rhino' by his *rheim*. The artful scoundrel apparently knew this, and took advantage of it, so charged. Not expecting such a reception, I slipped my foot, and fell, in an endeavour to get out of the way, fortunately beyond the prescribed limits of his captivity. Of course I got well laughed at, and deservedly so. I should have done likewise if the mishap had occurred to anyone else; but I certainly dislike very much playing the part of buffoon or low comedian for the entertainment of my dependants. I fear that I have often done so on this expedition, but it has been the result of not recognising danger soon enough, and also being hampered about my limbs with trousers, which much reduces a person's agility. The great Gordon Cumming and the Hon. Mr. Drummond, I have been informed, frequently dispensed with their nether garments when in the hunting *veldt*. They must have gone through a long course of preparation before they could comfortably do this, for a few minutes' exposure of my legs to the sun, invariably covers them with most unsightly and painful blisters.

The day after the death of the keitloa the lioness's carcass was found. The people had observed that all the carrion-feeding birds were hurrying in one direction, so they followed the course the vultures pursued—after the manner adopted by bee-hunters in search of honey—and so found the body. Unfortunately, the poor creature had died in a swampy reed bed soon after she was shot; thus the hair came out of the hide in handfuls, rendering it useless for all ordinary purposes.

CHAPTER XXVIII.

THE SOOTHING PIPE.

My narrative is not a diary, so the proceedings of some days have been left unrecorded. Thus the reader will not be surprised to learn that Dillon has now been absent two weeks. On his departure I did not contemplate his remaining half that time, so I feel uneasy for his safety. Probably I have no reason to do so, for if anything had happened to him some of the Zulus would have returned to inform me.

Sitting beside the camp-fire one night, I spent more than my accustomed time over my pipe and glass of grog. "It was a goodly night, and the cold winds had crept into their cave," for the breeze gets cool, even chilly, and ultimately dies away soon after sunset. The moon rose soon after I had finished my evening meal; her subdued soft refulgence possessed indescribable attractions from its contrast with the deep blue, cloudless sky, sprinkled over with innumerable glittering stars. To the south, but far up from the horizon, shone "The Southern Cross," enshrined in a perfect nebula of other constellations. It is easily distinguished by the dark and more unfathomable-looking space, situated almost equally distant from each prominent indicator that composes the group.

The night was particularly still, no wild beast's howl, for a wonder, was heard, but the voices of my men rose and fell in a full, rich, but gentle cadence. More contented, and, I think, happier beings there could not be. No wonder! they had plenty of food and their friends around them, so I envied their enjoyment.

Thus I commenced to get dull, homesick, and desponding, a state at all times far from pleasant, so indulged in an extra glass, and recalled the words of a song I had learned under most happy circumstances in the far Western continent. It was once a great favourite in California; doubtless it is now forgotten, so I trust to be pardoned for reviving it from the ashes of time.

> Contented I sit with my pint and my pipe,
>   Puffing sorrow and care far away,
> And surely the brow of grief nothing can wipe,
>   Like smoking and moistening our clay;
> For though liquor can banish man's reason afar,
>   'Tis only a fool or a sot,
> Who with reason or sense would be ever at war,
>   And don't know when enough he has got;
> For though at my simile many may joke,
>   Man is but a pipe—and his life is but smoke.

When the heart of man is distressed by care, when his surroundings are the primæval forest, when his associates are savages, and with his only friend in the country—his companion—possibly dead, yet, if alive, God alone knows where to seek him; it takes more than the cheery words of a ditty, or the solace of a soothing pipe of tobacco, to make the traveller feel amiable, much less contented. At my feet lay stretched a child of about three or four years—for it is difficult to tell these juveniles' ages correctly—whom one of my people had found starved and wandering in the woods a week or two before. The little derelict had immediately attached himself to me, and seems to dread to be alone with persons of his own colour. With the monkeys and baboons it is exactly the same, a captive animal of these species fears nothing so much as the presence of his *confrères* who are still free; thus this black waif of the human family scarcely ever permitted me to go out of his sight. At first I was far from flattered by his attention, for the child was suffering from skin disease; but regular meals, and plenty of food, with constant dressing of his sores with gunpowder and fat, had totally revolutionised his system, so that his hide now shines as if he had been polished with a blacking-brush. A feeling of affection or gratitude for what I had done for the little savage caused him this evening to draw closer and closer to me; at length he fell asleep, with his head—probably inadvertently—resting upon my feet. To remain long in the original position that I had occupied was impossible, for it cramped me. At length I moved my legs, when the sleeper opened his large black eyes and looked me in the face. His expression was a combination of fear, doubt, and affection; so to assure my little dependant that I was not cross with him, I gently patted him on the head. The intended kindness of this act he at once understood, moved his mouth, and gently said something I did not understand, and in a few moments more adjusted himself into a new position and fell asleep. In his sleep the poor infant talked; possibly his thoughts were running back to a time when he was surrounded by kith and kindred, for his features assumed a happy expression, which made them quite attractive. Mutual misfortune promotes fellow sympathy, and the sympathy that was engendered within me for the time being, partially dispelled the *ennui* and despondency that I had previously suffered from. It is strange, but nevertheless true, that the misfortunes of others often act as a sedative upon ourselves. This is possibly the result of comparing lots, and finding by comparison that we are not as hardly treated by fate as we might be.

While thus pondering, Sunday glided up alongside of me. His step was so silent and stealthy, that I started when I became aware of his presence. However, he made no remark, but took a seat upon the ground in my immediate vicinity, occupying himself for some moments in placing fresh fuel upon the now smouldering fire. Neither spoke for minutes. At length my man informed me that he and his people had been discussing the lengthened absence of Dillon, and that they thought that it would be advisable for some of them to go in search of him—not that they apprehended him to be in any danger, or that any accident had happened to him, for if such was the case, some of his attendants would have returned to inform us, but to bring him back, for he feared I was going to be ill.

"No, no," I answered, "I am all right—only a little dull, a little low-spirited."

"That's the way with white man before he gets the fever—no eat, no sleep, no hunt, and then in two or three days get very sick," he replied.

(Since then how true I have observed Sunday's prognostics to be. I have lost many friends in Africa by the fever common to the low-lying parts of the country, and the attacks they suffered from were invariably foretold by the symptoms mentioned.)

"I'll wait a few days more, and then if Mr. Dillon does not return we will bury the ivory and all go in search of him," continued I.

Sunday was not talkative to-night. I tried to lead him into a description of some of his wonderful hunting adventures, but the humour was not on him, so both relapsed into silence.

CHAPTER XXIX.

A SATANIC YELL.

IN this uncompanionable way we had been sitting for some minutes, simply engaging ourselves in replenishing or stirring the fire, when from the *copje* arose the most weird howl that I had ever listened to. In a few seconds another voice joined the first; it was equally horrible, but more spiteful and vindictive. It is no use hiding the matter; if this unknown yell did not cause me to be frightened, it made me feel very uncomfortable. Even the infant at my feet rose up, his eyeballs starting from his head, and with nervous force and great tenacity clutched me by the legs. It had scarcely died away, when numerous voices joined in, some deep bass others shrill and satanic, like the utterances of domestic cats when engaged in conflict with their fellows—"only a hundred times more so." I knew what were the originators of these hideous screams, viz., the baboons that had the rocks at the summit of the *copje* for their residence.

To be aware of what produces an unusually discordant noise deprives it of all its terrors. So Sunday, cognisant of everything, even the slightest whisper, that transpired in these wilds, sat unmoved both in feature and attitude. At length the weird yell was again repeated. No longer could I suppress my inquisitiveness, thus I asked him for information.

"Tigers (leopards) all the same as man and wife; both have fight, then make it up. He give woman whipping, woman scratch his hair out; we'll see in the morning."

These two fiends fought all night; their "skirrls" and yells disturbed the whole animal creation that surrounded them, even the owls and night-jars joining with the baboons in keeping up the lugubrious fracas.

My poor little derelict trembled and cowered closer to me. Who could blame the child? Even I myself had a strange quiver pass through me, as one is said to have when a person treads upon the place that is destined for his grave. I can quite pardon people for being superstitious when they can find no elucidation of strange and terrible noises, especially if they have the slightest resemblance to the human voice, and the yelling of these panthers certainly had this, but it was to that of a maniac's in his worst stage of raving. I suppose it was a break in the monotony that loosened Sunday's tongue, and led me to ask him regarding the superstitions of his countrymen. After a pause he narrated a wonderful story, an outline of which I had heard before. It was to this effect :—

During a terrible storm which took place all over Zululand, just previous to Mossuluketsi's secession from his country, several years ago, a white woman, with three attendants of the same colour, descended into the king's camp from the blackest thunder clouds, and in the midst of a terrific storm. Immediately after the stranger's arrival one of the attendants was sacrificed by the others, after which the lady commanded the storm to cease, when instantly the sun broke forth in all his glory. After a time this female's attendants wished to return to their own world. Their request being granted, they proceeded to the Umphilosi river, washed themselves in its waters, and dissolved—Sunday explaining, " the same as your sugar and salt "—when bubbles of air rose to the surface of the stream, floated down its current, and burst when in the full glare of the noonday sun. At this the new arrival blessed herself, and announced with joy that her comrades had departed for their own home. This woman still dwells with them in a *krantz* among the mountains beyond the Zambesi, attended by six Zulu virgins and a host of female witch doctors. To cleanse herself she uses fire as we would water, which is never allowed to become extinguished—in fact, fire plays the part in her toilet that water does in ours. This mysterious woman never eats, sleep is the same to her as food, and any of the male sex that attempt to intrude themselves upon her seclusion are handed over to the witch doctoresses for sacrifice after they have been permitted to gaze upon her lustrous beauty. Time has no effect upon her; her proportions are to-day as magnificent and grand as they were at the time of her advent, and the superb beauty of her features and hair have in no way diminished.

Of course this extraordinary romance is a fiction of the witch doctors, and is zealously disseminated to increase the belief of the Zulu people in their mysterious powers. That Sunday fully credited what he narrated was evident, so by neither change of countenance, nor movement did I indicate a doubt in the truth of his story. In after years I had an opportunity of discovering the grounds from which this strange fiction arose.

The *copje*, the scene of last night's disturbance, was visited soon after sunrise. There was enough hair lying about, yes, and blood with it, to indicate that no contemptible struggle had taken place. It seems to be inherent to all the cats, that when the sexes come together they have these desperate encounters. Possibly it is to test the superior courage and strength of the male; if so he has frequently to buy his bride dearly.

Although the panther never reaches anything like the size of the lion, it is quite as dangerous an animal, if not more so, to encounter, from its superior activity; the facility with which it also climbs trees gives it a great advantage over the other species in its methods of attack. It is as much dreaded by the Colonists as it is by the natives, for it has most eminently the gift of a crafty nature. Unlike others of the cat family, the panther is possessed of the forethought of the squirrel, thus will hoard food for a rainy day, so eats decomposed animal matter. This act of sagacity (hoarding) is unquestionably the reason that when it gains entrance into a sheep or goat kraal, if undisturbed it will make often a dozen or more victims before ceasing to slaughter. It is also said to suck its prey's blood, after the manner of weazels and ferrets. I am inclined to think this true, from an incident that came under my own observation a few years since.

I had a very sturdy, valuable, but diminutive hornless ox. On this last account, I suppose, he was fearfully bullied by his companions, so when at pasture he would stray off from the rest of the " yoke," and so occasionally get lost. When coming out of the high veldt, this valuable little beast was missing. So well had he retained his condition, and so willing was he when at work, that to leave him behind could not for a moment be thought of. After crossing sand-downs, covered sparsely with dwarf mimosa trees and *mapani* brush, I spied the object of my search heedlessly wandering among the bushes, about two hundred yards from the others, on the look-out for choice browsings. To facilitate driving the truant home I made a detour so as to get beyond him, for he was as active as a cat, nearly as fast, and enduring as a horse, and frequently very disinclined to return to the waggons until it was sunset. Poor little fellow, he had hardly become aware of my presence, and commenced to indicate a desire to avoid me, when a panther sprang upon his back. A less stout or well-conditioned animal would doubtless have broken down under the weight of its foe, although this assailant was far from a large specimen. The ox, with an evident and powerful effort, pulled itself together, and went off up wind at an astounding pace, considering its load. I returned to camp for assistance; soon after the bullock was found dead, with its jugular vein open, and the shoulders and neck otherwise disfigured with the slayer's claws. When the carcass was cut up, it was remarked by everyone that it appeared destitute of blood, although there was none around where the body lay. Was this the result of accident, or had the panther taken its victim's life by depriving it of the vital fluid? Unfortunately, at that time I had very few dogs, having given the choice of my pack to the up-country traders; thus, much to my regret, the despoiler escaped. The ferocity and courage of the panther is so well known among the Zulus, and, in fact, by all up-country races, that they instantly recognise the right of a man to the title of warrior when he has killed one.

CHAPTER XXX.

ONCE MORE AFLOAT.

To occupy time and prevent it hanging heavily upon my hand, I resolved to make a trip of some miles up the main river, and float down it upon a raft. This move was not relished by my followers However, I put the screw on, so if there were any murmurs of disapprobation among themselves afterwards, they were careful to keep them from my ears. Upon the heels of dawn a start was made, several of the Mantatees accompanying us; a refreshing breeze played through the trees, and the ground was in excellent condition for walking. Four trees I recognised, or thought I did so, from their close resemblance to those of India. If not identical as to variety, they are evidently of the same species. They are the *palas, mango, sal,* and *m'howa.* The timber of this part of Africa, and, in fact, of the colony, is generally very hard, and so possessed of little buoyancy, although there are, of course, exceptions; but no land, I believe, produces finer woods for turners, furniture-makers, or other ornamental mechanics.

The river also seems to shift its bed frequently, for in places I found the evidences of old watercourses, now densely covered with brush, reeds, and creepers, that were impenetrable to anything except buffalo or rhinoceri. In fact, it was evident that these coverts were the frequent haunts of such animals, from the trampled state of their edges, and the crushed and prostrate herbage that in parts bespoke their having been forced aside. The ease with which the soil is removed by the action of the water in this section of the world accounts, doubtless, for the *churs* and bars that make their entrance from the sea ever a matter of difficulty to even light-draught craft, and, probably, so it will remain even to the end of time. But for these impediments, the interior of south tropical Africa would long since have ceased to be almost a *terra incognita*. Scientific skill might be brought to bear upon such difficulties to navigation, but I fear not with permanent success. Whether or not I am right in these conjectures, however wealthy the soil might be agriculturally and mineralogically, it would take ages of fortunate commerce before the debt contracted for such a herculean work as constructing breakwaters would be paid off. These impediments, combined with the unhealthiness of the coast at certain seasons of the year, will, however, have one good effect, viz., it will long be a barrier to the annihilation of the noble big game of this portion of the world. The extermination that has been perpetrated upon the buffalo (bison) of North America, can, thank God, never be repeated here.

Where my approach to the margin of the river was uninterrupted, wonderful views were to be obtained. Within a distance of five hundred yards in either direction were visible numerous heads of schools of hippopotami, while I think that I have a right to conjecture that there were many of these huge beasts out of sight from being under the surface. Bird life was also particularly well represented—almost as much so as at the lagoon I have previously written of. My attention, however, was called to a little-known species of skimmer (*Rhynchops*) which were particularly numerous, and unwearying in their flight; so much so, that they at once recalled to my memory the Bosphorus, with its strings of sea fowl incessantly passing to and fro, which are reported never to alight, and are thus called "the spirits of the damned," sentenced to perpetual motion.

The general appearance of this skimmer has much resemblance to the tern, but it is separated from all other kindred species by the extraordinary shape of its bill, the lower mandible being prolonged at least two inches beyond the termination of the upper, and flattened out into a shape much resembling a spatula. The African variety's iris is dark brown, tarsus red, bill yellow at the termination, but bright vermilion from there to the junction with the head. The flattening of the bill is at right angles to the gape, so that when the bird flies along with the prolonged portion dipping in the water, it presents a sharp edge like that of a knife, which strikes the fish or crustaceans on which it feeds. The advantage which this arrangement presents is not yet quite understood.

Dr. Jerdon, the well-known naturalist, says in his "Manual of Birds in India" that the skimmer does not feed on fish. Dr. Darwin says, on the other hand, that it does, and that he has seen it capture them. The old adage, I think, is particularly applicable here, "When doctors differ, who shall decide?" As I have found the vertebræ of fish in their insides, with the latter I cast my lot.

On our tramp we came across fresh elephant spoor; its quantity showed that the troop was numerous, the formation of the footprints indicated that they were all females. Sunday, with a knowing look, remarked, "Where there's so many women, there's bound to be soon some men knocking about." A wise man is Sunday.

Having traversed about five miles of country, we again struck the river bank; it was at the tail of a rapid which descended into a long, sullen reach, the latter much resembling a gigantic ship canal, and margined on either side—although the banks in places were almost perpendicular—by giant reeds, fringed by water-lilies of the greatest beauty and size, over the leaves of which ran numerous jacanas (surgeon-birds), among the most beautiful, graceful, and active of the feathered creation. Of these there are two species common to this region, the larger and lesser (*Parra Africana* and *P. Capensis*); their habits of life seem to be identical, and quarrelling with each other their favourite pastime. In these little differences of opinion, they frequently lose or miss their footing on the lily leaves, but without an effort regain their supports. Like many of the plover family, when in a state of quiescence they jerk their heads about, as if nodding to each other, in terms of the greatest familiarity.

Soon my attendants had at the water's edge about thirty logs of a species of *geelhout*, or yellow wood. Remembering Robinson Crusoe's experience, I resolved to build my raft in the water, close to a shoal bar at the termination of the rapids. Vines were brought to bind the impromptu craft together, but I soon discovered that with such lashings there was evinced such an evident amount of instability that I resolved postponing my voyage till the raft was doubly secured by *rheims*. The reader need not think me timorous for thus procrastinating, but I do not see any fun in a swim among crocodiles, which, if it should terminate safely to my person, possibly would result in the loss of my rifle. So, soon after three o'clock, we started on our return for camp. Not half a mile from home I was attracted by the note, "toc toc toc tocko," of a yellow-billed hornbill (*Buceros flavirostris*), whose hiding-place, I was searching the upper foliage, to find out. Sunday and a Mantatee were at my side, the former carrying my rifle, the latter my shot gun. A shout of warning was heard, and at the same moment I perceived that the rest of my people were scattering and seeking shelter in or behind the surrounding trees. In a moment after I saw what resembled a tangled bush moving towards me; an instant after I recognised this to be a buffalo, over whose head and horns were suspended almost an armful of parasitic plants. There was no time to be lost. In an instant I had my rifle. No part of the brute presented itself for a fatal shot, for it carried its head high, almost parallel with the surface of the ground, so I let it have both barrels close to the bottom of the windpipe. This momentarily dazed the beast, but it continued the charge with only such deviation as to pass us within a few yards. I had not time to load, so seized the shot gun. I was not a moment too soon, for round came the assailant, made an almost imperceptible halt as if to assure itself of our position, and again charged. When about fifteen yards separated us, I gave it both barrels in the line of the face. Again our foe swerved, and went off among the trees, tail on end, finally cannoning against one, then another, several times falling, ultimately being brought up by direct collision with a large *boom slang* tree.

An instant after, all my attendants made their

appearance, assegai in hand, and soon had their weapons plunged into the irascible beast. Half the thrusts it got, any one would have supposed would produce instant death; not so. Bravely the poor wretch struggled on for many minutes before life was extinct. An African buffalo is as game as a wild boar, and that of a certainty is saying enough to attest to its pluck.

CHAPTER XXXI.

AN UNFORTUNATE CALF.

THE shots I had fired from my rifle, on account of the rapidity with which they had to be delivered, were made from the hip, a system of shooting which it is well to practise, as a fair amount of accuracy can be obtained in this way, with a little practice. It was not the last time that a familiarity with this method has done me good service. The unaccountable conduct of the beast, after receiving both barrels of the shot-gun, is easily explained—the charges had sufficiently spread to destroy both eyes. Altogether it was a narrow squeak, and far from pleasant while it lasted; but more credit for coolness is due to two of my boys than to myself, for, with nothing but assegais in their hands, they stood to me like regular "bricks."

The cutting up process I did not wait for, so hurried on to camp, where I found a half-grown heifer buffalo being dragged up to the cooking place. It had been killed by a lioness close by. The struggle and angry voice of the mother cow had attracted the people's attention, and when they arrived on the scene, the youngster was dead, but the cow had driven the slayer off to some distance. The shouts and formidable appearance of the darkies so discomfited both, that at length they were forced to take their departure. The cow that had just been killed was doubtless the parent, and the loss she had so ately sustained unquestionably accounted for her vindictive temper, and so for the unprovoked attack upon my party. No doubt the youngster had strayed some distance from its progenitor, and so come within the reach of its lurking foe ; otherwise I am certain it would not have dared to make an attack. A cow buffalo, even when unaccompanied by a mature bull of her species, is, in my belief, quite a match for a solitary lion. However, when two or three of the latter are together the tables are turned, as some will harass her in flank and rear till the victim lays herself open for a successful spring, after which combination in action completes her destruction. It is generally asserted by travellers that buffaloes are the principal prey of lions ; this I doubt, for the former animals are generally so gregarious in their habits, and so ready to give assistance to each other, when the note of danger is sounded, as to render them generally, comparatively speaking, safe. Moreover, the Cape buffalo is so ponderous, active, and courageous that, except in a rare instance, such as I have above mentioned, even a family of lions would hesitate very much in attacking a mature animal. With the larger antelopes, giraffes, and different species of the zebra family, it is quite another matter ; in fact, the last-named are doubtless the greatest sufferers from lions, as they are unquestionably their favourite food.

On inspecting the place where the young heifer had been pulled down, I found a large *mirouli* tree, easy to climb, and, from the spread of its branches at the fork, exactly suited for the building of a *machan*, so I at once ordered the calf to be taken back to where it had been struck down, and a suitable platform erected for myself, to enable me to keep guard over it, in case her ladyship thought fit to return. Sunday had a like perch made a few feet over my head, the object of this being that, if I should fall asleep, or not see the approach of the game, he should warn me by a string attached to my wrist. Although there was no moon, the night was wonderfully clear at first, from the innumerable stars that decorated the firmament. Unfortunately, however, later on, clouds drifted up from the south-east and banked overhead, which partially obscured the heavens. Jackals and hyænas soon found out my bait, but kept at a respectful distance, only testifying to their anxiety for a good meal by repeated yelps and howls. This was exactly what I desired; the voices of these carrion feeders would bring the lioness, or, better still, as they seemed loth to come close, her majesty might be at the moment close at hand, and so they dreaded rough treatment from her, if they took liberties with her prey.

In spite of all the attractiveness of such a scene

for the sportsman, I commenced to feel the awkwardness of my situation, and an irresistible craving for sleep. The latter I fought against for some time; at length nature gave way, and I slept—more than that, dreamed. From this happy state I was awakened by a pull at my hand. For some minutes I could not recall my scattered senses; at length a more violent pluck caused me to comprehend my position, and the object for which I occupied it. Now I could distinctly hear suppressed growls, and a rending sound, as if the flesh of the heifer was being torn from the bones. To get a better view of what was going on, I turned upon my couch, when every stick that composed it, most inopportunely seemed to crack. This untimely noise caused the feeders to cease their operations for a few minutes, as if enquiry was being made, who is the intruder? Silence, however, appeared to reassure the beast, for the sounds were renewed.

For the life of me I could not make out the outline of an individual animal. All seemed a black mass, but that mass very much larger than the bait could possibly be. I felt that it was utterly preposterous to fire under such circumstances, so waited; waited, ever inwardly praying that better light would be granted me. My patience was terribly exercised, and no wonder; within twenty yards were several lions, and I was perfectly incapable of harming them. About this time the sound of breaking bones was audible, a sign that the fleshy portions of the body had been nearly consumed, so there was every possibility that the feast would soon be finished, and the gourmands take their departure for their after-supper drink. I had commenced to express disgust at the hopelessness of the situation, and murmured inwardly, " Just like my luck, just like my luck," when a glint of subdued light threw itself across the scene. By it I could see the lioness and make out the outline of two cubs, each about the size of a large Newfoundland dog. Such a chance was not to be lost; in an instant I had my rifle aligned for the back of where I supposed the elbow of the shoulder of the parent to be. I heard the bullet strike, and in an instant after I put in a second shot; but to this was no response, except the deep guttural owh! owh! which the large *felidæ* make when suddenly alarmed and forced to beat a retreat. For good five minutes I heard this sullen sound repeated, till distance killed it. Then I realised that all my patience and inconvenience had been thrown away, nor could I find fault with myself in any way. Possibly my disappointment would have been more endurable if I could. It was the light, and the light alone, that was to blame.

In later years I have on more than one occasion known a good game shot miss even an elephant or rhinoceros when shooting from a *scherm*, at even a less distance than I made my bungle over. No; night shooting is very uncertain work, and a knowledge of this has made me practise it less than I otherwise would have done. Moreover, I do not think that it is a sportsman-like way of killing game, when other methods can be adopted. With the professional ivory hunter it is different, for his living depends upon the number of the beasts he slays. However, I would give him a piece of advice—never ascend a tree, but shoot from a *skerm*—a hole very like a grave, cut in the ground, and, if possible, surrounded with large stones or heavy boughs of trees, because, being low down, you can see the outline of the game's form, even in a very dark night, when your knowledge of the animal's figure will tell you pretty closely where to put your bullets.

When shooting after such a fashion as last mentioned, the best chance of success is to fix your eye steadily on where you wish to place your lead, and then fire a snap shot—in fact, do pretty much as you would when shooting rabbits in thick coverts.

Bed and camp I found very comfortable after the long, tedious, and uncomfortable wait; so, after a hot glass of grog, Sunday and self were soon sound asleep in our respective dormitories, although the chambers were only rush huts, and the pallets a thick covering of grass over the bare ground. So much for outdoor life and plenty of exercise.

CHAPTER XXXII.

FLOATING DOWN STREAM.

NEXT morning I started for the raft at the head of the same party as accompanied me yesterday, amply provided with buffalo rheims. The tramp was more enjoyable than heretofore, for it seemed to be chequered with more than the usual amount of interesting incidents. Sunday soon drew alongside of me, and narrated a strange story, that lionesses frequently suckled children which they had carried off from native *kraals* or surprised upon the *veldt*. My doubting the truth of this warmed him up to his subject. He asserted that he had not only heard of one case, but knew of several. I humoured him by requesting a description of what the captive looked like after a residence of years among such strange companions. In answer, he affirmed that they were covered with hair, went on all fours, had their elbows and all prominent parts of their figures covered with callosities, that they had lost the power of speech, but howled like their foster-parents, and moreover smelt exactly like them. In India I heard of eight or nine such cases, all of which occurred in the Province of Oude, but the nurse was on all occasions a wolf. Two or three of these Hindoo children had been sent to mission schools, and resided at them for several years. In character they were mischievous; absolutely refused to work, never recovered their voices, or lost the wild-beast smell. I know that many persons— people of education and social standing—are perfectly certain of the truth of these strange stories. In fact, I cannot say that I do not also believe in them, when the foster-parent is a wolf. Certainly it would be worth while, when another phenomenon of this sort is captured, to have a board of capable persons to investigate the case, and report their decision to the scientific world.

However, it is a widely different thing for a human being to be suckled by a lioness, to being nurtured by a wolf. Perhaps Sunday's narrative has its origin from the Hindoo belief, but that, there being no wolves in Africa, the next suitable wild beast was selected in its place, viz., a lioness; but it would be interesting to know by what means, and by what course, such a story could have reached Zululand.

It would be strange, after the passage of so many years, that what was always supposed to be the most arrant myth—viz., the suckling of Romulus and Remus by a wolf—turned out to be a possibility.

In a very sombre part of the forest we came across the evidence of the place having been just visited by a large drove of buffalo. Our experience of yesterday was not thrown away, so a sharp lookout was kept on all sides. The spoor of these animals led for half a mile or more directly along the route we were taking. At length a Mantatee directed Sunday's attention to something on the ground. My henchman, in return, called me up. What attracted both their visions was a long and distinct trail of blood. At first I was inclined to attribute this to the work of the king of beasts, but this impression was soon removed by the natives, who affirmed that the injury was the result of a battle royal between two bulls. That one of the combatants had got his death thrust I made no doubt of, and that his body was close at hand appeared a certainty; so I dispensed with the services of two of the Mantatees, on condition that they would go for aid, and take the better parts of the carcass, and hie to camp, which promise they most faithfully kept, I am glad to say; in truth, these savages have very much improved in cleanliness and obedience, and I almost suspect that they begin to see some virtue in honesty.

Afterwards I learned that at certain seasons of the year the natives procured a goodly portion of their food through the encounters that occur between the mature bull buffaloes. In North America I have several times witnessed most obstinate and protracted battles between two bull moose (*Alces malchis*) at the rutting season. They were very grand and terrific, but a combat of two mature Cape buffalo bulls, well matched in age, stature, and physique, with the arena clear of all impediments, would be a contest most truly magnificent.

The formation of the raft proved a more arduous and protracted job than I had expected, for the whole of the work devolved upon my shoulders. In America I have had lots of practice with the axe ; and among its easy-splitting trees, with the aid of an auger and notching, in two or three hours I could have made a float that would easily have supported the whole party. Not so here ; the timber was so hard and heavy that it had little buoyancy, while clamps and girders were required without number to give strength and cohesion. But for the buffalo *rheims* the whole structure must have been a failure ; as it was, when the machine was finished, it was nothing to boast about. True the raft was built in the water, but where the water was very shoal, so handspikes had to be employed to move it further from the shore. Half afloat as it was, it was nearly proving as obdurate as Robinson Crusoe's canoe. What distressed me most was, that when we " prized " at one corner, the whole structure changed shape, and, from an almost perfect square, assumed the outline of a meagre parallelogram. Elbow grease, when judiciously applied, accomplishes a very great deal ; so at length the raft slid into deep water, and as near as possible left us all upon the beach lamenting. The floating qualities of this craft we now discovered to be almost nil, so bundles of reeds were forced underneath it, then lashed there, with the result that it would now carry three, if they were not particular about wetting their feet.

CHAPTER XXXIII.

A LIFE ON THE OCEAN WAVE.

To be one of the crew was evidently distasteful to all; even Sunday winced when I told him to come along. The most intelligent of the Mantatees I selected as his companion, but no sooner did he see that my decision was come to, than off he bolted, with the whole hue and cry in pursuit. Soon he was brought back, shoved on board, and immediately afterwards there was no help for him but to grin and bear it, or swim. A pole and long scull were the implements I had to steer with, and they answered all purposes, although the bottom was exceedingly soft.

The expression upon the countenances of the crew, after a little experience, told plainly that they thought that they were having a "good time," but soon that was dissipated, when a hippopotamus rose close by, and took an exceedingly inquisitive, and impudent stare at us. I thought the brute meaned mischief, so I gave him a No. 12 bullet within two inches of the orifice of the ear. A little more struggling underneath the surface would almost have sent the river out of its bed; in truth, it swamped the raft sufficiently by the wash, to have made it appropriate to sing "A life on the ocean wave," but soon all was still again, while the carcass remained invisible. I confess to a liking to see and examine what I have shot at the time the deed is done, but with this kind of game it is seldom possible, for three or four hours have to elapse before it floats. Within easy rifle range were now to be seen many more hippos, but as I had already slain sufficient meat, I resolved not to fire at them, unless called upon to do so in self-defence. From the skin of the zee-koe (Boer name, literally sea-cow) being very thick, this animal bleeds very little externally when penetrated by a bullet; nevertheless, the vital fluid of my victim had escaped in sufficient quantity to warn the crocodiles that if they hurried up there was every prospect of their obtaining a meal of flesh. Such a hint was not thrown away upon such rapacious marauders; so, as far as the bend of the river would permit the eye to reach, these disgusting *saurians* could be observed sculling up stream with their utmost speed, an indisputable proof of the wonderful powers of scent that are attributed to them by the native population. Their tail seems their principal means of propulsion, it acting very much after the manner of an Archimedian screw to a steamship, while the velocity obtained is quite surprising.

It would be difficult to discover how rapidly a crocodile can swim, but I feel convinced that I may safely assert that twelve miles an hour is easily accomplished by them. All those that were in the direct route of the raft submerged themselves before they reached it, when their course could be distinctly traced by the large ripple of three waves thrown up by their displacement of the underneath water. I think that there is no animal on the face of the earth so thoroughly disliked by the human family, so I lost no opportunity of firing at these loathsome brutes when an easy or close shot presented itself. Moreover, they are such thorough cowards, that a wound never provokes an attack, but, on the other hand, causes them to seek safety in flight. In some rivers crocodiles are much more dangerous to our race than in others; this is the result of whether their habitat is, or not, abundantly stocked with fish, which is when obtainable, their principal food; nor is their size to be taken as a criterion of the mischief they can do to human beings, so a six- or eight-foot crocodile is as much to be dreaded as one double its length. Of course the struggle for life with a small one can be more prolonged; but if assistance does not arrive, or some unforeseen fortuitous accident occur, the result in the end is certain to be the same. Many assert that when they seize their victim they cannot afterwards release their hold. This is an error, for I have known cases that entirely contradict this supposition.

Saurians prefer their food in a state of decomposition; consequently they take their prey to some favourite haunt, there to remain till it suits their fastidious palates. Again, contrary to general belief, they have a small swallow in proportion to their size, so that the degeneration of the constituent parts of a body very materially facilitates digestion. This *penchant*, as may well be imagined, sometimes leads to fearful battles for the possession of a decomposing carcass, which doubtlessly accounts for so many of these reptiles being disfigured by fearful scars, or, not unfrequently, the loss of a foot, or a portion of their tails.

As we float downwards the nature of the banks becomes very much changed, for dense beds of reeds, often a hundred yards deep, margin the water, a certain haunt for buffalo and rhinoceros during the heat of the mid-day sun. As I fire shot after shot at the crocodiles, such immense flocks of birds arise from these water-loving plants as to darken the sky by their density and numbers. In their flight there is something familiar to me, and recalls very different scenes and associations. Yes! there can be no mistake, they are starlings, and, as far as I can at that moment judge, identical with our home beauties.

In Cumberland, both at Greysouthen and Whitefield, where I was in the habit of spending my juvenile holidays, enormous flocks of these birds used to haunt the adjoining plantations. In my boyish imagination, I used to think there was no place on earth that could show similar scenes, but they were not a patch on the hordes that now rose from the reeds, growing in the wilds of distant, little known, South-East Africa. They must have been literally in millions, and flushed as we reached a distance of twenty yards from them, when their evolutions on the wing afterwards, were identical with their *confrères* at home. The sight made me home-sick; I could not take my eyes off it, while memories that were intensely pleasant crowded my brain. Several times I shut my eyes to the surroundings, to let hearing alone be my monitor, and the result was identical, for as each flock swept down in our rear to reoccupy its temporarily forsaken resting-place, the tall reeds fairly resounded with the garrulous voices of these incessant chatterers of the feathered creation. I never see a starling now that does not recall that scene as vividly, as those I was then gazing at did the early autumnal evenings in Cumberland. In truth, it was a revelation of the past, a happy past, when the future was decked in visions of the most gorgeous beauty, and prospective life seemed to be one prolonged holiday of happiness and delight. It is sad indeed that there ever should be an awakening to such dreams.

A few days afterwards I procured some specimens of these starlings, and found that, although they were not identical with the home species in *contour* and colour, they very nearly approached them. They were well known by Andersson, the eminent South African naturalist, whose description of them is well worth quoting. " Like our European starling, which it very much resembles in manner and habits, it frequently collects in large flocks; it is comparatively tame and easy to approach, and is often met with near villages. Its food is very various, consisting of berries, seeds, and insects, and it is very destructive to fruit gardens. . . . This species forms its nest in the hollows of trees, lining the cavity well with feathers. The eggs are four in number, of a long oval shape, but tapering much more at one end than at the other; they are of a pale bluish-green, spotted all over with small dots of light brown. The iris is bright reddish-orange, the bill, legs, and toes more or less black."

Such is the Nabirop glossy starling (*Lamprocolius phœnicopterus*), the Latin synonym doubtless being taken from Sharpe's catalogue.

CHAPTER XXXIV.

ROBBING A CROCODILE'S NEST.

AFTER a mile or more of reeds, the view contracted in width, and the banks became sandy bluffs of various heights, none of them exceeding twelve to fifteen feet. My attendants had by this time become quite assured of their safety, so enjoyed the sail amazingly ; still their eyes were on the *qui vive* for anything that promised sport. Thus Sunday called my attention to a very large crocodile that was obviously intent on the occupation of scratching up the sand. My attendant and the Mantatee held a brief suppressed conversation, the result of which was that both concluded that the saurian had been laying her eggs, and was now covering them. There is nothing that a native regards as a greater delicacy, in the food supply, than these eggs, and, in truth, they are not bad when fresh, having a slight custard flavour about them far from unpleasant. As both my companions had no more idea of guiding a raft than they had of steering a steamship, the task of getting on shore devolved upon me. The sweep was lengthy, but cumbersome. the day a scorcher, and, as to myself, "not very fit." Moreover, the crutch I had fixed in which to work the oar was far from firm, so that when I used all my force the prop gave way, and with the mishap I went overboard. The ducking was but a trifle, but the vicinity of the crocodiles something serious, so I clambered on board with more than usual celerity. I don't think that there was danger in this episode, for the in-and-out was so rapidly performed; still, I will not deny that I was thankful to regain our frail craft without having had a nibble at one of my legs. After much labour we touched the beach, some distance below where we desired, and the solicitous mother for a time evinced no desire to give way; at length self-preservation overcame her maternal instincts, and she glided into the water with as little disturbance to its surface as would have been made, under similar circumstances, by an otter or seal. Her wake, however, was indicated by the ripples on the surface, showing at first an intention of crossing to the other side; but the reptile changed her purpose, made a wide sweep, and rose to the surface not twenty yards from where we stood. The brute was large and formidable looking, and the shot was tempting, so I aimed at the left eye. The distance was so short that the bullet flew high, but I could see that it had taken effect. Such a wound must have produced great pain; still the poor wretch did not desert her post of observation till a second bullet, better placed, doubtlessly penetrated her brain, for, in the brief struggle that ensued after receiving it, the unfortunate creature lashed the water around her into a framework of foam, then all was still, and the carcass disappeared like a foundering ship going down by her head or stern.

My men soon exhumed the anticipated treasures; they were thirty in number, which they would there and then, after the manner of all the natives, have commenced cooking, had I not peremptorily placed a veto upon such a course. A difficulty now arose regarding how they were to be conveyed to the raft, and thence home, so I lent my long Scotch woollen stockings for the purpose. They answered admirably; but blistered insteps resulted to me for my complaisance.

Sunday informs me that crocodiles have two nests, and that thirty-five is about the average of eggs deposited in each; that they take about two lunar months to hatch, when the mother returns and exhumes her progeny, leads them to the water, and remains in charge of them for such a time, as is necessary to pass, before the youngsters are able to take care of themselves. The reader will thus see that there are some "good points" even about saurians.

Again the river extended in width, and reeds and water lilies margined its edges. These fairly swarmed with coots (*Fulica cristata*), jacanas, and starlings, but the last-mentioned do not appear to enjoy a life of uninterrupted happiness, for hawks and falcons of numerous species were in close attendance upon the flocks, frequently making swoops from some place of vantage, which in nearly every instance seemed to be rewarded with a captive.

There is nothing that I could imagine on earth that would afford more pleasure to the sportsman, and naturalist than a sail upon the waters of one of these distant rivers, in a good roomy boat, provided always that the visitor was in the enjoyment of good health; in fact, this sail was a kaleidoscope of charms, in which each scene was more enchanting than its predecessor.

After having loaded my raft with the crocodile's eggs, once more we got afloat. The sun, which previously had possessed that hard uncompromising glare, peculiar to that luminary's appearance in Africa at mid-day, now lost much of its oppressive effect, the general result that follows when it gets well to the westward of the zenith.

The gentlest of catspaws, here and there, flecked the otherwise smooth surface of the water, giving a freshness to the atmosphere, which heretofore had been wanting, yet slight as this change was, it appeared to awake much animal life from its previous lethargy, and bring it forth from its retreats with renewed energy and vigour.

Martins, the fawn-breasted variety (*Cotyle fuligula*), were in immense numbers, and from their swift graceful flight, and the unremitting energy with which they pursued their insect prey—incessantly dipping and breaking the water's surface to obtain a fly—brought home to me many and many a scene in which these darlings of the feathered creation had played a prominent part.

This bird is not identical with the European species, but so similar to it that few could recognise the difference when either are on the wing. They build their nests in holes perforated in clay banks, or in crevices among the low rocks that adjoin upon the water edge. The home of their offspring is cup-shaped and fashioned out of clay; the eggs are generally five in number, white, tinged with a slight cinnamon shade, and blotched with dark-brown markings. In this species the iris is very dark-brown, so is the bill, the lower mandible being a shade lighter than the upper one; the legs and toes are also of the same colour.

It is strange what trifles bring back thoughts of the land of our birth; in this instance a little familiar-looking bird transported me in thoughts over thousands of miles of land and water. For the time being my surroundings were banished, and their place supplanted by the pools, stretches, and impetuous rapids of a favourite salmon river, on the banks of which I was in the habit during youth, of spending every spare hour of my leisure time. Travel and foreign experiences make home doubly dear when we are absent from it, but alas! it has another tendency, viz. : to render us dissatisfied with a permanent residence, even in the country of our nativity.

Strange as it may appear when the wanderer returns to the dwellings of civilisation, he forgets the hardships and trials he has suffered, remembering only the pleasures he enjoyed in the distant and barbarous lands he has visited.

Wherever I have been in Africa, the willow tree seems to flourish ; here it was in unusual abundance, more especially where the margin of the river was not fringed with reeds or water-lilies.

This is as fair a country as any I have seen in my multitudinous wanderings throughout this world, and in many respects resembles the blue-grass regions of Kentucky and Tennessee. Of course in making this statement I do not allude to the heavy-timbered alluvial lands that lay between my position and the Indian Ocean, but to the hills that form the watersheds of the numerous streams that flow to the Mozambique Channel.

On these foot-hills or high grounds, doubtless coffee, tea, cinchona, and superior tobacco could be abundantly raised ; while, by clearing away the forest on the vast wooded flats, the country would become adapted for the propagation of sugar, opium, indigo, rice, and even cotton. Nor do I think that there would be any difficulty in obtaining labour, as the natives appear most amenable to control, if treated with firmness and justice. Since my arrival at my camping place I have always had around me a fluctuating population of from twenty to fifty natives, and since my Zulus took the law in their own hands and chastised those that were disposed to be recusant, no further misunderstandings have taken place between us. These people are either an offshoot, or actually a portion of the great Bechuana race—although previously designated by me Mantatees—so are probably vassals of the Matabele King, having been, as well as the Makalakas, conquered by Mosoulikatsi, and afterwards by degrees incorporated with his Zulu followers into one nation. The Makalakas alluded to are a lying, good for nothing, idle lot; while the Mashoonas, to the north and east of them, on the other hand, are industrious, agricultural, and pastoral farmers; also, they are artisans of considerable skill, more especially in working metals. This is universally acknowledged by all adjoining tribes, so that their assegais and hoes have a wide reputation, from the upper waters of the Zambesi down to the southern limits of Bechuana Land. In fact I fear, I may say know, that many of the Mashoona race perish annually by the very weapons they have forged and tempered, and afterwards disposed of as articles of commerce. In our home hard-ware country, attempts have been made to manufacture the specialities of the Mashoona iron workers, but for some reason or other their efforts have failed, and a native will at once distinguish the difference between the foreign and native production, rejecting the result of Europe's skilled labourers, and paying high prices for what was fashioned and fabricated with a rock for an anvil, and a foot-worked bellows to keep the furnace in full blast.

It is strange that the Boers never took possession of this country, for many of the burgers of the Transvaal have visited it while elephant hunting, and so were fully cognisant of the value of this wonderfully attractive land; but these degenerate descendants of Holland knew well that such a proceeding would incur the wrath of Mosoulikatsi, or in later years Lobengulo, who would have thought nothing of "wiping" the would-be colonists, off the face of the earth. Again, a Boer is not an agriculturist, but a pastoral farmer; he has not industry for the former pursuits, and just sufficient indolence in his composition to attach him to the last mentioned occupation; but the tetze fly in sections of Mashoona Land, especially on the savannahs and low lying country, frightened him off from trusting his flocks and herds to the ravages of this pestiferous insect. However, in the hilly districts of Mashoona Land, large herds of cattle are to be found, and I venture to say that handsomer, better bred beasts, are not to be seen anywhere. True! they are small, very small, but the excellence of the beef they afford, is acknowledged by every trader and hunter that has travelled north of the Limpopo. A peculiar characteristic of these dwarf animals—which are nearly always black—is their playfulness of disposition, the children of the kraals where they are kept, regarding them more as companions than anything else.

Contrary to expectation, I find that the Portuguese are totally unknown in this country, except at one or two places on the sea-board ; they also have two or three stations on the Zambesi, where half a dozen traders of that nationality assemble at stated periods of the year for the purpose of obtaining slaves, ivory, and gold dust, for which privilege they pay large subsidies to the adjacent chiefs. Yearly the Matabele King despatches a formidable force to collect his rents, frightening the poor, decrepit, pusillanimous Portuguese, out of their lives, and making them scarcely dare to breathe freely, till the rearguard of the brave yet oppressive seceders from Zululand, are well out of sight in the forest, on their return journey.

Having alluded in a previous paragraph to the tetze fly, before leaving so important a subject let me make some further remarks upon this insect. The Portuguese designate it the elephant fly; this is a misnomer and likely to mislead, for, correctly speaking, it should be called the buffalo fly, for it breeds alone in the droppings of the last mentioned animal.

There are many places in Africa where tetze at one time abounded, and from which they have entirely disappeared, such as the vicinity of Lake Ngami and eastern Bechuana Land. The question may well be asked, what has caused this? answer: the destruction of the buffalo. Having from childhood upwards, an intense love of wild animals, a passion that has increased with my years, I really dislike to state that, by exterminating the buffaloes this dreaded opponent to pastoral farming can be got rid of. The African buffalo (*Bos kaffir*) is a grand beast, brave as brave can be, and in the sportsman's estimation affords the finest and most dangerous sport to be obtained on the African continent, but for all this, if its extinction is necessary for the benefit of the human family, then this " plucky," beast must be sacrificed. It is a well known fact that more white hunters are killed annually by this game than by any other, not even excepting the representatives of the cat tribe.

CHAPTER XXXV.

GAME WORTHY OF A SPORTSMAN'S SKILL.

THE river that we are drifting down must be the same as that designated in W. and A. K. Johnston's atlas, the Sabi, more properly Saabia, which enters the sea by several mouths about a degree of latitude south of Sofala. This river must not be confounded with another of the same name, which has its source in Zootspansberg, and flows eastward into the Limpopo, in the vicinity of Oliphants river. As we float onwards, the scene is constantly changing, although general characteristics mark the whole, viz., hilly and undulating land on the south bank even up to the water's margin, while the northern shore is girded by a mile of "savannah" before the country begins to exhibit a disposition to gaining altitude. Thus the river at our present position is tolerably free from aquatic vegetation on its southern brink; while to the north, dense reeds fringe its course. Occupied in admiring the beauties of the surrounding landscape, my attention was called by one of my attendants to the protruding head of a rhinoceros, which was evidently taking stock of the unusual sight of a raft supporting several human beings. The game was well worthy of any hunter's skill, the range short, and a vital point prominent; but I resisted firing, as sufficient meat had been provided for the wants of my encampment. The beast in question was a keitloa (*Rhinoceros keitloa*), a pugnacious and dangerous beast when encountered on land. It is as active as the *borèle*, and quite as vindictive in its disposition, but is superior in height and consequently in power of doing mischief.

As the sun was setting, we were near our landing place, a wreath of smoke rose perpendicularly from my encampment's fire, giving a home-like look to the scene that can well be imagined; moreover, every now and then rose and fell the mellow soft voices of the natives as they sang an accompaniment to their evening toil. Church bells ringing the call to vespers or tolling the curfew are loved by association, till you get too much of the monotonous clank, clank, clank, as, for instance, is the case in Malta, when the constant din becomes monotonous and annoying, subversive of rest, and destructive to ease; but not so with the native voice, for often as I have heard it, it ever seems to lull to repose, to speak of peace and good will.

If your attendants in Africa sing when they are about their labour, more especially when it be at the termination of the day, you can conclude that they harbour no ill will towards their employers; *au contraire*, appreciate their work, and enjoy their occupation.

An upheaval of the raft that threatened to sever

it, for the *rheims* that held it together had become stretched by submersion in the water, caused us considerable anxiety; what occasioned this approach to an accident resulted from a hippopotamus rising beneath our craft. It was a female with a youngster on her back. The old lady when she came to the surface looked wicked, and gave every indication that she would charge the obnoxious obstacle. Her distance from us was so short that it became necessary to take prompt steps to prevent such a *contretemps*, which would only have resulted in the annihilation of our raft, and the crew being sent swimming, so no alternative was left me but to fire, the result being that our would-be assailant disappeared under the surface of the water, with such energy and dispatch as to cause the wash produced by her descent to have a similar effect to that we dreaded from her attack. We saw no more of the matron, and right thankful I felt that such was the case, for a sea-cow, in its own element, is not an animal to be trifled with. By dint of sculling and poleing the raft soon after got ashore, and it was not without feelings of satisfaction and gratitude. Few persons have had the opportunities of enjoying field-sports in the perfection that I have; in my dreams incidents in them are often recapitulated to me, in my daily walks I frequently see—in memory, at least—the most striking occurrences of my experiences repeated, but I believe nothing ever impressed me more favourably with a day's pleasure, than did that journey down the wide and tranquil reaches of this south-east African river. As I stepped ashore I heard Sunday exclaim, "there is that d——d beast again." I turned round to learn the cause of this emphatic exclamation; an exceedingly large crocodile explained it. My man immediately afterwards added, "That brute means mischief; he wants some of our people. Give him a bullet, Bass," but before I could do so, the amphibion had sunk beneath the surface, in that undemonstrative way, alike peculiar to its race and the *phocidæ* family. My camp, home as I choose to call it, was in an unusually bustling state, for at least thirty visitors had arrived during my absence. They evidently belonged to a superior class from those who had up to this date been my constant attendants, being shorter in height, wore better carosses, and were more liberally decked with ornaments of metal and beads; moreover they were a much cleanlier people, and from the fine development of their legs, demonstrated that their homes were in a hilly, if not a mountainous country. A more urbane or more pleasant party of aborigines I had not previously encountered. Their countenances overflowed with good nature and animation, and while one spoke, he was never interrupted by another, unless I make this exception, that all repeated the last few words of a sentence being delivered by the spokesman. The cause of their visit was to sell ivory, which they placed but a trifling value on, and gold, which they evidently knew was a more appreciated commodity by the white man. This valuable metal they had stored in vultures' quills, closed with wax, each containing, on a rough estimate, upwards of half an ounce. Gunpowder was the chief object of barter they desired, still brass wire and beads were not without attractions. The gold was in small grains about the size of Nos. 6 or 7 shot, and almost in every instance perfectly spherical, clearly proving that it had been for some time submitted to the action of water, and that it had travelled a considerable distance from the *matrix* previous to its being exhumed from the watercourse in which it was found.

By this time I possessed as much ivory as I believed that I could find transport for, so was obliged to decline making further additions to my store; however, it was different with the metal, a pound, more or less, would go a long way, and could easily be carried about Dillon's or my own person, so that night, before I turned in, I had possessed myself of over ten or twelve ounces of it.

These new arrivals were excellent traders, and good natured withal; one, who appeared the head man, conducted the business of his companions, not, however, without permitting the principal to have a voice in the transaction. There never was a disagreement, not even haggling; what the head-man decided was done without objection or remonstrance.

CHAPTER XXXVI.

MY BLACK BABY.

MANY—so-called civilised—races would benefit by association with the Mashoona people, particularly if they followed their example in how they conducted trade.

On the morrow, soon after breakfast, my visitors again interviewed me; earnest and long were their solicitations that I should buy their ivory, and to my great regret I had to decline compliance with their request, although ultimately the price demanded for it was almost like giving it away.

While this chaffering was going on a fearful event took place close to the camp, which threw an air of sorrow and gloom over all its occupants; but I will commence the story from the beginning.

It will be remembered by my readers that my people had picked up a deserted child—a poor little starved waif, in the worst of health, and suffering severely from skin disease and other ailments that result from a lack of cleanliness. Good care, an abundance of food, and frequent ablutions had, in an incredibly short time, transformed the repulsive imp into a very attractive and precocious youngster.

A few days before I went up the river, a party of natives who paid me a visit, claimed my *protégé*, I have no doubt that they were the parents, so their offspring, screaming, biting, and kicking, was carried off by them, much to my sorrow, for he had become useful and very amusing.

The way this young elf would tease the juvenile rhino, and still keep beyond the length of the tether of this testy and most irascible termagant, was worthy of being seen many times, and not likely to be forgotten; moreover, I had constituted him my pipe-lighter, and nothing seemed to afford him more pleasure than to be sent for a coal, and to all but burn his fingers when placing it on the bowl.

Black children are far more precocious than white, and certainly much more comical.

Well, my boy was lugged off, and assuredly, I for one, thought that I had seen the last of him; not so. While I was absent up the river the juvenile toddled into camp with sore feet, an empty stomach, and altogether in a most pitiable state.

How far he had come, how he had found his way, how he had existed during the journey, and how he had not been devoured by wild beasts while making it, were all questions that might well be asked, but quite impossible to answer. This little episode in the young darky's existence had additionally endeared him to me, for it was an evidence of pluck, endurance, and skill, combined with affection for his white master that, deserved more than ordinary appreciation.

The edge of the river had always been a favourite resort of this youngster, frequent admonitions I thought had broken him from frequenting it; but not so. While I was engaged talking to the strangers, he had revisited the forbidden haunt, and was doubtless carried off by the great crocodile that seemed ever to hang about the ford. The perpetrator of this outrage was doubtless the animal that caused Sunday's remark last night, "that brute means mischief; he wants some of our people."

A piercing shriek was the only warning that any of the encampment received of the catastrophe, but the child could not be found, while on the margin of the river, on the soft mud, were the fresh indentations of the infant's feet.

A more excited or more angry throng than we were, when we assembled at the scene of the tragedy, it would be difficult to imagine, and many were the vows of vengeance then and there made against the assassin. I ordered a screen to be erected close by the place where this dismal tragedy had been enacted, that I could steal behind unperceived and so shoot from short range; but the murderer appeared to know what preparations were made for his reception, and never again afforded me a sight of his giant proportions.

On returning to camp I was again importuned to purchase the ivory; this led to the following conversation, which I think illustrates pretty plainly the position the Portuguese occupy in reference to this rich and extensive tract of country. Heretofore none of the natives I had encountered knew anything of Europeans residing near them; not so with the intelligent strangers who were now my visitors, and whose home, as far as I could judge, was several days journey to the north of my present position. Sunday acted as interpreter, and although far from efficiently he performed this duty, still, my guests having a fair smattering of Matabelu (Zulu), my faithful henchman was able to make himself intelligible, and to understand. "Why not take your ivory to the white men that live there (pointing to the north) and there (pointing to the east)? they would buy it," I enquired.

[By referring to a map of this section of the country it will be observed that I indicated as far as possible the direction of Tete and Sofala; the first, situated on the Zambesi River, the last, upon the western seaboard of the Mozambique Channel.]

After a great deal of jabbering and the exercise of much patience I learned the following. The Matabele having gone up to Tete to collect the annual subsidy paid by the Portuguese for temporary residence there, would be certain to appropriate their ivory, and not improbably take some of their lives for presuming to leave their country to trade in a commodity which was considered by their King as royal property. On the other hand, the journey to Sofala was difficult and very unhealthy, while the white men that lived there were not only dishonest in their dealings but frequently seized their visitors and sent them away across the salt water to distant lands, there to be fattened and eaten. This last belief, however absurd it may appear to us, is universally believed by all those races that, have been subjected to the slaver's brutalities, and all tribes that reside within a measurable distance of the Portuguese settlements on the south-east coast of Africa, have suffered much from this inhuman and cursed trade. In fact, it is well known that numbers of American, French, and Spanish ships were long engaged in this traffic, and that the efforts of our cruizers here were almost ineffective, from the numerous inlets and bayous that stud this coast, affording secreting places for loading, almost impossible to discover, from the intricate growth of the mangroves that hide their existence. As these settlements of Portugal are only held on sufferance, and all of them are in the most thorough state of decay, it only is necessary to let those races who reside in their vicinities know that there are other white races in the world besides the Portuguese, and that they will neither rob them of their hard-earned produce, make slaves of their women, or bondsmen of their children, and when such has been done these degenerate descendants of a once respectable race will soon find it desirable to seek other homes where they can practise their rascality. Goa and Macao are both familiar to me; no one who has visited them, and uses common judgment can, for a moment, deny that both settlements would be infinitely better off without the Portuguese; in fact, it is indisputably true that it is only Chinese stupidity and dislike to alterations that permit them to remain near Canton, and our own supineness that causes us to tolerate their presence on the peninsula of Hindostan.

What a change for the worse has come over the descendants of those bold navigators who first doubled the "Cape of Storms"! Reckless and unscrupulous they doubtlessly were; the age they lived in, and want of education made them so, but unquestionably they possessed one virtue to a pre-eminent degree, bravery, which is almost an unknown quality among the sparse Portuguese population that reside upon these little-known shores. To slavery and slavery alone must be attributed this utter degradation.

At Lorenzo Marquez a nominal Portuguese Government was found by me to exist, but it was an utter burlesque, and could at any moment have been annihilated by the adjoining native races; why such was not done is a question I can solve. The Zulu king forbids the Swazis and Secocomi's people from molesting them, for through their (Portuguese) agency he got European goods. Comparing the natives with the European intruders made the subject even more plain, for the former were a fine, manly, stalwart race, the latter, wizened up, blighted specimens of humanity, there being as much difference between the two as there is between the stalwart, manly Zulu and the pigmy bushman of Namaqua Land.

CHAPTER XXXVII.

A DISCOVERY IN NATURAL HISTORY.

The hippopotamus I had fired at last evening is reported to be ashore a short distance above the camp. I at once visited the body, and found that the head and shoulders only had grounded. Life had evidently just become extinct. The poor baby still clung to its mother's neck, but the discoverer of this mountain of human food had thrust his assegai through the little one's body, causing such an unsightly and serious wound that I felt it a duty to release it at once from further suffering. On receiving the shot that deprived it of life, and not till then, it released itself from its perch. Curiosity, and a desire to become conversant with all matters connected with natural history, induced me to examine the infant's feet, for it struck me that, without some unknown aid, it was morally impossible for a creature so young and helpless to retain such an elevated perch, more especially when the mother was passing rapidly through the water. Here is the elucidation: the ball that forms the sole of the foot was hollow, very soft and flexible, thus enabling it to act as a boy's sucker made of leather, which, with the aid of a string passed through its centre, empowers our youths to draw after them huge stones. When the young hippo reaches maturity, the ball of the sole doubtless becomes developed, therefore projects, and through use is hardened, so that it could not in mature years be employed in the same manner. Wonderful truly are the provisions of nature, yet how few of them cannot be elucidated by practical experience! The report of my rifle soon brought the whole camp to where I was engaged. The crowd seemed unusually jocose and larky. At first I thought that the prospect of a gorge upon the most succulent animal food Africa produces, was the reason of this friskiness, but soon I was undeceived; the demonstration was only a welcome to whom do you think? two of Dillon's Zulus. Grinning from ear to ear, looking so fat and sleek and well cared for, each advanced close to me, raised his right hand, and uttered the talismanic word, "M'kose." I could have hugged the swarthy, stalwart, affectionate creatures, but my heart was too full for some moments, to attempt movement, or speech, for I felt that again I belonged to a civilised world; that my countryman was within reach of me, and that an early reunion was in the immediate future. For truth to tell, for days I apprehended some catastrophe had occurred to my friend, and dreaded the return journey alone, as one does commencing an undertaking that he feels too great for his strength, and energy. A tear I know was in each of my eyes, but I managed to dispose of them, without being detected doing so, for I did not wish these warriors to think me capable of such weakness, a weakness that they would have scorned to exhibit; then I enquired if their Bass was in camp? On this each plucked from the hole in the lobe of his ear a reed; in both I found half a sheet of note paper, the inditement upon both was the same. " Come and join me here; capital country; good people; I have sent six natives with the Zulus. This is in duplicate, for the reason that their innate recklessness makes me deem it more than probable that only one will reach you. Come at once, there's good fellows; distance about five days journey; rivers low. Am in good health. Hope both of you are the same. Dillon." Here was a surprise in very truth. Go I must, for an option of refusal was not left me. The letter though brief was full of affection and thoroughness, just such as he or his compeers could only write, but he had yet to know of Selwin's death. Such impulsive natures as his do not suffer long, but the pain is intense while it lasts. What a shock it will be to him. These and similar ideas rushed through my thoughts, but action, up and be doing, worked upon me as monitors; so I ordered some of the sea cow's meat to be saved and jerked, the youngster to be cleaned and barbecued, loads to be made up, and finally inducements to be held forth to all our visitors to accompany me as porters.

Everything worked to perfection; there was as much order and discipline evinced in carrying out my instructions, as is so apparent in a well commanded regiment when it receives the route. At first the Mantatees made demurral about the distance they were going from home, and the hostility they might encounter on their return journey, but even these scruples were overcome, and the old camp was soon resonant with the voice of energy and good will, for its inhabitants strove to outvie each other in willingness to carry out the white man's will. The Mashoona were partly going my way, but they could not carry two loads, their own ivory and mine; so I made them a liberal offer for theirs on condition that they delivered it in safety at the termination of my proposed journey. This entailed a new sorting over of the precious animal product, and the rejection of much that I would have been pleased to have, but for superior being now in my possession. What I was unable to transport I buried, marking the place and an adjoining tree with the information what was to be found underneath, in case any white man, should at a future date come this way, in search of tusks; and moreover it might save the life of many a noble bull elephant. The paint I used to write these signs with was iodine, selected in the belief that it was the least indestructible substance from the action of the atmosphere, and the attacks of insects that I possessed. It is pleasant to have energetic servants about you, their assiduity speaks of good will, and kindly feeling to their employer; and when such is the case how rapidly is the most arduous labour accomplished, so before the sun went down that night everything was packed and ready to start. Till a late hour I sat and talked to the new arrivals; wonderful had been the success of Dillon, his daring and skill being the universal theme of their praise. But that I knew that rest was absolutely necessary, to enable me to go through the fatigue I should have to encounter on the morrow, I could have remained with pleasure by the watch-fire all night, listening to the eulogies so freely heaped upon my friend's prowess.

CHAPTER XXXVIII.

A RAT HUNT.

Up in the morning early; a farewell visit to poor Selwin's last resting-place, an application of the torch to the grass-huts which had for so long been our home, and all stood ready to shoulder their load to commence the coming journey. It was a grave moment, and the gravity was suited to the occasion; but in an instant all seriousness was dispelled, for from each burning wigwam rushed dozens of rats, or rather large mice, in the pursuit of which each of my followers took an active part, for these little rodents are considered a veritable *bonne bouche* by the natives. Not only had these little quadrupeds found a shelter among the litter which composed our beds and roofs, but a large *mamba*, a very poisonous reptile, common to Natal, issued among them from the flaming *débris*. This objectionable snake had doubtlessly found our camp a veritable happy hunting land, as it feeds principally on such "small deer" as my followers were now slaughtering. The serpent did not go far before getting its quietus. A few nights previously I could distinctly remember having placed my hand upon something that felt extremely cold, just before going to sleep; at the time I thought it was one of my boots, now I strongly surmise that it was the back of this dangerous snake. If so I had a lucky escape, for there is no reptile in South Africa, not even excepting the dreaded cobra or the puff adder, that distils poison more deadly to the human family.

While all this excitement was taking place, the young rhinoceros, by some means or other, broke his tether, and made off for the woods. His absence was not much regretted, as it would have taken at least four men to lead him, and such a number could badly be spared.

CHAPTER XXXIX.

ON THE LINE OF MARCH.

Our first day's march was through heavily-timbered land; at sundown, however, we again came upon open country, the continuation of spurs that pointed eastward from the "foot-hills," that led again from higher altitudes. These doubtlessly are the Lebombo Mountains. Here we encamped for the night, and, undisturbed by nocturnal prowlers, slept the sleep that generally rewards a day of toil.

Next day our journey was much the same as its predecessor, only the country was less wooded and more undulating; while our path was intersected by numerous water-courses, clear and bright as any burn descending Scotch hill-sides. Some of the pools that I examined were abundantly stocked with fish, each about a quarter of a pound in weight, but they much more resembled in appearance and manner the dace of southern English waters than the bonny speckled beauties so anxiously sought after by every wielder of the pliant trout-rod. If time had not been an object, I, doubtless, could have captured some of these fish by converting my mosquito-curtain into a draught-net, and thus had an opportunity of learning to what race they belonged, but *en avant* was our watchword, and not to be gainsaid as long as the patient heavy-burdened bearers refused to call out for a cessation of their toil. Many of the flowers which we passed to-day were of rare beauty ; one particularly struck me, it was a parasitic plant that covered a mimosa from trunk to summit, its flora was of the brightest orange colour, and so dense were the blossoms that they entirely hid the green of its foliage.

At first I took it to be a species of *Pirus japonica*, but closer examination told me I was mistaken, for the stranger's petals were much larger and far more fleshy than the well-known home production. Perfect swarms of sugar-birds surrounded it, whose beautiful metallic plumage made a startling but pleasing contrast to the deep coloured flowers from which they were obtaining their sustenance. Orchids also were most numerous and most gorgeous in their resplendent dyes. To-day I have seen no buffalo nor have I noticed any tetze fly ; however this is not proof that that objectionable insect does not exist in this vicinity. In fact it is well-known by travellers that where the tetze exists this year, it will not be found the next. Another strange circumstance in connection with it, I have learned from persons of vast experience in South African travel, viz. : that this poisonous fly will swarm on one side of a river, and not be known on the other. Even when the natives have killed game on the infected shore, and have transported the reeking flesh to the opposite side, not a fly would remain upon it after the transit had been accomplished.

Several small groups of natives as well as kraals were seen, but distrust, possibly fear, has so far prevented them from visiting us; but our party is so formidable numerically that it is apt to raise suspicion in the minds of a weak and comparatively sparse and unarmed population; however I have given orders that every overture of good will, and desire for their friendship, should be made to all whom accident threw within hailing distance.

My extensive experience of the American prairies and other well-known stock raising countries informs me that these foot-hills must at no distant time become a grand pastoral country. With an abundance of nutritious grasses, an unlimited supply of water, and plenty of shade to shelter your kine from the mid-day sun, how could it be otherwise?

The opinions I had formed against the salubrity of the country, I am much inclined to alter, for now that I am traversing more elevated lands than those that were in juxtaposition to my late camp, the air is quite bracing, in fact cold immediately after sundown, and this alteration of temperature would as a matter of course become more marked, the greater became the altitude occupied over the adjoining high grounds.

The lassitude and depression of spirits which I

had so lately suffered from had become already memories of the past, for now I felt fit for a tramp of twenty or more miles without the slightest dread of breaking down in the effort, a fear that had often haunted me in the days gone by; and no pleasant sensation it was, to have, in a distant uncivilized land, where transport would become a matter of great difficulty.

Every eastern-travelled Englishman is aware of the difference of climate that exists at the same season of the year, between the hills and plains of India; the same occurs in Zulu Land, and why should it not here? It certainly does, and from the propinquity of the Indian Ocean, I am inclined to believe even in a more marked degree.

Lengthened sojourns in nearly every habitable part of the earth have caused me to draw comparisons between the respective merits of each, and unless my limited experience here, has led me astray, I consider this land as near perfection as possible, for why? the majority of cereals can be successfully cultivated, all sub-tropical fruits, or many of them, could not fail to do well, while the great vegetable sources of wealth, which have been the main-stay of our Indian and Chinese merchants, such as cotton, sugar, indigo, opium, Peruvian bark, and tea,—as far as a simple temporary visitor's knowledge goes, would equal in their productiveness the crops they produce, even in their own native habitat.

Moreover, from the eastern lower spurs of these hills to the Mozambique Channel cannot be more than fifty or sixty miles, so no great outlay of money would be required to lay a tramway or railroad, through the unhealthy region to the seaboard, alike suitable for passenger or freight traffic; further, I am informed that there are many places along this coast where excellent harbours could be made, but I fear such would require more than a modest outlay. Moreover, the surf, more familiarly known by the designation of the "rollers," which commit such havoc with shipping in the vicinity of Algoa Bay, East London, and Durban, are almost unknown here, and then only in a most mitigated form. With the elements of such a population as has made Australia, New Zealand, Canada, and last, although not least, the United States what they are, located in this hill country, which is in my belief the eastern boundary of Mashoona Land, there could be no limits placed upon their prospects of wealth, and prosperity; for independent of the apparent richness of the soil, labour would be cheap, and those you employed for that purpose would be found an industrious, ingenious, and inoffensive people; further the valuable timber to be found on the alluvial low grounds could not fail to be a great source of revenue. The conclusion I come to in reference to the population is formed from the conduct of the party of bearers that I now have in my service. In fact, but for their effeminacy, they in many respects resemble the Zulus in obedience to control, who, although black, are the most perfect representatives of Mark Tapley's easy going character that, I have ever come in contact with.

Whether the advent of white men among this interesting race would not change all this, it is impossible for me to say, but any alteration for the worse, I should be disposed to place to the misdeeds, dishonesty, and overbearing of the immigrants. The Mantatees, those people that joined my camp soon after my arrival there, have on the other side to be controlled with a strict hand, and from the outset of your transactions with them, given to understand that, the white man intends to be master, that their fidelity will be appreciated, and the reverse conduct meet with the most condign punishment.

On settling in a new country, there are at first no understood laws, no scale of penalties for misconduct, no prisons, no police; thus the settler has to act upon his own responsibility, but in acting let him never lose his temper, and try to impress the delinquent with the belief that it is with sorrow he causes the transgressor to be punished. He who acts otherwise will soon find that he has raised a hornets' nest about his head, that will only be set at rest, by his leaving the country, and it will probably take considerable exercise of ingenuity to do that in safety.

I do not think that it is characteristic of the natives of this part of the world to harbour a feeling of revenge for a lengthened time, brooding over their wrongs and nursing them, till the sufferer becomes frantic, as is the case with a Malay, nor do I think that a Zulu or Mashoona would run "a muck" after the manner of the Eastern people mentioned. No! if they intended retaliation, immediate steps would be taken to accomplish it, and the hurricane of wrath that would be exhibited would be terrible to witness, but, like tropical gales, the very excess of the violence soon exhausts itself, and a placid frame of mind rapidly afterwards follows, when peace and good will can be firmly restored by a kind word or a trifling concession. Thus I think treachery, as the term is interpreted in southern Europe, is unknown among them as a means of avenging private quarrels. The stiletto, bowie-knife, and revolver, even if known here, would have an easy time, if they depended upon their special work for employment, and vendors of them would find these articles so little in demand, that it was unremunerative to keep them in stock. In spite of our boasted civilisation, we may from this learn a lesson that, deserves thoroughly digesting.

Here, another quiet night was passed; this may be owing to the large fires that were kept going throughout the hours of darkness, for I frequently heard a panther across an adjoining ravine, before I thought proper to seek repose. These large cats are not dangerous to adult human beings unless mobbed or wounded, when their extraordinary activity and strength make them most formidable antagonists. They are, nevertheless, a great pest to a *kraal* in whose vicinity they take up their residence, for they are alike partial to children, young cattle, and goats as articles of food, while their stealthy habits render their depredations particularly difficult to guard against. In hilly—especially rocky—parts of the country they are always most numerous, and are the last of the large game that disappears before civilisation; even at the present time they are far from uncommon in the earliest settled portions of the old colony of the Cape of Good Hope. Where guns have not been introduced they are generally killed by setting an arrow on a bow in the path that the marauder usually travels; a line lets the missile loose, and seldom ineffectually. In such arts the natives are wonderfully skilled.

CHAPTER XL.

A GRAND COUNTRY.

A MORE delicious bath than I had this morning it would be difficult to conceive; it was in a pool, very deep, and clear as crystal, with a fall of eight or nine feet in height at its entrance; the water felt very cold on making the first plunge, but that added much to the pleasure of the dip. Quite a large audience assembled to witness the performance, who at first, I believe, thought me mad, but when I dived from bank to bank, fetching up with me a couple of hands full of gravel, which I threw at the spectators, the climax was reached and the comedy universally declared "an overwhelming success." When I came ashore to dress, my skin was all aglow, and instead of a white man, as I formerly appeared to them, I stood in front of my people, a veritable red man; this seemed quite a puzzle to the Mashoonas. I believe that they would have been much less surprised had I come out black, for the reason that they would have explained the matter to themselves thus: "previously he was only painted, now the nasty stuff has been washed off and he is in consequence the same colour as we are."

It is a fearful nuisance that we cannot live without eating ; such was ordained, so all must submit to it. But for this law of nature, many an animal that I have killed might yet be roaming its native haunts in the full vigour of health and strength. The Creator gave us appetites which have to be satisfied to sustain our strength. He also doubtless sent the game to be utilised by man for that purpose. This is the best excuse I can find for taking the lives of so many graceful and magnificent members of the brute order.

The reason I write the above is that I am informed the Commissariat Department has come to the end of its supplies, and that fresh ones must be immediately sought for. I have ever found that when your breakfast or your dinner is dependent upon your gun, that instrument invariably takes an obstinate fit and refuses persistently to shoot straight, or possibly an empty stomach and an excessive desire for success make the hunter nervous, or fire too quickly, and so with uncertain aim ; which is the most probable cause, I will leave the reader to decide.

Having seen my *cortège* ready for the road— and let me say here, for the advice of future travellers, that no African porter on a long tramp should be asked, or expected, at the utmost, to carry more than thirty-five pounds—I took the advance, accompanied by a Zulu and a Mashoona. The morning was a glorious one and the scenery most attractive, just such a combination of circumstances as makes the pedestrian step out with such hearty will, and elasticity as to get him over the ground at a surprising pace. About half-past ten, when the heat was becoming perceptibly unpleasant, the Mashoona pointed out a black object under a tree, which at first I supposed to be a buffalo, but soon after learned was a "*blue vildebeest.*" The distance that the game was from me did not exceed four hundred yards, but to reduce that space and get to leeward of it required a *détour* of considerable extent. With due patience and ingenuity I made this circular advance, but when half executed, while I was wriggling myself over rather an exposed piece of ground, I all but placed my hand upon a puff adder. This *contretemps* disconcerted me, but not sufficiently to cause me to forget the object I had in view, so on I went till I thought I must be within suitable range. I had not only judged distance incorrectly but discovered that there was a kloof between me, and my prey of broken trap rock. To the edge of this I approached; the shot would be a long one, but I had been successful on many occasions at greater range, so I resolved to try. While giving the back-sight sufficient elevation, a clatter, as if produced by a dozen wild horses galloping, rose from the hollow beneath, and to my surprise, I found that the disturbance was caused by about a dozen Harris-bok or sable antelope. The beautiful and noble looking beasts were within seventy-five yards, a most desirable distance, so up went my rifle, and the ball struck an adjoining rock just over the leader's back. The left barrel I now put in with the same result. Astonished I certainly was, and angry too, for I let out one or two big oaths, and stamped around rather energetically, blaming the rifle and not for a moment attributing the failure to my want of skill. But the mystery was soon explained, and I don't think its solution at all acted as a solatium to my wounded feelings. The flap of the back-sight I had neglected to close after elevating it to shoot at the longer range.

There was plenty of game here, but as so often happens in Africa, the stampede of the alarmed beasts set all the others off; as far as I could see were to be observed zebras, elands, hartebeests, &c., in small parties, madly hurrying to join their numbers to this frightened and rapidly disappearing herd. There was no chance now of killing game in that immediate neighbourhood, so we cut across country so as to head the bearers.

In the afternoon I saw in the distance and far up the hill sides what both my attendants declared to be cattle, and, doubtless, they were correct; for on an adjoining hill, about half a mile further on, I could distinctly make out a native *kraal*.

I am afraid all would have gone supperless to

bed that night but for the porters having mobbed a young pig (Bosh-vark), which, although it did not go very far among so many, still assisted materially to allay the cravings of hunger. Near sun down, too, I had a slice of luck ; Sunday pointed me out a grand bustard or pauw (*Otis kori*), which, after a long and somewhat difficult stalk, I killed. When returning to camp after this success, I heard a koran (*Otis ruficrista*) calling ; after a slight search I discovered the position of this garrulous bird, and while endeavouring to get within range, flushed in succession, out of the long grass, three of the same species, all of which I bagged. As the specimen of the first-mentioned species weighed upwards of thirty pounds, and the korans were as large as hen capercailzies, I did not retire to my blankets hungry. A hint I would give to future travellers in Gasa Land : cook these magnificent birds as soon after they are shot as possible, otherwise they become tough. This is the secret of spatch-cock being such a toothsome dish in India.

The following day the appearance of the country materially changed, in many portions its characteristics being so similar to a nobleman's park at home, that when I gazed, it required no stretch of imagination to believe myself transported to the British Islands.

Spoor of game, from that of the mammoth elephant to the diminutive stein-bok, was everywhere abundant, and well it might be so, for the grass was short, crisp, and green, while water was in great abundance.

My people kept it up all night, as the new moon made her first appearance, and they had an abundance of their favourite food—zebra flesh. A little of this meat goes a long way with me, in fact I do not think that it would break my heart if I never tasted it again; but a black " brother " considers it fit for princes, and proves his belief by getting outside of so much of it at a sitting, that I have often wondered where space was found to stow it away. The native population, with few exceptions, are not given to great corpulence; thus, eating five or six pounds of half-cooked flesh at a sitting, to say the least, is likely to provoke astonishment. A city father I sat opposite to on one occasion at the Mansion House performed, I am certain, a greater feat; but then, his girthage being taken into consideration, I did not think the performance very wonderful, especially as several others in his vicinity at table were making a good race for championship of the " veteran food destroyer " stakes.

A quiet night passed, as far as prowling visitors were concerned, although I strongly suspect there were some of these gentry in the vicinity, as that pretty nocturnal plover called the "blacksmith"— from the metallic ring of its voice—kept constantly uttering notes of alarm, a certain indication that some brute or other had disturbed it by intruding upon its feeding place.

Soon after sun up some visitors arrived; they had seen our fires the previous night, so curiosity brought them to discover who were the strangers intruding upon their domain. Doubtless they had a long inspection before they exhibited themselves, but having recognised some of the Mashoona of our party, confidence was instilled into their bosoms, and they came boldly forth. There was nothing about their appearance remarkable to note; what I said of their countrymen from whom I purchased the gold, might with equal justice be repeated in their description. The natives are fond of paying visits to each other, and keeping up the ties of relationship, although they may be quite as many removes off as Scotch cousins. After harvest is gathered is the season for these reunions, and many are the weary miles that they tramp to keep up this good old custom. Hospitality is a virtue that is practised by the natives of South Africa to an extent unknown in other lands. The more destitute a stranger appears, the greater seems his claim, and the more rapidly is it acknowledged. Fortunately, some of the zebra remained, and the camp fire had not burnt itself out, so cooking was commenced with renewed vigour. I could not help observing what a happy, contented community they appeared; even the Mantatees seemed to have changed their natures, and vied with courteous rivalry who should do the honours of hosts with greatest liberality.

Through the assistance of Sunday I informed these people that I was desirous of obtaining supplies of grain or vegetables, for which I would pay a liberal price; after imparting this information, as time was no great object, I shouldered my rifle, and with the same companions as on the previous day turned my face to the lowlands in the hope of killing something of sufficient size to furnish my augmented party with an abundance of food for at at least one "good square meal." The breeze was from the south-east, and therefore suitable for my approaching wild animals without their winding me, a precaution quite as necessary to take here as in Scotland, when deer-stalking. To let yourself be seen is not half as antagonistic to your success in approaching game, as it is permitting them to wind you; I suppose they argue thus, better the devil they see, than the devil we are conscious of being near, but don't see.

We were some time in reaching the savannah lands, but the air was fresh and the walking comparatively good; what struck me with astonishment was the number of game paths, all running from east to west or *vice versâ*. These were old, and from the depth of many of the foot impressions must have been made in the rainy season. Still the action of the atmosphere had not destroyed the sharp outlines of the spoor ; thus I was able to discern that many a mighty bull elephant and unwieldy rhinoceros had honoured these thoroughfares by traversing them.

A mile or more off glistened the surface of a placid river, the banks of which were graced with an abundant crop of reeds, so towards it I directed my steps ; such places are always the favoured haunts of buffalo, especially during the heat of the mid-day sun. While debating in my mind what would be the best plan to accomplish my purpose without exposing myself to unnecessary danger—for I repeat, so as to impress it upon the minds of sportsmen, that I consider the Cape buffalo the most dangerous animal to be found in this part of the world—my attention was called to two of these animals lying down, just outside of, but on the margin of the reeds. The wind exactly suited, and several ant hills lay between me and them, ant hills not of the size of bushel baskets, but goodly structures between four and five feet high. Our approach was made with great stealth, the Zulu leading, your humble servant next, and the Mashoona at his heels. I was shooting with poor Selwin's rifle, which was a much superior weapon in precision to my own, when firing heavy charges of powder, while my Zulu carried my own weapon. Within forty yards of the cattle were two ant hills, both equally distant from them ; that to the left we selected for our ambush, and with little inconvenience and risk reached it. It was now necessary to get the brutes to stand up, as otherwise the length of the grass prevented certain work being done. My henchman was equal to the occasion; with his hands to his mouth he imitated the grunt this species utter when angry, and both of the game were on their feet in an instant, and gazing intently in the direction from where they supposed the sound to emanate. No manipulation could have placed them in a better position, so I aimed at the larger— a young bull—placing both shots about a couple of hand-breadths behind the shoulder. Down came the mighty beast with a crash. Still the other buffalo — an old cow — never moved; the Zulu placed the second rifle in my hand, and crack went my right barrel. On receipt of the bullet, the stricken beast sprang into the air in the position of a rearing horse, with an amount of agility worthier of a spring-bok, and not to be expected from so unwieldy a looking brute. On reaching ground again, after this aerial exhibition, at a pace almost equal to that of a racehorse she charged the ant hill —about which the smoke hung—and either by the shock of the concussion or getting her legs rather mixed by the resistance offered, over she went, evidently much to her consternation. Before the buffalo regained her legs, I fired my left barrel into her flank; this shot appeared a sickener, for she went off at rather a measured and by no means hasty step for an adjoining clump of reeds. Having reloaded both rifles, we followed up our game ; the piece of cover selected by the cow was not over a quarter of an acre, yet it was dangerous work to enter it. However, my Zulu would do so ; and the way he got chevied by that old female kept me in constant dread for his safety. My attendant's rashness afforded me a fresh chance to use my rifle, when the second shot proved fatal.

Having now procured meat in abundance, I turned my face towards home. On reaching the camp I found so many natives assembled as to make the place resemble a fair. These people had not been slow in obeying my behest, for each had brought for sale some commodity of barter, and all of value in their way. Their rice, tobacco, mealies, millet, gourds, melons, and ground nuts, for all of which the owners were perfectly willing to be paid in flesh, were a great blessing, as my supplies were getting low. The rice—that staple of food which I never tire to partake of—was the very best I ever ate ; and if prepared with the same knowledge and care as we do ours, would, unquestionably, have rivalled it in attractiveness of appearance.

The tobacco also was excellent, but stronger than I generally use ; this, I think, was the result of the method employed to cure it. It was made up in small packages of about half a pound each, bearing a strong resemblance in shape, to what is called "buffalo chips" in the United States. Some of the corn-cobs were almost as long as those grown in the valleys of the Mississippi and Ohio rivers; while the grain was plump, full, and abundant. The melons, although large and an extremely beautiful fruit to look at, had a strong astringent taste; nevertheless, they were very refreshing.

Both Sunday and Jim carried on a fluent conversation with some of these people, for being vassals of the Matabeles, they had picked up the tongue of their Suzerain, when on their annual visits to his capital to pay their yearly taxes.

Quite a touching little episode occurred here: among the strangers was an old man, a sort of petty chief, no doubt stationed among the Mashoonas as a spy upon their actions. In his youth he had left Zulu Land in the train of the dreaded Mosulakatze, and had passed through all the wars waged by that great warrior against Bechuanas, Mokalolos, Makalakas, Massarahs, and Mashoonas, and now he was spending his well-earned rest among these interesting people. A few words that Sunday said caused the veteran to recognise his nationality, when there ensued such congratulations, compliments, and enquiries as almost became nauseating to a spectator. The old man's delight was unbounded; to get news direct from the land of his birth, to hear of relatives still living, was a pleasure far over anything that he had ever anticipated. That night the old chief, with all my Zulus around him, sat from sunset till dawn, never for a moment permitting their tongues to rest. Thank goodness we had plenty of excellent meat in camp, and my henchmen did the duty of hosts in a right royal manner. Several times I went over to their fire to have a look at the happy party; all their faces beamed with good fellowship and the enjoyment of good cheer. Even under these circumstances, when remissness in attention to me would have been pardonable, Sunday never neglected his " Bass ;" in fact I think he took a delight in showing me off and singing my praises. The old chief even called me *n'cose*, the hightest salutation that they can bestow on a superior whom they respect. Happiness, I think, is infectious, for that evening I felt once more light hearted and far better than I have done since the death of Selwin. Gold I purchased here in one transaction to the amount of a pound in weight; a very old coat and brilliant colored shirt being the price I paid for it.

The old Matabele chieftain is, what you would call in our language, " a thorough good sort," and the favourable report that has been given of me by his countrymen has made him more than a friend; in fact, a person who would go any length—unless sacrificing his loyalty—to serve me. Too old to accompany me when shooting; lost time from my society he would make up for, by seldom letting me out of his sight when in camp; in fact, I may say that he almost haunted me. And fortune favoured me while here: quills of gold were being constantly brought me, and the demands of the owners for the transfer of their possession were the reverse of exorbitant.

The two-grooved rifle which I so much disliked attracted the old warrior's attention, doubtless, from its being so much ornamented. This resulted in his asking Sunday if I would sell it; of course I would, and be delighted to get rid of the beastly weapon at any price compatible with its worth in this distant country. As this intelligence was communicated to me, I was filling my three-pound shot pouch, so I responded: "If the old man will fill that with gold, he shall have the rifle." I may almost say this was said jocularly, and I thought nothing more of the matter; but in two days the veteran hero asked me to fulfil my promise, and the shot pouch was filled to repletion.

At this time I had a note from Dillon. This is what a portion of it stated:

"I fear we shall have difficulty in taking our ivory out of the country, as the Portuguese are *tabooed* in every direction. I have bought a considerable quantity of gold, and start nearly due west to Manica to-morrow. This province is peopled with an offshoot of the Matabeles, and are subservient to them, so are consequently Zulus. My own people assure me that there is no danger in the undertaking. If you have left the old camp when you receive this, bear about thirty degrees more to the westward than the guides would direct you, and we are bound to meet. Hurry up like good fellows, for I am most anxious to see you."

A consultation with the Matabele chieftain resulted in my learning that Manica was only three or four days' journey off, say, one hundred and twenty miles, that a near relative of his was Induna there, that this province was part of Mashoona Land, and that it annually paid a tribute to the Matabele King. What was more satisfactory still, the old gentleman proposed going with us, provided we did not travel too rapidly for his aged limbs.

The morning that we started was a most glorious one; all were in light marching order, for our ivory had been entrusted to the care of the head of a kraal, there to be detained, till further instructions in reference to its future destination were received. Still a shadow clouded my apparent prosperity. It was no less a cause than parting with the Mantatees. I scrupulously paid each his promised remuneration, and then gave all a present, after which off they went "happy as birds." These people belong to the great Bechuana race, I now believe, whose home is beyond the upper waters of the Limpopo and verging closely upon the great Kalihari desert. A more unattractive people than they appeared when first I met them I do not think I ever saw, but discipline and enforced cleanliness had worked a wonderful change in them, so great a change, indeed, that unless seen it could not have been believed. So much for a little wholesome correction, and imparting the information that, the white man is the superior, and therefore must and shall be master.

On the second day we entered what is designated the province of Manica; it is a hilly country, abundantly watered, and is said to be very rich in gold. It is asserted by many that this province of the Matabeles is the "Ophir" alluded to in the Scriptures.

Having wandered off a few miles to the westward of the route taken by my attendants, I came across undoubted evidence that civilised people had once dwelt here, for the crest of a hill was surrounded by a stone wall, in which were situated three lookout towers. This masonry was, however, now in ruins, but its contour much reminded me of the Genoese works that overlooked Balaclava harbour. I am not sufficiently skilled as an antiquary to fix any date for the erection of this work, so it may really have been constructed by Phœnicians, or any other of the enterprising nationalities that existed so long ago, that even history gives us little information about them.

However, here was a work of labour that could not have been executed in a short space of time, and only by the aid of innumerable labourers. I have little doubt but that gold, and gold alone, had been the inducement that brought the foreigners here, if foreigners they were, and not a race of human beings that have perished off the face of the earth. Excavating might disclose the secret of the early history of the place, but I had no means to undertake such a task. As Mashoona Land is a portion of the Matabele country now ceded to England, and is therefore in our hands, it is possible that such may be done at a future date.

The population of this country is much more numerous, than on the lands that we have formerly traversed; so many of the valleys are cultivated, and each hill top has a *kraal* perched upon it. From these huts, especially after sunset, I often heard soft music emanate; it was of two kinds: one resembling such as would be produced by an Eolian harp, the other being very fife-like in sound, and probably was the result of blowing into a reed.

The Mashoonas are a much superior, and less inquisitive race to any of the aborigines of Gasa Land that I have met, or their Matabele masters have taught them to attend to their own business, for those men and women that I passed, whether in the vicinity of their kraals or when engaged in agricultural pursuits, never attempted to follow me, and indulge their curiosity with an inspection of the stranger.

In the course of my walk, particularly in the immediate vicinity of rivers—not unfrequently even in their beds—I found excavations, undoubtedly made in searching for gold. These evidences of the presence of the precious metal were so numerous that large quantities must be annually obtained. Up on these spurs and foot-hills cattle were fairly abundant, proof undoubted that tetze does not here exist. As the sun went down I noted to the north and north-east two prominent ranges of hills, distant, I should think, two or three days' journey. Some of their peaks attained considerable altitude, say, six or seven thousand feet. Their crests were very irregular in outline, which I took to denote that their summits were rocky.

After sun-down I reached camp; around it was assembled a very large but orderly crowd. While taking a good view of the visitors I was saluted by Umpiqua, Jim being with him. Of course the first question was to enquire for his master; Dillon was over there with the chiefs, for the very "headman" that we had come to Manica to visit, had already become Dillon's host, and together they had set out to intercept us before reaching his principal station.

To describe our meeting and the anguish of my friend when he heard of Selwin's death, could scarcely interest the reader; let me only say that both were such as could be anticipated from one of his impulsive nature.

That evening we sat late; the two Zulu, or rather Matabele chiefs, were our companions, with

Sunday acting as interpreter, when our present and future steps were discussed. Dillon had already obtained a considerable quantity of gold through the instrumentality of the Manica Governor; but more was promised, particularly when we informed him that we would sell—with a suitable amount of ammunition—the three remaining spare guns. Further, that the two we retained should be returned to them by the porters they lent us to take our ivory to the port of embarkation as soon as we had completed our arrangements to leave the country.

It now became a serious and very important question which way we should select for the final part of our land journey. There were five courses open: first, return as we had come; secondly, proceed to Zumbo, and there take boat down the Zambesi; thirdly, go to Tete, and there embark upon the last-mentioned river; or to Senna, on the Zambesi, but nearer to the sea-board, and bearing from Manica about N.E.; and last of all, march nearly due E. to the petty seaport of Sofala, from whence it was probable we should be able to obtain passage for Réunion or Mauritius.

This last course was decided upon, for the reason that the distance was shorter, and that we were unlikely to meet any obstruction on the way from marauding bands of soldiers and hostile kraals; while Zumbo, we were informed, had been destroyed by order of the Matabele King, Tete had been sacked by a hostile chief from across the Zambesi, and Senna was held by a native force, till a large indemnity was paid for the privilege of trading, together with several years arrears of rent that had been permitted to accumulate. Of course to return as we had come was not to be thought of; but I cannot do better than add an extract from Doctor Livingstone's description of Tete, which in nearly every respect is equally applicable to Zumbo and Senna and the country intervening between them that lies upon the south side of the Zambesi.

"I was most kindly received by the commandant, who did everything in his power to restore me from my emaciated condition, and invited me to remain with him until the following month, as this was the unhealthy period at Kilimane. He also generously presented my men with abundant provisions of millet; and gave them lodgings in a house of his own, until they could erect their own huts, whereby they escaped the bite of the tampans, or, as they were here named, carapatos. We had heard frightful accounts of this insect while among the Banyai, and Major Licard assured me its bite is more especially dangerous to strangers, as it sometimes causes fatal fever. The village of Tete is built on a long slope down to the river, with the fort on the water's edge. The rock beneath is grey sandstone, and has the appearance of having been crushed away from the river, the strata thus assuming a crumpled form. The hollow between each crease is a street, the houses being built upon the projecting fold. The rocks at the top of the slope are much higher than the fort, and of course completely command it. The whole of the adjacent country is rocky and broken, but every available spot is under cultivation. The houses of the Europeans in Tete are built of stone cemented with mud instead of lime, and thatched with reeds and grass; they have a rough, untidy appearance in consequence of the cement having been washed out by the rains. There are about thirty of them; the native houses are built of wattle and daub. A wall about ten feet high encloses the village, but most of the native inhabitants prefer to live outside it. There are about 1,200 huts in all, which with European households would give a population of 4,500 souls. Generally there are not more than 2,000 people resident, for the majority are engaged in agricultural operations in the adjacent country. The number of Portuguese, exclusive of the military, was under twenty. There were eighty soldiers, who had been removed hither from Senna, a station lower down the river, in consequence of the mortality that prevailed among them there. Here they enjoy much better health, though they indulge largely in spirits extracted from various plants, wild fruits, and grain by the natives, who understand a method of distillation by means of gun-barrels, and a succession of earthen pots filled with water to keep them cool. The general report here is that, while at Kilimane the fever is continuous, at Tete a man recovers in about three days. The mildest remedies only are used at first, and, if that period be passed, then the more severe.

"The fort of Tete has been the salvation of the Portuguese power in this quarter. It is a small square building, with a thatched apartment for the residence of the troops, and though there are but few guns, they are in a much better state than those of any fort in the interior of Angola. The decay of the Portuguese power in this region is entirely due to the slave trade. In former times considerable quantities of grain—as wheat, millet, and maize—were exported, besides coffee, sugar, oil, indigo, gold-dust, and ivory. The cultivation of grain and the washing for gold-dust were carried on by means of slaves, of whom the Portuguese possessed a large number, and the natives of the interior, both chiefs and people, were friendly to the system, because they supplied the food for the sustenance of the slaves while engaged in gold washings, and thus procured in return a quantity of European goods.

"But when the slave trade began, many of the merchants commenced selling their slaves as a more speedy mode of becoming rich, and they continued this until they had no hands left either to labour or to fight for them. It was just the story of the goose and the golden egg. The coffee and sugar plantations and gold-washings were abandoned, because the labour had been exported to the Brazils. Many of the Portuguese then followed their slaves, and the Government was obliged to pass a law to prevent further emigration, which, had it gone on, would have depopulated the Portuguese possessions altogether.

"Rebellion followed closely on the decrease of the Portuguese establishments. A man of Asiatic and Portuguese extraction, called Nyaude, built a stockade at the confluence of the Luenya and Zambesi; the commandant of Tete armed the whole body of slaves and marched against this stockade, but, when they approached, Nyaude despatched a strong party under his son up the left bank of the Zambesi, which attacked Tete, and plundered and burned the whole town except the house of the commandant and a few others, with the church and fort.

"Having rendered Tete a ruin, Bonga carried off all the cattle and plunder to his father. News of this having been brought to the army before the stockade, a sudden panic dispersed the whole; and as the fugitives took a roundabout course in their flight, Katolosa, who had hitherto pretended to be friendly with the Portuguese, sent out his men to capture as many of them as he could. Another half-caste, called Kisaka, on the opposite bank of the river, likewise rebelled. He imagined that his father had been bewitched by the Portuguese, and he therefore plundered all the plantations of the rich merchants of Tete on the north bank, which is the most fertile, and on which the Portuguese had their villas. When these were destroyed, the Tete people were completely impoverished. An attempt to punish this rebel proved unsuccessful, and he has lately been pardoned by the Home Government. The Portuguese were thus placed between two enemies. Nyaude on the right and Kisaka on the left, the former of whom having placed his stockade on the point of land on the right banks of both the Luenya and Zambesi could prevent intercourse with the sea. The Luenya rushes with great force into the Zambesi when it is low, and in ascending the Zambesi boats must even go a little way up the former river, so as not to be carried away by its currents, and dashed on the rock which stands on the opposite shore of the Zambesi. In coming up to the Luenya for this purpose all boats and canoes that came close to the stockade were robbed. Nyaude kept the Portuguese shut up in their fort at Tete during two years, and they could only get goods sufficient to buy food by sending to Kilimane by an overland route along the north bank of the Zambesi. Commerce, which the slave trade had rendered stagnant, was now completely obstructed. The present commandant of Tete, Major Licard

T

having great influence among the natives, put a stop to the war more than once by his mere presence on the spot. Had I attempted to reach this coast instead of going to Loanda in 1853, I should probably have been cut off, as the war was still raging. My present approach was just at the conclusion of the peace; and when the Portuguese authorities here were informed that I was expected to come this way they all declared that no European could possibly pass through the tribes. Some natives at last came down the river to Tete, and, in allusion to the sextant and artificial horizon, said that 'the Son of God had come, and that he was able to take the sun down from the heavens and place it under his arms!' Major Licard then felt sure that this was the man whom he expected.

"On mentioning to the commandant that I had discovered a small seam of coal, he stated that the Portuguese were already aware of nine such seams, and that five of them were on the opposite bank of the river. As soon as I had recovered from my fatigue I went to examine them. We proceeded in a boat to the mouth of the Lofúbu, about two miles below Tete, and on the opposite bank. Ascending this about four miles against a strong current of beautifully clear water, we landed near a small cataract, and walked about two miles through very fertile gardens to the seam, which we found to be in the perpendicular bank of one of the feeders of the Lofúbu, called Muatize. On the right bank of the Lofúbu there is another feeder entering that river, called the Morongózi, in which there is a still larger bed of coal exposed.

"Further up the Lofúbu there are seams in the riverlets Inyavu and Makare; while in the Maravi country the coal crops out in several places, having evidently been brought to the surface by volcanic action at a later period than the coal formation. I was also informed that there are seams in the independent native territory, and, indeed, I have no doubt but that the whole country between Zumbo and Lupata is a coal-field of at least two and a half degrees of latitude in breadth, having many faults, made during the time of the igneous action. There would not be much difficulty in working the coal or in bringing it to market. The wages of free labourers, when employed in such work, is one braca, that is, two yards of unbleached calico, the only currency used. The carriage of goods up the river to Tete adds about 10 per cent. to their cost, the usual conveyance being by means of very large canoes and launches built at Senna.

"The gold-field, whence Tete draws its supply of the precious metal, lies outside the coal-field, extending in a segment of a circle from the N.E. to the S.E. In the former direction there are six well known washing places; proceeding to the N.W. we meet with the Mushinga range; then crossing to the S. of the Zambesi, near Zumbo, we hear of a station, formerly worked by the Portuguese, on the river Panyáme, called Dambarári. Then follows the unknown kingdom of Abútua, once famous for its gold. To the S.E. of this lie the gold washings of the Mashóna, and still further those of Manica, where gold is found much more abundantly than in any other part, and which has been supposed by some to be the Ophir of King Solomon. I saw the gold from this quarter as large as grains of wheat, while that found in the rivers which run into the coal-field was in very minute scales. The inhabitants are not unfavourable to washings, but at present they only wash when they are in want of a little calico. They know the value of gold perfectly well, for they bring it for sale in goose quills, and demand twenty-four yards of calico for one penful. When the rivers in the district of Manica and other gold-washing places have been flooded, they leave a coating of mud on the banks. The natives observe the spots which dry soonest, and commence digging there in firm belief that gold lies beneath. They are said not to dig deeper than their chins, fearing lest if they did so, the ground should fall in and bury them. When they find a *piece* or flake of gold they bury it again, from the superstitious idea that this is the seed of the gold, and, though they know the value of it well, they prefer losing it rather than the whole future crop.

"Besides gold, there is iron in this district in abundance, of excellent quality. In some places it is obtained from what is called the specular iron ore, in others from black oxide. The latter has been well roasted in the operations of nature, and contains a large proportion of metal. It occurs generally in rounded lumps, and is but slightly magnetic. The natives become aware of its existence in the beds of rivers by the quantity of oxide on the surface, and they find no difficulty in digging it with pointed sticks. They consider English iron as "rotten"; and I have seen a javelin of their own iron curled up by a severe blow like the proboscis of a butterfly, and afterwards straightened while *cold* with two stones. So far as I could learn there is neither copper nor silver. Malachite is worked by the people of Cazembe, but, as I did not see it nor any other metal, I can say nothing about it. A few precious stones are met with, and some parts are quite covered with agates. The mineralogy of the district, however, has not been explored by anyone competent to the task.

"The scenery of the country surrounding Tete is picturesque, being hilly and well wooded. The soil of the valleys is very fruitful and well cultivated. The plantations of coffee, however, are now deserted, and it is difficult to find a single tree."

While with the Manica chief we were abundantly supplied with meat, and finer beef than that obtained from the little handsome Mashoona cattle I never saw or ate. The people also were wonderfully hospitable, and Kaffir and honey beer was given us in such quantities that it was impossible to consume it; while the produce of the country could be purchased at such trifling prices as really to be laughable.

With the valuable and all-powerful support which we had, still there was a difficulty in obtaining porters, and several days' delay took place in consequence. Our own Zulus, to a man, stuck to us, and their laudations, combined with the chief's power, ultimately resulted in success, as we finally obtained fifty-nine able-bodied bearers, so, with our own people, at forty pounds to a load, I calculated that we should be able to take out of the country about two thousand five hundred pounds of ivory, which, at six shillings a pound—the then current rate on the East coast—would realise something over four hundred pounds sterling. This was not more than half of the valuable commodity that we had collected, but for want of porters it was of necessity left behind. With the gold that we had obtained, however, we should be able to repay ourselves all our outlay, and still leave a handsome profit to be added to our credit.

The veteran chief accompanied us two days march, so our start for home was made under most favourable circumstances, which continued till the sea-board was reached. About seventy miles from Sofala a second line of hills was traversed, but presented no formidable obstructions to pedestrians or cattle.

Game still continued abundant, buffalo and elephant spoor being found in every direction; but Dillon only shot five of the former and one of the latter, all being for food; however, he never went any distance from the line of march.

At Sofala we had a slice of luck: a small brig had the blue-peter flying at the foretopmast head. Dillon communicated with the skipper, and induced him to delay his departure for Réunion for a couple of days. This gave us time to pay off our people and make the necessary arrangements for the voyage. Our Zulus had resolved to return to Manica, and from there proceed to their countrymen in Matabele Land, before returning to their own homes.

I was truly grieved to part with them all, for more faithful, honest, and courageous men never served a master.

Of Sofala I have nothing to say, more than that it has a dozen or so fairish houses with several "go downs" scattered about it; the rest are miserable wattle and daub shanties. On the sea-board there are some attempts at fortification, but quite inadequate to prevent the landing of a hostile force, while the soldiers, I was told, were all convicts; whether or not, they were as sorry a crew as I ever looked at. I think the garrison consisted of about forty men.

During our voyage we had fine weather, but it was extremely tedious; however, the cooking was fair and the skipper—a Frenchman—made himself agreeable.

From Réunion we shipped to the Mauritius; from there Dillon sailed to Bombay, and I for home.

With sorrow I have to state that my friend's vessel was lost at sea, for neither he nor it was ever afterwards heard of.

Thus terminated the most successful shooting trip—in a pecuniary sense—that I ever made into Austral Africa.

LIFE ON THE HIGHT VELDT

AND

COUNTRY WEST OF MATABELE LAND.

THE heading that I have selected for this article has been duly considered. Why I choose it, is that under it I have scope to have a growl at the rising generation of sportsmen.

Half the men who hunt with foxhounds in modern times do so for the sake of galloping, and do not care a jack-straw whether pug is killed legitimately or not. Very much the same kind of charge I might bring against the wielder of the gun, in *anno domini*—well, the present period of my life.

The foxhunter and the shooting man of to-day are as much behind their progenitors as the liquor-besotted red men of the present date are inferior to those Sioux and Blackfeet who made themselves a terror to every paleface that entered their hunting grounds.

A man on a three hundred guinea horse can, if he lets his beast have his head, be in at the death after thirty minutes of stiff going, and yet know no more about hounds and hunting than a pig does of a whistle. So it is with the majority of shooting men of the present day, for their adage at home is, "kill all the birds you can," possibly and probably to make a boast of their slaughter, but not unfrequently to balance their poulterer's bill with the outlay their sport has cost them.

Then there is another class of shooting men, who desire to turn their setters and pointers into French poodles or showman's trick dogs. Bah! with a bleat of double emphasis; I would sit upon or rub out such canine teachers. Sellers of dogs, exhibitors of dogs, and doggy men in general, do these things, but who but an unfledged heir to an estate, or a numskull who knows not the value of the coin which has been amassed for him, would call such persons sportsmen? Certainly I would not call such men sportsmen, although they attend country fairs clothed in laced boots and leggings, shooting-jackets covered with pockets, and possibly a whistle at the end of their watchchain instead of a locket. No, thrice no. Give me the sportsman of a quarter of a century back, who would neither sell his game nor turn his kennel into mountebanks; who would listen and gain instruction from those who have shot abroad as well as at home, and after dinner, and even before it, feel that if fortune had sent him to foreign lands, he could have done as the narrator did—yes, and possibly have beaten him.

I trust I have put the above intelligibly before my readers, for they were about the feelings that actuated myself and companions before we started for a country in which to enjoy field sports which a man did not require to be heir to an estate, his mother's darling, or a successful speculator in stocks and shares to participate in. No, no, the land I was bound to penetrate was one where the best man led the way, where the rifle took the place of the bird gun, and the milksop, as well as the robust, often died.

A few years ago Bamanwato was the *ultima thule* of civilisation in South Africa. Here I found myself, after a tedious and trying journey along the edge of the Kalihari Desert.

Poker and *vingt-et-un* helped to put in an otherwise desultory fortnight, while the waggon was being re-fitted and fresh oxen obtained. Specie was scarce among the traders of this "jumping-off stone of the world," and if they had not gold, they had its equivalent in blood-feathers, and ivory, either of which was as good as coin the moment their possessors reached Algoa Bay or Capetown.

I cannot give names, for possibly both my most redoubtable foes in card contests are still alive. For several days the fickle goddess, Luck, appeared to have no partiality, so that a settling would not have made a difference of fifty dollars either way. But Fred D——, the trader, direct from the Diamond fields, arrived at Shoshong, and among his articles of *vertu* he had what was believed to be seven dozen of champagne and cherry brandy, with which to purchase hunting veldt from Lubengulo, for that august monarch considers a mixture of these admirable drinks the only thing fit for a lubricant of his royal throat. Well, the King of the Matabeles never got that liquor, and Fred never got any further up country.

A more remarkable circumstance occurred after this last arrival's cargo was broached, viz., that poker became as much indulged in by daylight as it had been after the sun had set; and, instead of ostrich feathers and ivory changing hands, "chits" did. "Chit" is a Chinese and Indian word; in this instance it represented an I O U, and not a friendly note.

Fred D—— got his return load without going further north, for his champagne and cherry brandy sold well, although the former was New Jersey cider, and the latter Angostura bitters; but what mattered the difference of appellations? None of the Bamanwato *coterie* were particular as long as the flavour had a smack of the Simon Pure, and there was a "bite" in its swallow.

At length the last of my antagonists (for the others had retired disgusted) called out, "Double or quits." I accepted the challenge, and won. Again I was asked to "give the loser a show." I did so, and was victorious; a third time the same was the result. So the deck of cards was thrown upon the table by my unfortunate rival, and we adjourned to have a drink and settle amicably.

People were not particular in paying debts or collecting them in that locality, so after all the fuss I only found myself richer by three hundred pounds, which was represented by ivory, blood-feathers, and two horses. Both these nags were good-looking, serviceable beasts; in fact, one appeared as if he could gallop, but I neither got nor asked for a warranty with them. No, Bamanwato was a happy-go-lucky place, and there people do not condescend to be "dirty particular."

Where the habits of the white population were so primitive and arcadian, my natural modesty prevented my inquiring the character of my new horses. Moreover, I did not think that their past records mattered much, for I was egotistical enough to believe that I could ride anything, from a grasshopper to a mud-turtle. So when I trecked out of Shoshong, the capital of Bamanwato, I scarcely knew more about my lately-acquired nags than that one was a strawberry roan, and the other a black chestnut. "Jordan is a hard road to travel." The author who wrote this piece of information obviously never trecked round the southern and eastern side of the Bamanwato Hills, or he would have quoted that locality instead of Palestine's river. For the next three days there was no improvement in the travelling, for when out of sand veldt in we dashed into a sand river-bed, the track always so heavy that the lower felloes of the waggon wheels were six or more inches out of sight. However, in due course of time Tchakani and Limooni vleys were passed, and soon after I was outspanned at Palatswe river, where water was found by digging.

Here I met the son of a Yorkshire horse-dealer who was going up country on a trading expedition, and, as lions had killed his horse two nights previously, he wanted another nag. My newly-acquired black or dark chestnut struck his fancy; so, if he rode him and liked him, he would pay me £50 for the animal and take him without a warranty for being *salted*.

Short a time as I had possessed the beast, I did not like him, that's a fact, for he had kicked me once pretty near the region of the abdomen, and taken a piece out of my shoulder with his teeth, and all this exuberance of spirits was testified because I had gone, prompted by a Christian spirit, into his vicinity, to see whether his halter rope was secured and his proper allotment of mealies doled out. No, upon the whole, I think I would sooner have been without that horse; his demonstrativeness and playfulness of character did not suit my usually staid disposition.

One of the boys saddled and bridled the beast. When led out with his trappings on, a gayer or more corky-looking mount could scarcely be seen, although he showed a little more of the white of his eyes than I desired to look at.

The Yorkshireman, who considered himself equal to any rough-rider, mounted, and turned the animal's head from camp; but as the black did not evince readiness to leave its locality, the rider jogged him with his spurs. Whew! Buffalo Bill's best buck-jumpers, whether it was Brick Pomeroy or Delirium Tremens, could not have excelled the black in their performances. So friend G—— rapidly found himself on his back among the mapani brushwood. However, the would-be purchaser was not to be thus intimidated, so he mounted again. This time he was shot high enough to go over a telegraph wire, so he refused to continue the exciting pastime.

I chaffed him on the exhibition he had made, so he badgered me to get on my horse. I did so, but did not remain long there. However I thought I would make another try, and postpone dismounting so abruptly; but my views on the subject I was unable to carry out. So we both turned into the waggon and tapped a bottle of "square-face."

Among a hunter's retinue of servants there are certain to be ambitious characters. I had several of that sort with me, so all of this disposition had a try with the black, and the result was the same, save that one nearly broke his neck, and was in consequence on the sick list for a week. So this "poker horse," for so I called him, having won him at that interesting game, was not sold then; but I trusted to find a purchaser on a future occasion among the coloured aristocracy of the land. I have heard it said that money won at cards never does any good. Certainly this horse, won by these means, did not promise to be of much service to me.

At Gokwe I was joined by a number of natives who were returning from the diamond-fields. Among them was an unmistakable Hottentot. My cook told me that he came from Basutoland, was a good horseman, and would like to ride the black. It was all for amusement and pleasure that he would do it. No, he did not want any saddle; a blanket and a surcingle was all he required, except possibly I could spare for the occasion my handsome silver-mounted *jambok*. The Tottie's trifling request was acceded to, for I expected some fun, and that he would not go far.

With his customary amiability Poker was mounted; the yellow imp gave a yell, and at the same time laid on with vigour the *jambok*. At such treatment the black was evidently taken by surprise, for he forgot to buck-jump, but went off into the veldt at a swinging gallop, that far excelled in pace any speed that could be shown by the other horses about the waggons.

At length rider and horse began to grow beautifully less in the distance, and ultimately disappeared. I began to regret that my animal was having so much taken out of him, and the longer his return was delayed, the stronger were my regrets.

At length the sun went down, and at length the sun rose, mid-day arrived, in due time sunset, and only then could I understand, or bring myself to believe, that the confounded Tottie had stolen my nag, the new blanket that had been strapped so tightly under the surcingle, and my handsome silver-mounted *jambok*.

If we, my Yorkshire friend and self, had used a cutting switch instead of spurs we might neither have been thrown; the punishment inflicted with the former Poker evidently was used to and dreaded, for possibly he was bred among niggers, who, like the Boers, seldom or never make use of a spur.

One would have thought that I had seen the last of Poker; not so. When riding through some heavy timber, near the Seribi river, not above thirty miles from Tatin, I came across seven giraffes. I singled out from among them a splendid cow with a calf at her heels, about ten feet high, and pushed them at my horse's best pace. At the time I was mounted on the very flower of my stud, an animal that could gallop. At first I rapidly gained upon the game, but afterwards, getting into a dense scrub, I began to lose ground. However, I dare not slacken my pace, for that meant losing the meat I had set my heart upon; so hoped for smoother riding and fewer impediments. After a time I got my desires, but it was too late; my willing horse was pumped out, and could go no further. Already he had made several flounders ominous of coming on his head, and my reins were tightening on the bit to pull him up, when, to my surprise, a horseman dashed in after my game over a hundred yards to my front. It only required a glance to tell me that the new comers were Tottie and Poker. Oh! but it was a gruesome sight, more than any Christian man could stand; so I jumped out of the saddle and put up my two hundred yards sight, with the hope, you must know, of hitting the horse, but I was out of breath, and made a clean miss; at three hundred and four hundred yards I did the same, so quit shooting. Then I thought to follow up the chase, and capture the horse thief, but my horse was so blown that I dared not urge him beyond a walk. I was beaten, fairly beaten, and, worse than all, the scoundrel would doubtless secure the meat I had worked so hard for.

There was nothing for me to do now but return to the waggon. To William, my driver, I narrated what had occurred, and also that I would give ten dollars, so many strings of beads and pounds of brass wire, for the capture of the thief and horse. Immediately afterwards he had a consultation with some Massara Bushmen who were with me, and they, with my factotum, soon departed in pursuit of the delinquent, leaving me alone to chew the cud of anger and disappointment.

About midnight they returned. Poker was with them, but the Tottie had escaped. They said that he had heard them approaching, so scuttled into the bush. Nevertheless, however hurried was his departure, he had taken with him my new blanket and silver-mounted *jambok*. I feel convinced they let him off, believing that blood is thicker than water. It was probably better so, for what could I have done with the miscreant but flog him?—a summary course of justice I much objected to. After this adventure I often rode Poker, and a better or more enduring beast seldom looked through a bridle.

HUNTING FAVOURITES IN AUSTRAL AFRICA.

IN my life I think I have made acquaintance with all the great hunting grounds of the Old and New World, and can assert, fearless of contradiction, that the southern portion of Equatorial Africa bears the palm from all others in this speciality, for it is the home of the lordly elephant, of the giraffe, rhinoceros, hippopotamus, eland, hartebeeste, khoodoo, zebra, lion, panther, and smaller game too numerous to mention. Several times, of late years, I have visited this paradise of the sportsman, and seldom am absent from it for a short period, but that I wish to return. The reader must not imagine, however, that in this distant land all is *couleur de rose;* no! far from it; but the sweets far outbalance the bitters. Indian *shikaris*, I fear, will not feel disposed to have Hindostan placed in a second position to this country; but I have no hesitation in doing so, as I know both, and therefore can judge of the pretensions of each.

The African elephant, on an average, is quite eighteen inches, often two feet, taller than his Indian congener, and male and female alike bear ivory, while, in our Eastern Empire, few males possess tusks, and the cows are always without them. Again, the lion is a much nobler and heavier-built animal than the tiger, nor is he the skulking rascal that the latter is. Hear the king of beasts roar at night when he visits the vicinity of your camp; his approach may be made on silent feet, but if so listen to the bass voice that proclaims his presence, and you can well feel satisfied that the utterer of those deep toned notes does not dread any other denizen of the forest or *veldt*.

Further, the giraffe and hippopotamus are only found in Africa, while the varieties of antelopes common to this continent are too many to be enumerated, and in the majority of instances far excel in stature any representatives of their species that are to be found in any other part of the world.

The truth of the above remarks is known to so many that it is unnecessary to add further to them, so we will at once proceed to the table lands between the Limpopo and Zambesi, definitely named Mashoona Land, where, not a long time back, stood my hunting camp. A part of this plateau is nearly five thousand feet above sea level, so, although it may be intensely warm there under the vertical sun, night and early morning are cool and invigorating; quite sufficiently so, in fact, to brace you up after the lassitude you may have suffered during the previous noon-day heat. Then no inconvenience or worry from mosquitoes is experienced, unless your halting-place be in the immediate vicinity of marsh or stagnant water. The country here is, moreover, not the same uninteresting dead flats, covered with nought else but grass, peculiar to the Orange Free State, portions of Griqualand, and the Old Colony, but a constant succession of rolling hills well supplied with wood, while water in localities is abundant. Of course, droughts occur in Southern Equatorial Africa as they do elsewhere, but they never have the same lasting and deleterious effect that they produce in the territories adjoining the great Kalihari Desert. Thus the constant anxiety that is experienced by the traveller in the South and West of Africa, for fear he shall not reach water by a certain time, or possibly not find it at all, is done away with. An excess of water may be the cause of many ills to the human family, but the want of it is simply death, not only to man, but to every live creature with him, and on whom his progress and comfort depend.

But where my camp is, and where I wish the reader, in mind at least, to accompany me, there is no fear that we shall suffer from want of the above necessary of life, and the appearance of my servants, horses, dogs, and cattle will soon convince the visitor that such is the case. It is not necessary for him to be a judge of condition to be satisfied on this point, for comfort and contentment reign over all, from the herculean Matabele to the pigmy bush boy; from the powerful wire-haired greyhound to the vicious Skye terrier; from the wary, ever watchful baboon, to the little black-faced grey monkey or sleek domestic tabby that purs in contentment on his favourite seat, the dissel-boom or pole of one of my bullock waggons.

Plenteous and nutritious pasture here abounds, while the whole landscape over is dotted with numerous trees, many of which are fruit bearing. But fruit in its wild state never equals in size and flavour what has been cultivated, for, as a rule, the stone will be found out of all proportion in size to the edible part. The preponderating species of trees will generally be found to be the boabab, the meruley, Indian fig several varieties of mimosa, the different kinds of euphorbias, and the African banian, whose pendent tendrils from many a limb aloft, swing to and fro on the pressure of the slightest breath of wind.

The boabab, the first mentioned, although far from lofty, is supposed to possess the largest trunk of any vegetable production known, a circumference of one hundred feet being far from rare when measured a yard or two above the ground's surface. For thirty or more feet the trunk is bare, but at that altitude the branches strike out to an immense distance, at right angles from the parent stem, covering with their shadows a vast area. The individual leaves are very large, and in shape like those of the horse-chestnut, while the fruit resembles a large cocoanut when the husk is green. From this the natives and the few Europeans that are acquainted with the boabab make a refreshing acid drink, which is considered an unfailing specific against fever.

To the researches of the great naturalist, Adanson, we owe our first knowledge of this wonderful tree, hence it has been scientifically called *Adansonia gigantica*. He supposed that the large specimens to be found at the present time existed before the flood. Whether this be so or not, you cannot destroy it by water, or kill it by fire, unless the stem be utterly consumed. The trunk is invariably little more than a shell of a foot in thickness, and consequently the interior forms a large chamber, frequently made use of for a dwelling-place by the natives. But, if man makes use of its lower portion for a shelter, nearly all the birds of the air do the same with its branches, and it appears that all live at peace with the others in these commonwealths, however contrary their natures may be. I am under the impression that as this tree has such a vast circumference it cannot be ascended by the tree-snakes, the enemy of all the feathered family; and that, therefore, on this safe and neutral ground family quarrels or dislikes are temporarily laid aside.

The meruley tree, which is also likely to be unknown to the reader, seems to be a cross between a green plum and a walnut or hickory, the leaf, stem, and general characteristics having all the special peculiarities of the latter, while the fruit is externally like the greengage, but internally a nut. Its size is about that of an ordinary ash, say thirty-six to forty inches in circumference, so not too large for the mammoth bull elephants to sway to and fro till the sweet, acid fruit falls. It is well known that elephants will travel very long distances to districts where this tree abounds, at the season when the fruit is ripe. Well do the Massara bush people know this, and so make many of these *gourmets* pay their lives for their gastronomic *penchant*. The next two families of trees are common enough to be known to all, but not so the euphorbias, which in every variety are intensely foreign to European eyes. Frequently they grow upright to the height of seventy feet or even more, at other times they might almost be deemed creepers; the bark, however, is always deeply annulated, and the surface and wood extremely spongy and full of sap, which is a deadly poison to all cloven-footed animals and horses.

The natives, being aware of this circumstance, use this juice for poisoning the rain pools and small *vleys*, which results in their killing large numbers of antelopes and zebras annually.

Having thus given a brief description of the principal, and, at Home, least known, trees that prevail about my camp, so as to enable the reader to have a good idea of its surroundings, we will suppose it to be that time in the morning when darkness is giving place to daylight. Lighter and lighter as it becomes in the east, so the surroundings become more clearly defined, till the numerous details that constitute my camp equipage are revealed. The lumbering Cape waggon, with its snow-white tilt, has been so often described since the Zulu war that it would be superfluous for me to do so here ; suffice it for me to say that I have two, and that they are drawn up parallel to each other about twelve feet apart, the intervening space between them being covered over with a large heavy canvas sail. Under this temporary roofing are two or three portable chairs and a table, this constituting my sitting and dining-room, but not my dormitory, which is inside one of the waggons, under either of which, or both, my coloured servants and hunters sleep. But there, also, others of my retinue pass the night—viz., the dogs; and it is wonderful in what a small space they stow themselves away, and how unobservable they become, for, whether for warmth or protection, they secrete themselves in twos or threes alongside of each black man—an arrangement which ever appears to be alike satisfactory to biped and quadruped.

Although the sun is not yet up, my body servant soon produces for me a hot cup of strong soup, made from kooran, pauw, or buck, the savoury mess having been left to simmer over the fire the whole of the previous night; and rare stuff this is for a pick-me-up at that time of day, especially if thickened with some onion, rice, and broken biscuit. But eating and the smell of the viands attract the dogs, about twenty in number. Some, as will be observed, are well bred, others out-and-out curs, but all are useful. The former are six imported greyhounds and a pointer; the latter are nondescripts, with more or less greyhound blood in them, and picked up anywhere, and from anybody, since I made my start from Griqualand West, at an average price of one pound each. The large brindled animal that takes precedence of all the others is a three-quarter bred greyhound, his other parent being of the breed at present so fashionable, and called the "big Dane." This is my favourite, and my most frequent attendant. He possesses both courage and strength to attack almost anything, yet knows how to take care of himself—a matter of no small importance—and has such an admirable nose that wounded game seldom escapes him, for he is possessed of great speed and bottom, but his temper is uncertain, so that I seldom chastise him without fear that he will turn upon me. With his companions he is simply king, and with corresponding dignity so treats them. He has long won his spurs, for in single combat he has killed striped hyæna, a serval (the largest of the lynx family), and a huge baboon, this last performance being almost without precedent. As to springbok, duykers, steinbok, hares, and jackals, all the other dogs have had a turn at them and similar small game, and have acquitted themselves with credit. After distributing among the hungry pack a few pounds of biltong (sun-dried meat), I proceed to inspect the rest of my belongings, followed by the entire pack. By this time the sun commences to show his ruddy, burnished face amid a retinue of clouds as brilliant in colour as himself. This is the most delightful portion of the twenty-four hours in Africa, and I affirm that in no part of the earth have I seen such sunrises. Their beauty word-painting could never do justice to, although the landscape artist might be more successful with his brush. But would such a work be saleable? No! I say, for our connoisseurs and stay-at-home authorities upon such matters would unhesitatingly condemn it as unnatural. Once in New York I was charmed and delighted with a painting, which in no way exaggerated the marvellous colours of American autumn foliage. A noble lord, closely allied to a house reputed to possess one of the finest collections of paintings in England, actually walked past this acknowledged irreproachable work of art with the remark, " Preposterous! Colour was cheap when that was done."

But as I advance to the front of my waggons, a short, sharp click attracts my attention. Again and again the sound is repeated, each time more impatiently than the first. "All right, old man, all right," I call out; "no need of hurry, old man;" and in a moment after I confront the cause of the noise, a very large baboon, sitting on the top of the waggon tilt just over the front box. This is Boanerges, so called from the depth of his bass voice, which, when heard, is not easily forgotten. He is sociable and kindly, although a wee bit selfish with his master, dislikes black men as an American does an Indian, and assuredly would be dangerous to native women and children if they were unprotected. With the quadrupeds he is on fairly good terms, but his disposition to play tricks or take liberties often causes a break in the *entente cordiale* that ought to exist. Moreover, he is a wise brute, not only in his own conceit, but in the opinion of others, for there is none in my menagerie that can catch him asleep or play tricks upon him, except my pet monkey, to whom the reader will be introduced in due time. Why, I may be asked, do I keep Boanerges? For the reason that he is one of the most useful animals in my whole retinue. But how? In keeping guard at night he is far more wakeful than any dog, while his sense of smell and powers of sight are marvellous. Let any strange animal approach the camp by day or night, and it will at once be challenged by a " Who's there?" that will be heard in still atmosphere for nearly a mile. This warning puts the dogs on the *qui vive*, when, whether the intruder does or does not steer off, his "little game" is checkmated for that occasion. Neither is my baboon destitute of courage, for I have known him attack a hyæna, mobbed by the dogs, with such ferocity and science as were most effective. But his method of assault differed entirely from that of his allies, for, watching the harassed antagonist that was standing at bay, he availed himself of a chance, and seized it by one of the hind legs, which he drew from under it, and completely disabled by ham-stringing, at a single bite. Again, if fresh vegetables are wanted, which is not a rare occurrence, Mr. Boanerges is turned loose, and it is seldom long before he discovers a large tuber, not unlike a turnip, which is generally a foot or more under the soil, and, consequently, would have been passed without our being aware of its existence. Presenting my valuable friend with something edible, I move on to inspect the bullocks. By this time the heat, having become sufficiently effective, all are on their legs, standing in the order in which they treck the waggon, to which each belongs, for all sleep tied by strong rheims around their horns to their respective yokes. The driver of each team makes his report, pointing out the footsore and sick, if any such there be. Then the ailing are examined, and if nothing serious is the matter, all walk off under the guardianship of the *voor-looper* in search of the most nutritious pastures to be found within easy distance.

Now, however uninteresting an animal an ox may appear, I assure all that " there are bullocks and there are bullocks." Your leaders and after-oxen must be possessed of certain qualities, and these qualities are the result of specialities of character, and the more you study and become accustomed to them, the more you will find to appreciate in them. Of all things, if you want them to serve you well and willingly, do not resort to the whip unless absolutely necessary. In 1882 I had a pair of after-bullocks and leaders which never required more than the voice to hasten or direct their course, and as the intermediate animals follow the example of those in front, an occasional show of whip was ample for all purposes.

Well! there go my means of again returning to civilisation; they appear to know pretty well what they are about, but watch them for a few minutes and, you will be certain of it. A well-known and trusted member of the herd lows, the others answer, and straight as a bee line, all follow the first speaker to the best pastures or water, whichever they may be most in need of. Again, at night, when they are brought home, each stands facing the driver, and submits to have the rheim placed round his horns, when, without resistance, they walk to their own yoke to be tied up. This docility is particularly noticeable when they are in a country where large carnivorous animals are numerous. In such submissive conduct does it not appear that they are aware that their safety depends upon such a course of procedure? Undoubtedly I think it does; so, take my word for it, bullocks are gifted with no small amount of intelligence. The more distant, and therefore more uncivilised natives, admire the ox so much that they try to resemble it, and the better to do so, knock out their front teeth in the upper jaw. Now, there are no keener observers of animal life, and none that note their good and bad qualities so correctly, so if they thought the ox a fool they would not wish to be like him. No, the bullock is no fool, but he is obstinate, and extremely sensitive of abuse. Thus, if you are always punishing him with *jambok* and whip, you will soon have evidence that cruelty is far from the best policy.

Love of offspring is another marked characteristic of the bovine family. No cow, however young she may be, will desert her calf, and if the youngster be attacked, even by the most formidable beast of prey, the mother will sell her life to save the youngster's. What other animal, even proud man himself, could do more?

But now I pass on from the too generally abused treck oxen to the most popular and esteemed servants of all man's animal dependants—the horses; but these must not be expected to be found the sleek, well-conditioned, well-groomed favourites that the English eye is accustomed to rest upon at home.

For beauty and speed there unquestionably is no horse that rivals the Arab and our own home-improved breeds, but, for disregard of exposure, power of enduring thirst and scantiness of food, I will back the Cape horse against any of the equine family that I have found in any part of the earth. About Capetown and the oldest settlements very pretty little saddle and harness horses are to be seen, but the true old stamp is not common until the Orange River is crossed. Of course, this stock was brought there by the original Boer seceders from British rule, who made their exodus from the colony when slavery was abolished by us. Thus, I am inclined to believe that the Basuto, Transvaal, and Bechuana Land bred horses are descended from a cross between Dutch and barb progenitors, for they have more or less, the marked external characteristics in form, of both. Although this breed seldom exceeds fourteen and a-half hands in height, they are wonderful weight carriers, very good tempered, and remarkably easy in gait, all great advantages in the hunting *veldt*. Their withers, however, frequently appear disproportionately high, their necks unusually long, with an ungainly falling off towards the rump; but if they are able and willing to do the work demanded of them, what does this matter? It is a common expression in interior South Africa, " never buy a big horse if you can get a little 'un;" and in this expression there is a great deal of truth, as I myself have proved. But here are my stud, three in number, waiting for their morning feed of soaked mealies, each shaking with impatience his empty nosebag, in which their muzzles have passed the preceding night. Why so? may be asked. To keep them from inhaling the night air, for the canvas bag acts as a respirator, and as such I have found it useful and a great preventive to horse sickness, one of the most fatal diseases that this family is subject to in any land.

A quarter of a patent bucket of swollen corn is given each morning and evening, and, when not required for use during the day, the nags are turned loose till near sundown under the charge of one of the boys, to enable them to fill their stomachs with the nutritious but coarse grass which abounds. It is customary to knee-halter horses when doing so; but if they are fed regularly at certain hours they are sure to return to the waggons at the specified time to look for their night meal. When not troubled with *lampers*, which is not very prevalent here, these up-country horses are greedy feeders, and, at such times, disposed to be very spiteful to each other; thus they should invariably be tied some distance apart. Grooming, of course, cannot be practised thoroughly when leading such a nomadic life, still, a rub over with a wisp of rushes or coarse grass, with an after-dressing with a hard brush, will always be found conducive to the health and comfort of your horses. The first of my beauties is a bay with black points, and of undoubted English pedigree. He has a great turn of speed, and, over ordinary ground, can with ease overtake a giraffe; no mean performance, I can assure the reader, for these long-legged, spotted gentry can go a tremendous pace. He also can jump well, which I proved to the astonishment of some Boers in Marico, where I rode him back and forward over a brick wall, just under five feet in height. I never saw men stare and look so crestfallen as these Dutchmen did, when I offered to repeat the performance, provided they doubled their bets. But these gentry do not easily part with their coin, so satisfied themselves by exclaiming, "*Mein Got!*

mein Got! vat a verdam'd Englander." But this was not by long odds the most remarkable of my bay's performances, as you doubtless will think when I narrate the following :—

I left Kania, in the country of Hasesheba, at 6 p.m., and reached Lininkani (the distance being seventy miles) before six the next morning. Over part of the country traversed there was no road, and I lost myself for quite two hours, the night being very dark, while the latter portion of my journey was exceedingly stony. After fourteen or fifteen hours I was again in the saddle, and reached the diamond fields in Griqualand in five days, the last distance covered being two hundred and forty miles, and some of it over the most villainous loose sand imaginable. As I was travelling at night, to avoid meeting marauding parties of Boers, then invading Monsewa's and Moncoran's country, I was only able to procure grain twice for my own mount and that of my after-rider.

This after-rider was said to be a son of the redoubtable Nimrod, Gordon Cumming, and was the only red-headed black man I ever saw. He rode a small, black stallion, purchased by me from a trader who had captured it from the Boers, and I seriously affirm that this far from good-looking horse seemed to freshen up to his work the further we progressed. Now, as both of us were six-footers, and each weighed close on twelve stone, this I hold was a wonderful performance when all the surroundings are taken into consideration. On another occasion I rode this bay horse from Sechele's to Molemo's, a distance of over seventy miles, in about fourteen hours, having spent at least two of them in stalking a springbok and hartebeeste, and two more hours during the time I was twice "*off-saddled*," yet my dear little bay arrived at his destination apparently as corky and full of life as he was at the time of starting. Proud I am of this beauty, and I think he knows it, for, whether loose on the *veldt*, or tied up, he ever greets my approach with a welcome whinny.

Yes! and so does " the old moke," the next in seniority, a thorough type of the best class of Boer horse, once an iron grey in colour, but now getting very white along the flanks. A better hunting horse than "the old moke" never looked through a bridle, and only one fault does he possess that I know of, and that is, if walking at a slow pace he appears to have the same failing as Mr. Wardle's fat boy—going to sleep, and consequently stumbling. But when the rider is aware of this, it is not difficult to prevent its occurrence However, on the grass or bush velt there could not be a safer animal to sit on when going the pace.

Once he was ridden by a friend of mine, no light weight, I can assure you ; but I had probably better begin the story from the start. It happened in this way. We were out-spanned near Pitsani, in West

Bechuana Land, and had settled to have a long hunt on the morrow. Big game, such as hartebeeste, wildebeeste, and quaha (*Anglice*, quagga), are not now plentiful in this neighbourhood, although small bucks, bustards, florikins, partridges, sand-grouse, and hares abound in every direction. Lately we had feasted *ad nauseam* on the minor-sized trash, so resolved not to use our rifles till something worthy of a Martini-Henry bullet was found.

On a stony ridge of undulating hill, about an hour after leaving camp, my companion whistled to attract my attention. Turning, I saw he had dismounted, and, doing the same, I proceeded to join him, as silently as a veteran can move through brush when leading a horse.

When I reached his position we left our horses, and made a sharp detour to the right, not only to render the wind better suited to our purpose, but to gain ground less obstructed by brush and such like impediments as might interfere with our aim. In our calculations we were perfectly correct, for through a glade we saw a hartebeeste cow, quite as high as an ordinary ox at the withers, unsuspiciously cropping the lower leaves of a mimosa tree. This antelope, although probably, with the exception of the ostrich, the most wary of game in South Africa, was evidently quite unconscious of our presence. My friend's opportunities for killing the larger species of game not having been at all equal to my own, I waived the honour of first shot, in his favour. The range was, say, one hundred and twenty yards, and sharp on the report came the ominous drum-like "thud" sound, that told decisively that the object aimed at was struck. Still the hartebeeste never moved, or indicated in any manner that it was alarmed by the sound of the discharge, or even was aware of our presence. Soon another cartridge was placed in the breech, and the same episode was repeated, but with the difference that the game broke into a gallop on receiving the bullet, and would soon have disappeared had not my comrade sprung into his saddle and followed in hot pursuit. Not deeming for a moment but that the chase would be short, quick, and decisive, I ascended a neighbouring acclivity to observe what took place. When I again saw the principals in the drama, they were nearly half a mile off, in comparatively open country, but going at their best pace, and, extraordinary to say, which looked the heavier handicapped was hard to decide. My comrade was not remarkable for his horsemanship, and a very substantially-built gentleman; still he was a bold rider, so well I knew that the hunt had developed itself into the question of who could last the longest, and in spite of what my ears had told me of the bullets going straight, I commenced to question their accuracy. But, contrary to the habit of this game, which is to go right away, it kept doubling and turning, making my position almost the central point upon which the whole adventure was being enacted. After about twenty-five minutes of this work the hartebeeste gained some low bush and halted in it. In another moment my companion was on his feet and about to fire, when the game again broke into a gallop, apparently as fresh as ever, but was stopped before going many paces with a shot so effectually delivered, that, large as it was, it dropped as if felled with a pole-axe.

On skinning and cutting up the quarry we found that the first shot had gone through the lobe of the heart and split it up for the distance of quite an inch; an illustration of the extraordinary vitality possessed by all the antelope family. If it had been a lion or a leopard that had received such a wound, it never would have moved ten paces from the place where it was struck.

A person cannot hunt long in Africa before he discovers that all vegetable-feeding animals are possessed of very much more vitality than those that subsist on flesh. But the above is narrated to show what endurance "the old moke" possessed, for if he had gone one, he had gone eight or ten miles at his best pace over very rough ground, with at least fifteen stone on his back, and at the termination of the run, excepting a little flank action, showed no visible indications of fatigue. Dear old horse! I am not likely to see your equal again, either for companionship, utility, or a knowledge of what to do or how to act under any circumstances that arose, for you loved your master, gave your heart to your work, and never quarrelled or kicked at the most presuming or intruding of your comrades.

But Strawberry, although a lady, I introduce last. To excuse myself for so doing, I may state that she is the youngest and least experienced of my trio, yet she has all the qualities (barring temper) that will make her most valuable. In company she is a little jealous, and a little fiery, and apt to presume on the good temper and skill in equitation of the rider whom she does not know. When she came into my possession she had never had a saddle on her back, and her powers of buck-jumping were of no mean order, but now she will bring an antelope home on her back with the utmost *sang froid*. Her courage, too, is marvellous, and you may ride her up close to the most dreaded of carnivora without her showing the slightest nervousness, let alone fear. She reminds me very much of my dear old charger, Tommy, which I rode from Petermaritzburg, Natal, to near here (the situation of my present camp), and back again to my starting place, without being sick, sore, or weary during this terribly long and tedious journey.

But, to return to Strawberry, if she was turned loose at any time, unless driven off, she would not leave camp, where she would have her nose into everything edible, or otherwise, that excited her curiosity ; as for my reading or resting, when she is about, it would be quite out of the question. If she had not me to plague, she would devote her time to the cows, goats, or dogs. The baboon she has an intense dislike for, and if that wise beast did not take shelter on the tilt of the waggon, she would soon settle scores with him. This feud commenced from the day Boanerges took her by surprise, and stole from her a head of mealie corn. However, with the cat it is quite different ; that sleek gentleman frequently sits on her back, and invariably makes it his haven of safety when the baboon is loose. An onion will tempt the baboon to do almost any reckless action to get possession of it, but even that will not entice him to go to the mare's bucket if she be feeding out of it.

Sugar-cane is also a great favourite with both, but if a stem be given between them, unless Boanerges gets his end between the spokes of one of the waggon wheels, he is not likely to enjoy more than a small share of the luxury ; but should this occur, then there is a regular game of " pull devil, pull baker," till at length the superior weight of the mare gains the day, when Mr. Baboon, sulky, but still chattering, retires in high dudgeon to his favourite retreat.

One trick that is objectionable I cannot break her of, viz.. biting the buttons of my coat. I have known other horses to do the same. The charger of General Cliffords, A.D.C., did not only this to its master, but to any person that came within its reach. So my mare's offence is slightly mitigated, for others have done likewise. "Two blacks don't make a white," I am aware; but then, Strawberry is my baby, and consequently, I suppose, just a little spoilt.

Having got thus far, my principal servant announces breakfast. On non-hunting days this meal is made an event of, for all the good things the waggon contains are hunted out to do it honour. An Indian or Chinese cook I give the palm to, but a Kaffir or Zulu, with a little instruction, will not be found far behind, and as regards cleanliness I think that the African certainly deserves preference. But while I am enjoying my meal there is a visitor who puts in his appearance, whose appetite demands gratification, and who has no objection to show that such is the case; this is young Master Jumbo, a baby elephant, a few weeks back made prisoner by some of my bush people. Already he has become quite tame, and appears to have entirely forgotten his loving and devoted maternal parent, who sacrificed her life to save young hopeful from capture. Alas, as it is among men so it is among beasts—how soon are forgotten kindness and favours bestowed! As far as I can judge I should imagine young Jumbo to be about four months old; his height now is a little over three feet, but he is already as strong as a

Shetland pony, in proof of which I have had three young darkies on his back at the same time. It is absurdly amusing to see with what complacency he permits this liberty to be taken with him, not for a moment exhibiting the slightest impatience till he is induced to carry his load, when in detail he takes each of these black mites of humanity by the leg, and, as we would say in Scotland, "coups them clean off." This performance is never done hurriedly, but with a gravity thoroughly ludicrous to behold; taking down the great *genus homo* a few pegs evidently tickles his fancy. The history of this poor little beast is rather a sad one. Cigar, my head huntsman, was out looking for giraffes when he came across the spoor of a large and small elephant. This he followed up for a few miles, when he overtook the parent and child, the baby not being able to travel fast and the mother refusing to desert it. As is invariably the case under such circumstances, the old cow was exceeedingly vicious and chevied her pursuers in every direction, thus making it totally impossible to capture the youngster. Such devotion and resolution displayed in so good a cause, one would have supposed to be reason enough for giving up the intention of kidnapping her precocious progeny. But Hottentots are not sensitive or particularly thin-skinned in reference to perpetrating deeds of barbarity, so they turned to, and destroyed the life of the self-sacrificing parent. But this was no easy matter. A *vley* of water was at hand, in which both took refuge, and it was not until the hide of the elder one was so covered with assegais as to make her resemble an irate porcupine that she succumbed, her last and dying action being to embrace her well-loved offspring. Cigar and his party had some difficulty in getting Master Jumbo to camp, but in a very short time he forgot his affectionate mother, and appeared desirous of supplying her place by brute and human friends. When at meals he is a fearful nuisance, for his trunk is into everything, and though he is constantly getting scalded and meeting with numerous mishaps and indignities, still it appears impossible to correct the little scoundrel's proclivity of prying, and discovering for himself whether what he finds is edible or not. Sugar is his favourite delicacy, but biscuits or mealie porridge are also much-loved viands. Soon after his capture his skin indicated that he was suffering in health, and that not improbably caused by change of diet; but now he appears to have regained his pristine state, which I partially account for through his having a bath twice a week, on which occasion he is abundantly lathered with carbolic soap, after which he is lubricated, the oil being rubbed thoroughly in by the elbow grease of a couple of stalwart Massara bushmen till he shines like a piece of black indiarubber. The performance of this operation gives Jumbo an immense amount of pleasure, for he submits to be turned and pulled about and placed in every conceivable position without the slightest objection.

It is more than amusing to see this task executed; it is absolutely ridiculous, for he has as spectators all the children of my retinue, several of the dogs, Billy, my pet goat, and Boanerges, who not unfrequently has in his arms the little monkey, which evidently enjoys the novel sight as much as any of the others. After the shampooers have thoroughly done their work, the young elephant considers himself entitled to a game of romps, on which occasion, his excess of animal spirits, causes him to be anything but a gentle playfellow, as many of the young darkies can attest. When this exuberance of spirits becomes too manifest, the picaninnies fly for shelter under a waggon, from which retreat he often drags out one or the other by the arm or leg. On one occasion I had to come to the rescue, as he had caught a little girl round the neck with his trunk, and appeared to be in a fair way to committing homicide.

When enjoying my *dolce far niente*, Jumbo will frequently steal quietly up to me, and the first indication I have of his presence is finding his trunk searching in the depths of my numerous pockets for hidden delicacies. Nothing edible that he thus obtains is despised, but, *au contraire*, appears to be more appreciated than if it had been given him.

Wild elephants at liberty in the jungle will frequently, when tormented by flies, break off limbs of bushes and fan themselves with them. This proclivity I have turned to use by making him perform that service for me. At first, through carelessness or mischief, he did not hesitate to give me a switch across the head or shoulders, which, from his strength, was far from pleasant; however, after a due exercise of patience, he was induced to give up this objectionable practical joke. How this was accomplished is worth being explained. It was in this way. Causing Cigar to sit down, Master Jumbo was instructed to fan him, when, if he struck him, my man would pretend to cry, and give evidence of pain, I commiserating with my servant in such baby language as appeared most suitable to the purpose of impressing the delinquent with the enormity of his offence. A few such lessons secured the object in view, and for more than a week I can safely say he has scarcely touched me with even the tip of a leaf. At night my motherless charge is never tied up, but sleeps wherever inclined; his favourite resting-place being close to the fore wheel of the waggon I use as my dormitory. When on the *treck* he follows the *cortège* with the other loose animals, but he will occasionally deviate to the right or left, to gather wild fruit or other dainties that his keen senses of smell and sight tell him, are in the vicinity. Nothing appears to afford him a greater amount of satisfaction than a good bath in such *vleys* or water-holes as we may chance to come across, when, if they are sufficiently deep, he will submerge himself till nothing but his trunk and forehead are to be seen. If teased at such times by the children, he will blow water at them for a distance of several yards, and almost with the force of the discharge from a small steam-engine, a feat intensely relished by the performer, but objected to by those operated upon. I have a small musical box, which I frequently carry in my pocket, after having wound it up and set it going. The tunes evidently caused Jumbo great room for thought and curiosity as to how the noise is produced. At first, he appeared afraid, but fear has now been supplanted by pleasure, for, if capering can be called dancing, then my pet certainly does dance. This performance is far from graceful; still, the regularity with which he moves his limbs indicates his intention of keeping time.

A HOTTENTOT PATRIOT.

IN 1879, a Hottentot, named by white traders and hunters Cigar, saved my life when I was endeavouring to enlist men among the Bechuana tribes for service in Zululand; but as I have elsewhere narrated the matter, I will pass it over and tell how he again did so only a few years since.

As soon as Great Britain had resigned control of the Transvaal, and withdrawn her soldiers into Natal, those dissatisfied with the former British control at once turned their attention to punishing the native tribes that had been loyal and true to the Imperial Government, especially such as had their residence along the frontier of Bechuanaland.

Persons that live at home can scarcely credit or believe the frightful scenes of carnage and spoliation that were then enacted in this unhappy part of Africa. They are too horrible to relate, too dreadful to gain credence.

Cigar had heard, from some Griqua hunters on their route to the Zambesi, that I was again in his country. No sooner did he obtain this information than he travelled many days' journey to meet me, and render me such assistance as lay in his power, for well he knew that we were both living in perilous places. Nothing could have been more opportune for me than this resolve, for I was about to enter the debatable ground that, for nearly a year, had been the daily scene of tragedies, horrible even now to think of. The dangers anticipated by me were twofold : first, from the natives who had been driven desperate from the incursions of hordes of freebooters ; secondly, from the freebooters themselves, whose animosity to British subjects was, if possible, more vindictive than even towards the natives.

Frequent and protracted wanderings in the interior of Africa had long enabled me to do without a guide; but it was not a guide I wanted now, but an advance guard to prevent me coming in contact with persons of any description whatever, till I was through the dangerous locality, and if I had searched the world over, I could not have found another person so suited for this purpose, as my tried and faithful old friend Cigar.

The earnestness of his greeting on meeting me, and the manifest pleasure he exhibited at being once more my companion, told me, as plainly as words could say, that in my absence I had not been forgotten, and that time had not one iota diminished his regard for his old employer.

By day and night he hovered about me, in fact his attentions in this way were at times somewhat troublesome; but woe betide the man who treated me with lack of courtesy, or dared to raise his hand against me, if my friend was present. Several times I had appointed a date for my departure, but insuperable delays forced me to postpone it. At length I decided, whether my business was settled or not, to leave the day after to-morrow.

The evening I came to that resolve, soon after midnight Cigar paid me a visit. His object for doing so was to inform me that a party of marauders had made up their minds to waylay me near a *kloof*, about thirty miles distant, when, to simplify matters and prevent my return to England with the knowledge I possessed of their depredations, I was to be shot down from behind one of the adjoining boulders or trees that thickly edged the path, through the ravine I contemplated taking.

From various circumstances that had occurred, I could not doubt the correctness of my informant's statement; but there was only the one route open for me that I knew of, and delay did not promise to make a journey over it more secure.

"Well, what would you advise, old man; for go I must, let the risks be what they will?" I inquired.

"I have thought of that; do as I tell you, and you will get through safe and sound. My plan is this. Take your servant with you; don't tell him a word of what your intentions are, but profess you are only going for a ride. Start about half-past three in the afternoon, keep a course about due south for five miles, when you will find a road that runs through a large mealie-garden; at the edge of it, and close by where cultivation commences, you will see a woman gathering sticks; pull up your horses and follow her till she hands you over to the guidance of another, who will take you where I have instructed her, then you will know if Cigar, the old Hottentot, is not as good as his word, and as true to his old Bass as ever he was."

To the letter I carried out this programme. I

left the station at half-past three, found the woman gathering fuel, who at once turned off into the woods, and led us at a rapid pace till long after dark, when we again entered open country. Here our conductor was joined by a young man—not a female, as anticipated—but before he took charge of the cavalcade I had time to recognise in the first guide one of Cigar's wives, in the other his eldest son. Fancy the return journey this poor woman had alone, at night, through a country not destitute by any means of wild beasts, and scoured by men infinitely more savage; but the native women of Africa have ever been a power when patriotism has been demanded of them; in its cause they have never hesitated to risk their lives.

Under our new leader the pace was considerably sharpened, for the ground was comparatively free from stones, while there was a distinctly-marked path. After traversing about fifteen miles of this description of country, my conductor made me dismount and follow him. You may judge of my surprise when, after walking about a quarter of a mile, we came on the road I had intended travelling, the sandy surface of which was marked by the fresh spoor of a number of horses.

This was evidence enough, in all conscience, of the truth of Cigar's statement; and, to make the results doubly sure, the would-be murderers had taken time by the forelock so as to have untired horses for any unexpected emergency that might occur, and thus to place as much distance between them and the intended scene of their atrocity, as to make it look impossible for them to have been the perpetrators.

Silently we rejoined our horses, directed their steps more to the eastward up a rocky defile, on to a table-land that in daylight must have overlooked the country for miles. Here our guide uttered a long whistle in imitation of the red-legged plover, which soon was answered, and immediately afterwards Cigar was by my side.

As may be imagined, he had plenty to tell. The party so interested in me had arrived several hours before, by the usual waggon route. They had partaken of their suppers, knee-haltered their horses, and were now sleeping, conscious that they had matured a splendid plot, which scarcely could fail, and that they would be enriched by it to the tune of two first-class horses, rifles, saddlery, &c., with a considerable round sum in gold; all this, mind you, to become theirs for the firing of a well-directed bullet—a mere trifle to such characters—nothing more.

The horses and my servant were despatched to a distant ravine where mealies in abundance awaited them, while Cigar and myself kept watch over the freebooters, who were only a few hundred yards beneath us. How the old fellow regretted that we had not with us two or three mutual friends he named, for, as he forcibly expressed it, he was hungry for a *salted* horse and a breechloading rifle. But such things were not to be, and much better so. I told him; but the response he made showed that he was not a convert to my ideas.

"To-morrow you will be gone and safe, but my family and self will be at the mercy of these brutes."

My old attendant was not communicative that night; he had too many grievances to think of, to make him a talkative companion.

At break of day the marauders were moving, the first thing they did being to inspect the boulders behind which they intended to fix their ambuscade, and no place could have been more admirably situated for their purpose, for from it they could perpetrate their despicable business at easy range, and without being seen.

Soon after mid-day a couple of these worthies left the main body, and followed the back track they had taken yesterday. Their business doubtless was to report my approach. An hour after, all the horses of my foes were collected and saddled; but their future conduct I cannot report, for Cigar insisted upon an immediate start. So perfectly were his plans organised that we had no fear of surprise, for he ordered his son to the top of the nearest peak of hill in the vicinity, with instructions that if the enemy changed their plans and made a move in the direction we were going to pursue, a fire was to be lit upon it, the smoke of which by day and blaze by night would give us ample warning of the necessity to adopt new measures.

Before taking an adieu of my pursuers, I again went to the edge of the cliffs to have a final survey of them. In doing so I surprised a koodoo, which, in bounding along the face of the ravine, detached a stone, which rolled down in close proximity to their camp. One or two of the younger men rushed for their arms; but the older heeded not, believing, doubtless, that it was the work of baboons.

Before next morning I had travelled good sixty miles from the scene recorded above, and the time had arrived for Cigar to bid me good-bye. Our parting took place on a hill-side which looks over one of the loveliest countries in Africa or any other land. My Hottentot friend, who is remarkable for the size, fulness, and boldness of his eyes, appeared sad indeed; but he spoke not, for his heart was too full for speech. At length I said to him:

"What a sin it is that such a splendid country should be the scenes of the exhibition of all that is bad in the white man's character."

"Yes; but they are not your countrymen. Would that they were back here again; but that will never be now. Once I had hoped they would remain with us; but that is over since the day you gave back the Transvaal."

"Come, come; cheer up, old man! You'll see me again, and that before long," I said.

But with an incredulous smile upon his face he bid me an abrupt adieu, and, without waiting for reward or thanks, turned off among some adjoining "*kopjes*," where he was immediately lost to sight. Naturally I concluded that I had seen, for the time being, the last of this devoted friend. But such was not the case; for a few hours after I lost my way, and, from the rough and irregular nature of the ground, seemed unable to recover it. Hazardous as the step was, in a fit of desperation I went to an adjacent cattle *kraal* for information or a guide. My reception was anything but assuring. The lads in charge of it would scarcely answer me, and threats or bribes, usually effective means, were for a time utterly thrown away.

At length I produced a sovereign. Its glitter and value bore good results, for the oldest of the party, after much hesitation, led the way and I followed. Thus we had travelled about an hour and a half, when my guide, who was a few yards in front of me, was felled by a stone thrown by an invisible hand. I thought the lad was killed, for he did not move after he fell. The reason of the assault was a mystery, unless the missile had been intended for me, and if so, I might look out for a second one. So I drew my revolver to be prepared for any emergency.

To my surprise, a voice from an unseen speaker addressed me: "Put up your revolver and come this way."

I obeyed the latter order, but not the first. In a moment after I was confronted by Cigar, who, without question or preface, addressed me:

"You have had a narrow escape; in another hour you would have been in H——'s *kraal*, where there are at least fifty of the freebooters and their followers at this moment. How much would your life be worth among them? After you left me I had a fear come over me that you would lose your way where you did, so came across the *kloof* to put you right. Queer that I should think that you would lose your way, for you know the country as well as I do; still, something told me that you would go astray. Come, let me take your bridle, and I'll put you on a waggon-track in an hour."

So correctly did my hero reckon time and distance that the space was covered in the allotted time.

Before we parted I said: "I fear that lad is killed by the stone you threw. Why did you treat him so roughly?"

"Roughly did you say?" with great astonishment, adding with vehemence, "Why, he knew that he was deceiving you, and that you would lose your life through him. Killed! not him; he is only stunned, and that is what I intended to do, for if the young scoundrel had seen me, my own life would not have been safe this side of Bamanwato. Killed him! what does it matter while you are safe. You have fought for us, and you are the only one who will try to bring us protection from these accursed Boers; and somehow I think you will succeed."

"Succeed, yes; if in mortal's power," I replied.

With a shake of the hand and a blessing he again glided from my side, and the bushes and rocks immediately shut out from my view one of the truest patriots I ever met, and he was a Hottentot. How faithfully I have performed my promise to him, many thousands of my own countrymen, as well as my old follower, now know, for without the assistance I afterwards rendered the Bechuanas against the freebooting Boers, their country would not be British territory, nor the trade route from the Cape of Good Hope to the interior of tropical South Africa open to our commerce.

FEMALE HEROISM.

AMONG a race of people who have only lately become conversant with caligraphy, of course there are no written laws, and therefore precedent seems to be without value, the chief and elders deciding upon all cases that are brought before them strictly on their merits. Thus we may say that the Bechuanas are governed by a Court of Equity, unbiassed by any technicalities.

The majority of their disputes arise in reference to the possession of gardens and cattle, trespass, or conjugal infidelity, and the penalties awarded are invariably by fine.

When a member of the tribe considers himself aggrieved, he reports the matter to the chief, when, if the complaint is considered sufficiently serious, a day is appointed for its hearing.

The defendant is ordered to attend at the *Kotla* on the date fixed, and to bring his witnesses with him. On such an occasion the chief, or heir to the chieftainship, supported by a numerous staff of the elders, listens to the complaint and defence.

The elders then decide upon the merits, the voice of the majority invariably ruling. A stranger witnessing one of these trials could not fail to be struck with the vehemence, volubility, and powers of oratory these uneducated people possess, and to admire, if not to laugh at, the deep and cutting sarcasm frequently displayed, as each cross-examines his opponent and his witnesses.

The Bechuana language is wonderfully melodious, yet capable of being used with great force, while the gestures displayed are frequently most striking and are perfect specimens of pantomimic art. In spite of all this, the people never lose their tempers, and ever appear impressed with the sacredness of the tribunal before which they are arraigned, and the majesty of the inclosure within which all such affairs are decided.

A verdict once obtained is final and cannot be appealed against, and when once the fiat goes forth, not another word, not even a comment, is heard upon the subject. No stay of execution is ever asked for, for it would not be granted, and there and then the fine must be paid, or security obtained for its payment.

As specie was little known and less used in this country until a very late date, oxen, sheep, or grain were the legal tender. In rare instances, where the unsuccessful litigant has failed to find security for the fine, he has been sent to work for his successful opponent for a shorter or longer period, according to the gravity of the offence.

During my numerous visits to Bechuanaland, I never knew but one case of capital punishment, and the victim in this instance might have easily escaped her doom, if she had thought proper. In fact, everyone hoped she would do so.

It was a sad affair from start to finish, but I may as well narrate it from the beginning.

When at Kania, I had often heard of the beauty of one of the girls, who, twice daily, after the manner of her tribe, visited the spring for water. Several times I went to the pit with the hope of seeing her, but it was some time before my curiosity was rewarded.

At length fortune favoured me, and in all my journeyings I never saw a more perfectly developed figure. At that time she was about fourteen years of age, and, therefore, just entering into womanhood; her colour a rich brown, her skin possessed of a lustrous polish and smoothness, ever indicative here of good lineage and being well fed and cared for. Where there is so little clothing worn, none of her figure was concealed by drapery. Thus, I was aware at a glance, that I looked upon a bust, waist, and limbs that would have done honour to any artist's model.

Her face, too, was remarkably attractive, her nose being straight and thoroughly Grecian, eyes large and brilliant, mouth possibly a trifle too full, while her carriage was equal to the grace of the far-famed belles of Andalusia. Alas! all these charms had a terrible obstacle to contend with: viz., an enormous *coiffure* of black, frizzled hair, abundantly daubed with mica and rancid butter. Here, as elsewhere, young ladies engage in numerous games of romps, the only peculiarity that I noted in the Bechuana maidens being that they were a trifle more boisterous than their European sisters, and the subject of my narrative appeared to out-Herod Herod in hilarity and feats of activity.

To say that these girls can run is scarcely sufficient, for I have known them defy half-a-dozen white men to catch one of them, while their doublings are almost equal in abruptness to those of a hare.

In course of time I got upon speaking terms with this bronze-coloured Venus, and not unfrequently obtained a beaker of water from her pitcher as I met her threading her way from the wells to the station. Thus I took more than an ordinary interest in her. Soon afterwards I heard that she was betrothed and about to be married to one of the oldest and most opulent men of the tribe. This report created a good deal of sympathy with the young creature, as her future spouse was very decrepit, very parsimonious, and already possessed of many helpmates.

Not only this, but it was currently reported that she had fallen in love with a young Barolong, of reputed courage and handsome physique.

Now would have been the time for the girl to have eloped, and all, doubtless, would have ended satisfactorily; but, either she could not find the opportunity to leave her home, or her inamorato had not the pluck to take the responsibility. Day by day the attentions of her fiancé became more and more repulsive. But what could she do? Her parents favoured the match, and, to suit their views, she was to be sold into bondage far worse than slavery. However, the girl was not without courage, for, as a last resource, she appealed to the chief; but, in spite of her tears and entreaties, he refused to interfere, and at length the marriage took place.

Three months afterwards, the aged bridegroom, accompanied by his child-wife, visited a mealie garden, some distance from Kania, in which there was a solitary hut. Next day the old man was found murdered, his body being fearfully mutilated. It was evident to all, from the nature and severity of the wounds, that they could not have been inflicted by this girl unaided, but that she must have had an assistant, or more probably still, that the crime was the action of another, and that she took no active part in its accomplishment.

After a patient and lengthened hearing, in which every effort was made to compel her to reveal the name of the assassin, the girl was condemned to death. However, no restraint was put upon her actions. Her hut remained unwatched, and every opportunity was afforded her to fly the country. But this she would not do. Times innumerable the old chief and his attendants visited her, promising her her life on condition that she would reveal the name of the person who had committed the deed. This was of no avail. Days drifted into weeks, and weeks into more than a month, when one chilly morning two executioners and a superior officer came to her hut. The last-named placed a noosed rope round her neck, and led her away to the rocks at the back of an adjoining *kopje*, the rear of this fearful cortége being brought up by the last executors of the law. There was no shriek, no cry for mercy. Many witnessed the child-wife being led away to her doom, still she asked not for aid. Brave in heart, and brave in limb, she followed her dread leader without resistance.

On reaching the place of execution she was once more entreated to confess, but again she was equally obdurate.

Still loth to take the life of one so young, a final appeal was made to her, on which she broke out into a torrent of abuse, charging her executioners with cowardice and fear to take her blood. All means to save her had now failed, and reproach was returned for sympathy, so the powerful *knobkeeries* of the executioners were dashed upon her head, and in a few minutes life had departed, the body being left to feed the vultures and jackals.

Whatever may have been the faults or guilt of this unfortunate girl, she met her death in a manner worthy of a heroine, and I doubt if in history, an instance of greater stoicism and resolution can be found than that displayed by this Bechuana belle.

Cases of wife-beating in this country I never heard of; in fact, they cannot take place, otherwise, I should have done so. This is not to be accounted for by the introduction of the Christian religion among a small minority, but by an innate knowledge that woman being the weaker, it is beneath a man's dignity to raise his hand against her. Still the women do all the manual labour in the fields, and gardens, carry water, grind corn, gather thatch, and make crockery ware, but never are permitted, on any grounds whatever, to take a part in the care or management of cattle.

This, with hunting, sewing *karosses*, manufacturing weapons, attending upon their chiefs, and soldiering, constitutes the occupation of the males, although I should not forget to mention, that I have seen many of the women take a very prominent and active part on the battle-field.

It is not for a moment to be supposed that because the women work in the fields they have not a word to say, in reference to household affairs! on the contrary, if their special premises are interfered with by the husband, or he should in any way forget the dignity of his position, he will soon be made aware of their disapproval of his conduct in language pointed and forcible. A Bechuana scold, I imagine, is quite equal to her sisters in any other part of the world, and when several wives combine, which they often do, to vent their indignation, the lord and master, like a wise man, invariably finds the neighbourhood too hot for him, and makes a bolt for a neighbour's kraal, there to remain till the wrath of the bellicose ladies has "simmered" down.

It has never appeared to me that the Bechuana women object to bigamy, in fact, I think they rather approve of it, while the more wives a man possesses, the less work there will be of necessity, for each to do. In all establishments there is a chief wife, and her offspring, whether she be number 1 or number 3 in the order of marriage, is heir to the father's position in the tribe. It also ought to be known that each wife and her children have a hut to themselves; their habitations being separated by a small fencing. Each woman has also a garden, and not unfrequently cattle, which she keeps for the individual use of herself and her husband, none of the other wives having the right to interfere with, or possess themselves of these supplies.

BELIEF IN GHOSTS.

THE reader, on perusing this, will doubtless say, "the interior of Africa is a strange place for ghosts to have got to." No doubt the ghost-yarns that are to be heard there, owe their origin to a European source. Whether or no, Hottentot and Boer, Griqua and Colonial trader equally believe in them, and so thoroughly is this credence in supernatural beings ingrafted in them, that to express the smallest amount of scepticism of their truth would inevitably entail upon you a storm of indignation.

Whether I believe in ghosts or not, it is unnecessary here to state, but I will say that I have never yet seen one, although nurtured and brought up in a country where they were stated to be particularly numerous. But although I have never been interviewed by one of these visitors from the spirit world, I will be honest enough to acknowledge that I have listened to the narratives about them of my seniors with awe, that I have felt my hair rise almost perpendicular upon my head, and my pulse become slow and interrupted, while a clammy damp gathered on my hands and brow.

As I sat devouring what had been seen and might be witnessed at the corner of a lonely lane, or by the rock where deeply eddied the dark waters of some silent river, or where the road was closely shadowed from the light of moon and sun by intertwining branches of elm and beech, I have emphatically thanked fortune that, by such places I had not to pass on my way homeward on blustering dark nights.

If I may be permitted to express an opinion upon a subject on which I am not an authority, I would say that ghosts did well and wisely to seek the silent *veldts*, the rocky *kloofs*, the darkling forests, and the rugged and cavernous mountain sides of the southern portion of the African continent for a habitat and resting place.

In canny Scotland, some terrible deed of violence,

such a crime as has never previously been heard of for brutality, and reckless disregard for human life, is generally believed to be the cause of the spirit of the victim refusing to be pacified, and thus haunting the scene of outrage, to wreak vengeance upon the murderer, his children, or relatives.

Such being the case in "Caledonia stern and wild," a hundredfold more should it be accepted as the reason for ghosts being abundant in South Africa; for find me a *Kloof*, or *Vley*, a *Kopje*, or *Krantz* that has not been the silent witness to Bushman or Bechuana, Kaffir or Hottentot being done to death, by the unerring rifle of the early Boer invaders of that land.

It was in the month of April, approaching the end of the South African autumn, that I outspanned in that extensive district of bush that lies to the westward of *Monkoroane's* country, Southern Bechuana Land.

Our journey had been slow and tedious from the heavy sand that we had passed over, and, as the bullocks in consequence were more than weary—dead beat in fact—and as heavy, massive, ink-coloured clouds were rising rapidly to windward, indicating either rain or wind, or both combined, I gave orders for the canvas sail of my waggon to be drawn over the tilt, secured by double lashings, and everything, in fact, made tight and ship-shape for a dirty night.

Our camping ground was picturesque, in close proximity to numerous *kopjes*, from the *krantzes* and rocks of which hung suspended wonderfully distorted veteran trees, in many instances loaded with such a growth of moss, as to give them the veritable appearance of great age among aged surroundings. Those trees, however, that grew upon the flat were of a more youthful character; still many a year must have passed over their heads from their height and development of trunk.

This camping ground had a bad reputation, for near it three members of the Griqua Land Police Force had at different times disappeared, and in spite of the most assiduous search, not a remnant of their bodies, clothing, or equipment was ever found.

Bushmen, lions, and leopards are still to be found in this locality. Wiseacres, of course, asserted that the gallant troopers had succumbed under the poisoned arrows of these pigmy and baboon-like representatives of the human race. Less experienced persons scouted the idea of Bushmen being the malefactors, but laid these mysterious occurrences to the door of *feræ naturæ*. Who was correct has never been decided, but, strange to say, in each instance the trooper's charger returned unscathed.

If the weather had been more propitious, and the cattle less fatigued, I, doubtless, should have listened to the entreaties of my attendants, more particularly to my Hottentot driver, not to outspan in such an uncanny spot. However, I was wilful, and had my way; and well it was so, for scarcely had the tent been made secure over my waggon, when down descended one of those torrents of rain characteristic of the place and season.

With the rain came the wind, which fairly screeched in wrath, as if complaining, with angry protest, that aught on earth dared to oppose its progress.

Excessive violence in the elements never lasts long. As in man and woman, such ebullitions in nature soon exhaust themselves. So, ere the vermilion lines of light in the west, that told the place where the sun had disappeared, had been totally deprived of their brilliancy, wind and rain had passed to leeward, and calm but natural stillness usurped the place of the raging elements.

Hunger—what a matter-of-fact thing it is, and how, in spite of adverse circumstance, will it, with tyrannic power, assert its supremacy. Thus, my attendants were soon busied over the flesh-pots by compulsion, and the blaze of the camp fire ascended brighter and stronger as the last remnants of daylight disappeared.

Still, my people were not happy; the driver's air was nervous and suspicious, whilst the subordinates indicated by their movements, a dread of going the shortest distance from the waggon, in search of the necessary fuel for the fire, which all knew to be the grand protector from the mysterious beings with whom their imaginations had peopled the locality.

With good appetite I ate my piece of roasted kid. With better appetite the natives stowed away an enormous potful of mealy porridge.

Hunger satisfied—speaking for myself—feeling at amity with all the world, I reclined on my "*karosses*," lit my pipe, and in the everchanging puffs of smoke saw or recalled memories of the past.

In this state, if I had not been interrupted, I might have remained till my big load of tobacco had burned away; but I was interrupted, for my confounded followers, although redolent of the *bouquet de nègre*, would keep crowding closer and closer upon me. Such a proceeding was unusual with them, so I remonstrated, but to no purpose.

I have often thought the black man, in his original state, like a child, for white children I have seen act exactly in the same way as my followers were doing, when they have imagined themselves in an uncanny place.

The storm that had passed away was soon followed by another, less violent possibly, but still sufficiently powerful to make the old trees creak and groan under its mighty influence; and now the night birds found their voices and added their weird notes to the other discordant noises. A skulking hyæna, moreover, had smelt our fare, and, from the shelter of an adjoining shadow, complained sadly that he had not been permitted to join in our repast.

The example of this animal was infectious, for a family party of jackals answered his wail and appeared to confirm him in his belief that he was a much abused animal in not being invited to participate in the good things of this earth. But these are minor noises, for from the kopje sides comes a deep sonorous bay that would do honour to the deepest-voiced hound that e'er followed a disciple of St. Hubert. It is the "all's well" of the sentinel baboon, perched upon the summit of an adjacent *krantz*.

My Hottentot driver was telling a story to a most interested body of listeners, of how a great chief had been murdered by his people in a most dastardly and treacherous manner, and how he had returned to avenge himself upon his assassins, in the shape of a man-eating lion, when the narrator's voice ceased, and his and every eye was directed to the westward, whence came the distinct sound of a horse's footfall, such as is made when the animal is passing over wet ground. The black men heard it, so did I; they evidently looked for a supernatural apparition. I, on the other hand, murmured to myself, "It is a dirty and unpleasant night for any poor fellow to be on the road."

In a few minutes the unknown appeared through

the circle of light that bounded the fire. In a second or two afterwards he dismounted, when I asked him to accept the hospitality and shelter that my waggon could afford him.

Let me describe the stranger. He was a tall, powerfully-built man, but not possessed of a superfluous ounce of fat. Determination and energy were stamped upon his countenance, while the big sinews and veins that showed themselves in his neck and hands told plainly as words could say, that he was possessed of strength almost superhuman. From his complexion (which was what the Boers call " rooi ") and his voice, to an observant person there could be no doubt but that he hailed from the old country. That Africa had known him for years was equally certain from his sunburnt throat and hands. Such a man would be expected to possess a wonderful horse ; the stranger's animal was to the equine family what he was to the human—in fact, such a beast as could cover a hundred miles in twenty-four hours and be willing to repeat the same operation next day, provided he had an occasional good roll in the sand and half a bucket of mealies every twenty-four hours.

While my guest was doing justice to my larder, the Hottentot driver returned to his story, upon which I abruptly and uncourteously shut him up, desiring him to cease frightening his listeners by such absurd narratives.

Hereupon the stranger turned to me and said in few, but pointed words, "If you don't believe in ghosts, I do. Yes! smile if you like. I am not ashamed to own it; and the place where I became converted to a belief in the supernatural is not above four hours by horse from this spot. Disbelieve it! how could I? and my after-rider saw it as well as myself, while old Erasmus Swartz and his *vrow*, with their folks, have seen it many times.

"Come, if you don't want to turn in yet, make the niggers put some more wood on the fire; give me another *soupje* of *square-face* in my beaker, and after I load up my pipe I'll tell you the yarn. Believe me or not, as you like, it matters nothing to me; but I shall remember and believe what I am about to tell you to my dying day.

"About this time last year I was buying cattle in an adjoining part of the country, and had occasion to call at Uncle Erasmus Swartz's house. The weather had been fearfully warm, without a breath of air stirring. All Nature seemed affected by the oppression, even the very cattle stood listless chewing their cud, absolutely refusing to leave the shelter of the homestead and cattle kraal. When I got up to bid the old folks good-bye, the old vrow said, 'You had best stay where you are, there's a storm coming, and a pretty "testy" one it will be while it lasts.'

"But I had business to attend to elsewhere on

the morrow, and, much as I might have desired it, I could not remain, so ordering Jansey to put the saddle on Dopper — the horse that I am riding to-night—I and my after-rider started.

"If you have ever travelled that neighbourhood you will remember that after you leave old Swartz's farm, the country in front of you going westward is as desolate a district, as any to be found in South Africa; rocks piled upon rocks, till the *kopjes* assume the magnitude of hills, and scarcely a bush or bunch of grass to be seen upon them. I had only proceeded five miles before I received warning of the bursting of the storm. Large drops of rain began to fall, and sudden brief gusts of wind to wail among the adjoining *krantzes*. The ravens and vultures wheeled their flight high aloft, giving utterance to their harsh and repellent notes, as if warning the dwellers upon earth of coming evil.

"The further we advanced, the storm increased in severity, till the rain became a torrent and the wind a hurricane. Jansey, pale as a Hottentot could be, now rode up alongside of me, and begged me to turn off the trail and seek shelter in a *krantze* adjoining our position. This I refused, but he persisted. While doing so, he pointed with his hand to the front, and exclaimed. 'For the love of God, Bass, what is that?' I stared in the direction indicated, but from the drift and rain could see nothing, and told him so most emphatically. 'Nothing!' he whispered, in a voice overcome with fear; 'look there, right in front, just entering the kloof, straight ahead, look—look—look!'

"I shaded my eyes with my hand, the better to protect them from the rain, and, true enough, just entering the *poort* of the *kloof*, I saw what I deemed to be a party of Kaffirs, with baggage-oxen, in single file, evidently pursuing the same road as ourselves.

"Turning to my after-rider, I said, 'It's only a party of natives, you fool.'

"'No, Bass,' he answered, "it is the ghost of Morocco, his son and their wives, who were murdered in this kloof forty years ago this very month.' Here Jansey, who was a good Catholic, in spite of his fears, found time to cross himself.

"During breaks between the drift and the rain, I managed to see more of this mysterious *cortège*.

"It consisted of ten persons, five of whom appeared to be women, and with them were ten dun-coloured oxen, half of these animals being loaded with the usual odds and ends that compose a Kaffir's household gods. Certainly, it was a most mysterious looking procession, each human being that composed it, keeping with the utmost regularity his or her allotted place, and more mysterious still was it that, all the cattle should be the same colour, and that a most unusual one.

"Jansey kept close to my heels. I could, during

breaks in the heavy gusts of wind, hear sufficient to know that he was praying.

"The exit and entrance to this "*poort*" are as gruesome and uncanny-looking as any I know, the sides being a hundred feet or more in perpendicular height, while immense boulders hang, apparently, so insecure that the slightest vibration must of necessity detach them. Once this "*kloof*" is entered, there is no exit possible for a human being except at the far end. Knowing this, I pushed on my good horse, Dopper, to overtake the travellers, but, strange as it may seem, for the first time in his life, he gave evidence of being an unwilling servant. True, he had an almost blinding torrent of rain in his face, and the wind was so strong that it was difficult to stem, while lightning descended in incessant streams, and thunder belched forth in deafening cannonade, but, in spite of all these adverse circumstances, Dopper's duty was to obey, and with no gentle spur I let him know that I was master.

"My horse is swift; still, I did not overtake the bullocks and their attendants. 'Mysterious,' I thought to myself, and again pushed my mount to his best pace. He seemed neither to gain nor lose distance.

"A strange feeling came over me; at once I comprehended its meaning: '*I was, against my will, becoming a convert to a belief in the supernatural world!*' But against this I fought, so made one determined effort to solve the extraordinary enigma before me.

"The unknown and inexplicable procession was just leaving the *kloof* at the further *poort*; in fact, the leaders had turned the corner and were out of sight when I pulled Dopper together, drove both spurs deep into his flanks, and dashed forward to intercept at least the last of these mysterious travellers. But I was too late; all had turned the corner and disappeared behind the rock-projecting barrier. With renewed energy I myself turned it, expecting to see the string of natives before me. To my surprise and astonishment, all had vanished.

* * * *

"Forty years before the adventure I have narrated occurred to me, to the very day, mark that, the Boers murdered Morocco, his son, their wives, and their attendants in the most inhuman manner, and worse still, under a flag of truce. The Baralong race, to whom they belong, well remember the circumstances, and the scene of the massacre was Asvogel Kloof, near old Erasmus Swartz's farm, in Griqua Land West.

"Now, I would ask you, friend, are you surprised that I believe in ghosts?"

HARRISON AND SONS,
PRINTERS IN ORDINARY TO HER MAJESTY,
ST. MARTIN'S LANE.

www.ingramcontent.com/pod-product-compliance
Lightning Source LLC
Chambersburg PA
CBHW020236240426
43672CB00006B/551